ROOTS OF totalitarianism:

The Ideological Sources of Fascism, National Socialism, and Communism

J. Lucien Radel

Crane, Russak & Company, Inc.

NEW YORK

Roots of Totalitarianism

Published in the United States by
Crane, Russak & Company, Inc.
347 Madison Avenue
New York, N.Y. 10017

Copyright © 1975 Crane, Russak & Company, Inc.

Library Edition   ISBN 0-8448-0374-X
Paperbound Edition   ISBN 0-8448-0600-5
LC 74-80978

Printed in the United States of America

Contents

PART IV

Introduction–The Substance of Utopia–The Roots of "Early French Socialism"–Jean-Jacques Rousseau–François Fourier: Evolutionary Socialism–Pierre-Joseph Proudhon: Theoretical Anarchism–Louis-Auguste Blanqui: Revolutionary Socialism–Immanuel Kant: The Nature of Human Duality–Georg Wilhelm Hegel: Alienation of the "Spirit"–Ludwig Feuerbach: The Alienation of "Man"–Karl Marx: German "Scientific Socialism"–Lenin's Application of Marxism.

Charts

Preface

THIS book presents what one might call a comparative re-interpretation of the theory of Modern Totalitarian Dictatorship, viewed through its three major forms—Fascism, National Socialism, Marxian Communism. Instead of the usual, most frequently used approach of observation and description of the institutional and functional features of these three forms of government the main emphasis is here placed on the *motivating factors* behind the emergence of such regimes.

One must point out in that connection that contemporary comparative political research, which relies heavily on surface observation in order to analyze the assembled information, might possibly lead to erroneous conclusions if one does not look with special attention upon the impact of psychological incentives as a primary, preparatory phenomenon in the formation of group attitudes. Most likely, such erroneous conclusions will not be a result of the frequent insufficiencies in the necessary data (the latter are usually packaged for the analysis of the structural and functional features in the political activity); they would mainly stem from a condition which from the beginning excludes the most *fundamental,* the "mind-forming," or, if you will, the psychological "grass roots" data from the analysis. The inclusion of such data, however, will, in fact, provide the foundation for such research, would facilitate and eventually allow an analytic penetration into the formulating process of totalitarian thought; hence it will subsequently bring into focus the motivation of the *entire* totalitarian process. In other words, consideration of the psychological mind-forming factors, along with observation of the resulting structure and activity of totalitarian regimes, will bring about an *explanation* of their particular phenomena, rather than a mere discovery and description of their features.

This book does not shy away from the domain of conventional comparative political studies. While it does not deal exclusively with traditional forms of government, its subject matter is *comparative* political theory, somewhat simplified by a reduction of the general diffusion of material (which characterizes that particular branch of political science). The book thus focuses on the concrete domain of *modern totalitarian* theory. It seems that the most suitable avenue for analysis would be the *comparative approach,* as it is used in political science—though in the beginning it may not be applied with the greatest degree of precision. In fact, comparative precision would seem unnecessary in Part I, which is devoted to a broad discussion having the primary purpose of laying a foundation for later comparisons. However, in spite of the elementary nature of Part I, special care has been taken to avoid distracting or distorting generalities.

Use of a somewhat more sophisticated—in fact, aspect-by-aspect—analytic function is gradually introduced in an applied and integrated fashion on the more advanced levels, where the study enters into an analysis of narrow and in some cases isolated aspects of the theories of Fascism, National Socialism, and Marxian Communism. An example is the comparative evaluation of these regimes' "exportability" (pp. 97–99 and 140).

The primary purpose of Part I, therefore, is to display and blend the contemporary perception of elementary values and norms of modern Democracy into a solid ideological platform against which later to contrast the forms of totalitarianism by categorizing and decategorizing (associating and disassociating) particularly pertinent characteristics. Thus, this procedure should aid in developing the common framework of three separate, but concurring, kinds of theoretical comparisons: (a) between Democracy and Totalitarianism; (b) between the three specific forms of Modern Totalitarian Dictatorship; and (c) between Democracy and each of the above forms of Modern Totalitarian Dictatorship.

Thus, the purpose of Part I is to set forth the notion of Democracy in its most fundamental and theoretically elementary, even idealistic, conceptual form; to contrast it with the particularities of the concept of Absolute Autocracy, while tracing the latter's evolution; and, finally, to use the framework of all this material as a suitable vehicle for comparisons among the theoretical features of Fascism, National Socialism, and Marxian Communism.

Parts II, III, and IV, while tightly integrated in order to maintain a compact comparative evaluation, are devoted individually to each of the above forms of Modern Totalitarian Dictatorship, hence each regime can be studied independently from the others. The purpose of these sections is to highlight the essence, similarities, and differences between the regimes' most typical *ideological* features—features which conditioned and subsequently created the enthusiastic group mentalities in Italy, Germany, and Revolutionary Russia that supported the respective dictatorships.

Valuable help, during the various stages of development of this work, was graciously offered by Professor Frederick J. Carrier, who took time to read the entire manuscript and to give sound advice on points of intellectual history. Professor André LeJules, of *l'Ecole des Hautes Etudes Internationales* and *l'Ecole des Hautes Etudes Sociales,* in Paris, and Professor Vaclav Beneš, of Indiana University, helped me, at the time of the research phase, with their inspiring comments regarding a number of comparative political ideas principally dealt with in Parts I and III of the book. Special gratitude should also be given to the French Institute for Polemological Research under the presidency of Professor Gaston Bouthoul of the University of Paris, and under the sponsorship of the French Ministry of National Education and Scientific Research. Equal recognition is extended to Professor René Carrère, the Institute's Vice-Director of Research whose cooperation—in offering the use of the Institute's facilities—and inspiration, created the opportunity to assess the perspectives of a number of psychological causes for ideological conflicts. Professor A. James Gregor, University of California-Berkeley, and Professor Sven Groennings, formerly of Indiana University-Bloomington, contributed individually through their constructive criticism and valuable comments, mostly related to the social and political aspects of National Socialism. Finally, Mr. Steven Lamb, a very diligent graduate student and research assistant in political science, undertook the heavy task of helping me put together the entire manuscript. However, all responsibility for liabilities in this work is solely mine.

My deep gratitude also goes to the undergraduate and graduate students at four different universities in the U.S. who chose to attend my conferences. Reference is made to those who, at different times, enrolled in my courses "Totalitarian Patterns of Government," "Government and Politics of the U.S.S.R.," "Conflicting Political Ideologies," as well as to the students who took my seminars on the "Development of Socialism and Marxism," and on "Anarchism." They all truly inspired me (through their stimulating interest, questions, and expressed opinions), scrutinized my arguments, and created a genuine incentive, and comfortable atmosphere, for the undertaking and progress of this work. Thus, this group became a most powerful source of motivation. I thank all these students for thus helping me to complete the task, and I take this opportunity to dedicate this book to them.

J.-LUCIEN RADEL
University of Wisconsin
Oshkosh / 1975

Part I
The Foundations

The Idea of Democracy

Our times are characterized by continuous evolutionary—and in many instances—revolutionary changes. In fact, serious attempts are being made to modify the ideological premises of various political regimes. All these modifications are intended to revise ideologies in order to update them and accommodate them to modern societal needs and realities. These endeavors have brought about a new dimension which has almost completely displaced the peaceful, traditional, legalistic, and voluntaristic proposals of political theories in the past. The resulting ideological dynamism, therefore, could make it difficult to argue that Democracy is a way of life related to a clearly defined structural framework which follows from an established sociopolitical and economic order.

In light of such prevailing conditions, all traditional attempts at a definition of the notion of Democracy may appear vague, incomplete, and unempirical. The assertion that Democracy is a government "of" the people, "by" the people, and "for" the people may become unsatisfactory even to laymen. In fact, each element in this trio might be severely questioned as to its functional validity.

Thus, the traditional definition of Democracy may not have today a tangible empirical character, that is, being a collection of elements flawlessly applicable to modern societal conditions, relationships, and sociopolitical interaction. Therefore, the democratic concept does not have a traditionally expressed, and at the same time, contemporarily valid, clear-cut framework with finite boundaries.

One functional characteristic of Democracy, however, may be easily established, namely that Democracy is an *attitude* observed in group activity or relationships. One may also assert that the democratic type of attitude is based on an established mentality, varying from one cultural group to another which is likely to recognize certain values and norms of behavior and consequently, directs most of the group activity in recognition of these values and norms. Moreover, one could even say that only some of these values and norms are known and well established in relation to democratic attitudes, and that so far, all traditional attempts to define Democracy have been based on the observed information which ends at this point. This is to say that the traditional U.S.

1

definition, that is government "of" the people, "by" the people, and "for" the people, has been constructed only upon *some* of the available information on democratic attitudes, that portion that has been observed procedurally, and that has become known and established. But if one looks on Democracy primarily as an "attitude," rather than an established procedure—whose needs are changeable from era to era due to diverse circumstances and fluctuating human desires according to different cultural mentalities—then one can discover the second important characteristic of Democracy, namely, its unlimited flexibility derived from rational, as well as *emotional* factors.

It is this latter, pliant aspect of Democracy that cannot be included in positive terms in the traditional definition, a lack which could easily invalidate the functional capacity of the entire definition. In addition, a goodly number of the elements of Democracy are not only changeable, but some of them are not even foreseen, or, for that matter, thought of as yet; therefore, some are close to incorporation within a total definition, while others remain quite distant. However, it is imperative that allowance be made for the inclusion of *all* pertinent elements in a totally comprehensive definition.

While it would be virtually impossible to achieve such an inclusion in positive procedural terms, it would be possible today to elaborate a set of relationships containing a number of unknowns, an endeavor which eventually could serve as no more than a *basis* for further elaboration of a viable definition of Democracy. Such relationships would group, in one unit of a possible equation, all of the observed and functionally proven, long-established elements which are known to be a part of the practically operative democratic societies, while the other unit would contain all of the unknown and intangible—sometimes disputed—elements of Democracy with an allowance for anticipated but as yet undiscovered data.

On a quite different, primarily sociological, plateau, a group of political scientists (Professors G. Almond and S. Verba could be a good example) have attempted to define Democracy in terms of the degree of "input-influence" by the population on the governmental decision-making process. This group maintains that the greater the "input-influence" by the population on the governing process, the higher the degree of Democracy in that given politically organized society. Undoubtedly, a proper balance in the correlation will result in the establishment of the correct degree of *self-governance* of the population in question. However, will it simultaneously establish in a viable contemporary form a degree of Democracy psychologically commensurate to the *current perception* of Democracy, i.e., is that all there is to be considered in a governmental system *today* in order to qualify it as Democracy?

It appears that if one conceives the essence of the term Democracy in the ancient Greek sense, the above premise would be not only satisfactory, but it would also be a very significant empirical advancement over the Aristotelian approach. However, current societal needs and our understanding of *functional* Democracy, as *perceived* by modern individuals in terms of Democratic *attitudes*, rather than a procedure establishing the degree of "self-governance," appear to have changed significantly the meaning which was given earlier to that term. While the above premise would necessarily provide for a nice and convincing, clear-cut argumentative logic, and even a formula for measurements, in regard to "population-government relationships," it would neglect at the same time the fundamental *modern rationale* as to what exactly a man primarily is looking for today in his relations to his government and his peer group in order to classify the system as democratic or authoritarian. As a matter of fact, through that premise, instead of evolving freer relations, the matter appears as ordained for him. The shortcoming of that premise will possibly become apparent when one attempts to ascertain whether modern individuals are, indeed, looking for a high degree of their own *input* in the governmental process, or whether they are, more importantly, perceiving Democracy as a system of government under which they expect to be left progressively alone to make their own decisions with only a minimal number or eventually (and idealistically) no rules and restrictions. The former premise could theoretically be invalidated, and the latter advanced, simply by the fact of frequently demonstrated "apathetic" electoral attitudes in modern democracies, where important problems are usually "solved," or at least decided upon, by 30, 40, or even 50 and 60 percent of the popular vote. In the best of these cases there would be a significant 40 percent of "apathetic" attitude, hence that great a *lack of desire* by the population (for whatever reason) to assert their own "input-influence" on the decision-making process of the government. A psychologically-coded research design asking primarily "why" a certain percentage of people have abstained from the polls, rather than the usual "what" income, professional, educational, sex, and age levels have displayed apathetic electoral attitudes, would appear to have much more contemporary flavor amidst confirmed democratic societies. It would attempt to penetrate *directly* into the people's "frame of mind" created by the current conditions of the actual environment, instead of venturing into loose interpretations of it, or ascertaining the model of a mere registry resulting from these conditions.

It might be appropriate, then, at this point, to relate the following incident in order to clarify further how ordinary modern men begin to perceive in a probably subconscious but practical sense, the evolved meaning of Democracy in their informal daily life. The following is an actual account.

Two visiting professors of political science, recently arrived at their new temporary place of work, at a major Midwestern university, met in mid-semester in my presence during a time of determined efforts to achieve more faculty participation in the governance of the institution.

One of them asked his peer: "How do you like it here?"

"I like it very much," came the answer.

"And why do you happen to like it so much?" the first one continued.

"Because nobody seems to direct me; I can develop my work in terms of my research and my teaching the way I want to," was the reply.

"But how about you, are you satisfied with your new position?"

"Oh, yes! Nobody bugs me either; it is a genuine Democracy here. We've got a really good central administration!"

"It is a Democracy, all right, compared to the institution I come from," agreed the first one.

No mention was made by either participant in the conversation of the notion relating to faculty *input* in the university policy-making process, although this incident occurred at the end of a very lively meeting which had just passed a resolution demanding more faculty participation in the university governance!

The hereby proposed alternative premise to the sociological "input-influence" concept would take into account the reason as to *why* contemporary man continues to organize himself on the basis of a government—and would only then attempt to contribute to the definitions of Democracy and Authoritarianism. Within that framework, Democracy would *not* be basically defined in terms of people's "input-influence" on the government, but in terms of governmental regulations and restrictions imposed (by whatever means, democratically or not) on the individual. In that regard, one could allege that the greater the number of rules and restrictions affecting the life of the individual in a given politically organized society, the lower the degree of Democracy in that particular society. An interesting feature of the above correlation would be that it would *not* permit the display of separate systems—one of them democratic, the other authoritarian—but there would emerge only one continuously floating indicator which would be capable of presenting momentary changes within a single system, in some aspects and instances democratic (to a determined extent) and authoritarian in other aspects, times, and circumstances (again to a certain extent).

This approach could also solve once and for all the old normative dilemma involved in the interpretation of whether a government is democratic if the people have consciously, willingly, and freely elected an openly pronounced authoritarian political group to national office and desire to maintain it there. The history of the political development of nations is replete with cases of popular outcries for Authoritarianism; they have been heard as recently as in the 1800s in such a sophisticated and by-now traditionally democratic country as France; also noteworthy is the strong popular support given to Hitler in the Germany of the 1930s, not to mention the two decades (1922–42) of unquestioned popularity enjoyed by Mussolini in Italy.

In order to narrow the entire proposal to an attempt at a system definition, one may begin with the *elementary,* the most unsophisticated and idealistic premise of the democratic idea, instead of "furthering" the study beyond its allegedly achieved higher level of contemporary understanding. By doing the latter, one risks becoming a victim of possible current misconceptions of Democracy by unwillingly incorporating into the new product a large portion of what probably has already been misconceived. The former alternative, however, implies a start from scratch, that is, a consideration of the most elementary and idealistic concept of modern Democracy.

In the earlier suggested set of relations, *all* of the elements of Democracy—the known and unknown alike—can be divided into two categories according to two distinct characteristics: firstly, those of legal and constitutional nature, and secondly, those of moral and spiritual nature.

The Legal and Constitutional Characteristics of Democracy

These characteristics are at least nine in number; most of them descriptive, elementary, and unquestionably related to the notion of Democracy. They illustrate those factors which normally lead to the formulation of the "input-influence" conception used for the currently understood definition of Democracy and have hardly emotional substance.

Representative Government reflects the important correlation between universal suffrage and the governing process on the executive level. A government is regarded as a representative agency of the people only if it comes into being and assumes office as a direct result of freely expressed universal suffrage. In addition, the suffrage is the cornerstone for the modern understanding of a legitimate government as against the formerly used, but still not far distant, principle of dynastic inheritance.

Right of Discussion suggests that processes of evolution are intrinsically basic to Democracy. There should not be any claims that a qualitative excellence has been achieved by the adoption of a particular form of government, and that such form of government alone reflects the permanent or absolute political desires and goals of the people; nor should there be claims that such goals have been achieved in the static sense. Thus, Democracy is a continuously fluctuating phenomenon; its evolution relies on free and unobstructed discussion without which the searching, innovating, evolutionary process would be impossible.

Majority Rule evokes the proposition that in Democracy, the government can be truly representative only if it emerges as the result of majority wishes and is sustained by continued majority support. This characteristic expands on the principle of "Representative Government."

Minority Rights is a concept very closely related to Majority Rule. The unobstructed existence of the political minority is an all-important factor in Democracy. The minority should be regarded as having not the same power but the same *intrinsic value* as the majority. Basically, the rights of the political minority are based on a fundamental principle without which the concept of Majority Rule alone would not have any democratic meaning; the political arrangement then could transform itself into a dictatorship, or a "tyranny by the majority."

According to the principle under discussion, all majority rights are guaranteed, including the right of existence and of "peculiarities in attitude." The simplified rationale for this characteristic is that all appropriate ideas should be paid attention to and freely discussed because of their particular and probable suitability to a given society. In a politically organized community the ideas of the majority are usually regarded as appropriate, that is, "good" for that community, because they have been confirmed in free elections. However, according to democratic principles, the so-called "poor" and inappropriate ideas should also be carefully heeded and openly discussed because only then can they be classified as inappropriate.

Limitations of Governmental Power implies that only certain actions prescribed in advance can be undertaken by a government. Usually such powers are delineated in a constitution or in some other basic legal document. According to democratic theory, there are always certain areas of public life in which the government should not interfere.

Governmental Responsibility to the People implies that the government, on the executive level, when acting within its prescribed areas of public life, should be fully responsible for its actions to the people. However, a number of obstacles of a practical nature seem always to prevent the direct assumption of such responsibility, hence the existence of an institutional machinery is necessary to guarantee its achievement. Parliaments are practical *instruments* for the achievement, to a highest possible extent, of such responsibility. They provide a body of elected people's representatives from whom the executive level of the government seeks final direction for its policy making, and to whom it accounts for its actions. Even civil servants appointed by the government are held responsible for their actions under laws which are, in turn, elaborated on and approved by those same people's representatives. Appointed judges are also subject to these same legal provisions.

Rule of Law prescribes that in a democratic state, the government is a government of *law*. All individuals, whether members of the majority or the political minority, are equal under the law. The same principle pertains to the government itself, whether taken as an institution or as a group of individual citizens.

Established Principles and Means reflect the notion in Democracy emphasizing that not only the established goals are important for the maintenance of democratic values; the means used in achieving these goals are *equally* important.

Indeed, there should be a very close *correlation* between the means and the ends sought. Only certain means are acceptable in a Democracy. No means may be applied which might harm the well-being of an individual whether as a member of the political majority or of the minority. Also, under no circumstances may non- or anti-democratic means be applied in sociopolitical life, even if they might be aimed at increasing the degree of Democracy or, at making it more appropriate to the particular society. Thus, the emphasis on means and ends should always be even-handed in democratic societies. In the Anglo-Saxon world the "goals-means correlation" is allegedly applied through the principle of "techniques and procedural rules."

Right to Revolt appears most often in highly controversial form, especially when the importance of the "goals-means correlation" is asserted. As a result it is less identifiable with Democracy than the previous norms. The foundations of such doubts have largely been attributed to the frequent speculation made by leaders of the governments of totalitarian states upholding the Right to Revolt as justification and legalization of their own regimes. Theoretically, however, democracies are based on the right of the population to revolt against a government which does not serve the interests of the individual citizen as expressed in the "majority rule—minority rights correlation." Within this theory, the right to revolt should be used only as *a last resort* when no other means of control are available to society in order to correct the activities of an unacceptable government. The following analogy could easily be made for defenders of the right to revolt: revolt is to internal politics as war is to international relations, and, consequently, it may be used (as in the latter case) only as a last resort. However, the fact still remains that revolt is a contradiction of the principle of equality asserted in the "goals-means correlation."

The two basic documents upon which the U. S. system of government is founded provide an illustration of the uncertain status of the right to revolt. These are the Declaration of Independence and the Constitution. While no mention of the right to revolt is made in either the Constitution or the Bill of Rights, this same principle is very clearly indicated in the Declaration of Independence.

The Moral and Spiritual Characteristics of Democracy

These characteristics are particularly capable of motivating the irrational impulses of the individual, hence of determining, in a psychological sense, its overall extent of fulfillment or frustration. Through its moral and spiritual principles Democracy takes into account and makes allowances for various circumstances which involve the interacting sociopolitical forces of *emotional* substance. In spite of the obvious primary role of rationality in decision-making processes, an extremely rational society would appear to be incompatible with

Democracy. Most likely, it would result in an over-organized and over-bureau-
cratic society with state agents being, for all practical purposes, nothing but
robots in their function of enforcing laws and regulations. Orwell's *1984* projects
a stark image of such a society. Individual and group attitudes cannot be
democratically based exclusively on a legalistic foundation, or contractual relations, that is, on the simple notion of only using one's rights and fulfilling one's
obligations. Although it is more difficult to precisely characterize the values of
this category, one may say in a general sense that they are more dynamic, more
functional, more unpredictable than the norms of a narrow legalistic nature and
of a broad constitutional prescription. Thus, their ranks are frequently modified.
Many of them can rightfully be listed as intangible or unknown characteristics of
Democracy, preferably suitable to the unit containing the unknown elements of
Democracy in the earlier suggested possible equation related to the proposed
basis for the definition of that phenomenon. The discussion of two characteristics, namely, *human relations* and *individualism*, will suffice to illustrate the
illusiveness of the moral and spiritual elements in these relationships.

Human Relations refer to a Democratic concept which takes a position of
unlimited optimism in regard to man's nature. Man is considered a rational being
capable of *independent* use of his powers of reason and judgment and of
applying these abilities to sound decision-making in regard to the betterment of
his own life. According to the concept of Democracy, this fundamental rationality is the basis for most human relations. This supposition implies quite
idealistically a *moral* aspect: that man, in default of rules and regulations, will
voluntarily limit his natural impulse for freedom in order to promote freedom of
development and expression for others. Conversely (and more realistically), man
also, as a measure of self-protection, limits himself in order to elicit respect for
moderation from other men as they express themselves. But whatever the case,
Democracy involves numerous kinds of voluntary compromises supposedly
drawn from man's ability to reason but tied to the expression of his *emotionally*
motivated attitudes.

Individualism is usually regarded as a characteristic belonging to a very highly
developed and sophisticated form of Democracy. It attributes an enormous value
to, and reliance on, the human being. A layman could easily become confused
when categorizing Individualism because it is associated not only with Democracy (in its highest form) but, in a philosophical sense, it is the primary motive
of Anarchism and also of Karl Marx's second stage of Communism. The relation
between these three ideological types is so close, in their fully evolved form, in
regard to Individualism, that if either Anarchism or fully developed Marxian
Communism, or both, could become a reality, they might be regarded as very
high forms of Democracy.

The fundamental principle of Individualism is that each man in a given society has more intrinsic value than the entire state institution with all of its hierarchical machinery. Thus, in the state organization, he deserves *all* the respect. The individual was the most important element in the philosophy of the ancient Greek Stoics of Jewish Monotheism—which proclaims that all men are children of God, and hence asserts that man has divine value—and lastly, he is the cornerstone of Christianity. In the eyes of individualists, government and the institution of the state should be regarded only as a means to maintain order *in service* of man but never as a goal or achievement of high authority. Once the state is conceived as a separate entity, merely as an instrument for man's convenience, society and the individual are regarded as entirely different phenomena which can never be identical to each other or to the state. The state's function is to serve man; it can by no means impose itself on either the individual or society. In theory, Individualism assumes that the human element has top priority in the organization of national states. The priorities are: a) the individual, asserted as the most important element; therefore, the state machinery should be ready to serve *him* in an exclusive manner; b) society, for the reason that it is composed of individuals; c) the state institution with its governmental machinery is rated at the bottom because, theoretically speaking, its *raison d'être* is uniquely singular: to serve first the individual and then society which is composed of individuals.

In summary then, one may suggest that Democracy is primarily an *attitude* which, in turn, is a function of known and unknown elements placed within groups of rational, emotional, legal-constitutional, and moral-spiritual characteristics. Thus, the above-mentioned proposed set of relationships—attempting to contribute to a modern, up-to-date, and comprehensive foundation for the definition of Democracy as *perceived* by the individual today—may be expressed as follows:

$$\text{Democratic Attitude} = F \left\{ (K[(r,e), (l,m)] , U[(r,e), (l,m)]) \right\}$$

with K and U being used as the Known and Unknown characteristics of Democracy, while r, e, l, and m reflect the factors of rationality, emotion, legal-constitutional aspects, and the moral-spiritual values respectively; or one could attempt to tie the relationships more closely together by the use of the following equation:

$$\text{D.A.} = F \left\{ (K[(r,e), (l,m)] + U[(r,e), (l,m)]) \right\}$$

However, these relationships might appear suitable only to the most modern (one might even say "futuristic") meaning of the democratic concept. If applied universally, this equation would be likely to present a certain insufficiency (as a matter of fact, it would present, conversely, the very same kind of shortcoming as the one regarding the simple "input-influence" conception) when it comes to communities which are still adhering to the ancient Greek idea of the democratic phenomenon, namely, those which are still involved in a struggle for the organization of an effective "self-government."

In the sociopolitically developed world the concept of self-government (with substantial "input-influence" by the individual on the group decision-making process) has achieved, for many, a high degree of sophistication and it is regarded as a mere routine, with a role performed periodically (during elections) by the individual, who in many instances does not worry about petty details of political safeguards. In fact, he takes them "for granted." This state of affairs may account (at least in part) for the previously mentioned "apathetic" electoral attitudes in modern democratic societies.[1]

On the other hand, the populations of newly emerging or still developing states are substantially below this level of political routinization. They still appear to be primarily concerned with the modes of selection of aspects and practices of self-government, which are well established as routine political forms in the developed world, or with the successful and advantageous adaptation of these aspects to their particular cultural-political milieu. In other words, their level of social evolution has not yet achieved the degree of political relaxation which one can observe, in regard to the individual, in Western Europe. Of this the Fourth Republic of France and the current democracies of Italy, Belgium, Switzerland, Holland, Denmark, are, with some variations, good examples. In contrast, this fact accounts well for the individual voter's tense political interest, his determined drive for participation in government, and his vociferously expressed arguments relating to political affairs in the newly emerged or still developing states. Judging from the intensity of popular interest in various political achievements, it appears that one can formulate a hypothesis showing a negative correlation (compared to the developed world) between a given country's degree of social evolution and the drive for political participation by its individual citizens. It seems thus: the more intensive and enthusiastically violent the drive for political participation is in a given country, the lower is that country's degree of social evolution. In such cases, the social evolution is still primarily concerned with its *political* aspects.[2]

Thus, a genuinely comprehensive, and also realistic, attempt at a definition of Democracy should take into account all types and degrees of social aspiration, as

---

[1] J.-Lucien Radel, "A Developmental Perspective for Socio-Political Evolution," in *Administrative Science Review*, Vol. VII, March–June, Dacca/Bangladesh (1973).
[2] *Ibid.*

currently observable in the various parts of the world. For this reason, one must still take into consideration, *in part,* the "input-influence" concept until such an ideal and probably distant time when the degree of social evolution in all parts of the world reaches the stage of social organization in which its political aspects would be seen only as a mere routine in a well secured and flawless performance.

In reality, however, it would be difficult to blend the two proposed concepts into a single set of relations because of the various degrees of social evolution. It would, indeed, be obvious that the greater the development of a given community, the less consideration should be attached to the "input-influence" conception, and vice versa. Nevertheless, with that explicit caution, we may present, in this regard, the following equation:

$$I + F \left\{ (K[(r,e), (l,m)] + U[(r,e), (l,m)]) \right\} = D$$

where I and D would stand for Input-influence by the individual and Democracy, respectively.

The Idea of Autocracy

The above theoretical and elementary characteristics of Democracy may be regarded, from a methodological point of view, as the necessary foundation on which to contrast the important principles of Modern Totalitarian Dictatorship. Since the latter represent only a quite narrow idea of Autocracy in general, a similar treatment of that phenomenon should increase the precision of the comparisons and thus provide a more lucid analysis. This kind of systematization is all the more necessary because Autocracy has many political varieties, easily changed by influences reflecting the social, economic, political, and emotional circumstances of the times. Indeed, many political regimes have been based on Autocracy, but only one of these is the Modern Totalitarian Dictatorship. It is the latest and most sophisticated expression of the idea of Autocracy.

The notion of absolute Autocracy has passed through at least five distinct and major stages of development. One can classify them as follows: a) Tyrannic Stage; b) Theocratic Stage; c) Royal Autocratic Stage; d) Traditional Authoritarian Stage; e) Stage of Modern Totalitarian Dictatorship.

The fifth stage in the evolution of absolute Autocracy represents the *focal point* of this entire work. The sociopolitical and economic forms known as Fascism, National Socialism, and the contemporary application of Marxian Communism are manifestations of that stage. However, a brief introduction to the first four stages are, nevertheless, necessary in order to provide the reader with background and perspective for our discussion of the fifth stage.

The Tyrannic Stage has been considered by man long before the recording of history. Greek antiquity produced a variety of definitions of Tyranny which express different aspects of the concept. Aristotle's understanding of the matter was quite simple. He thought of Tyranny as a *degeneration* of earlier monarchy. It is easy to understand why the ancient tyrant had to be, in more than one sense, similar to both a monarch and a modern dictator. However, the early Tyrannic regimes should not be confused with recent dictatorships or monarchial forms of government. Tyranny is a product of a substantially more primitive stage of sociopolitical development. For instance, Tyrannic systems, although containing many variations, were all closely linked to the cult of the tyrant. Under Tyrannic rule no development whatsoever of social and economic systems occurred. Finally, Tyrannic rule was not based on, or connected in any way with, an ideology, whether of political, social, or other nature.

The Theocratic Stage is distinct from other sociopolitical forms of government by the fact that among other characteristics the top national ecclesiastic leader is, at the same time, the absolute political ruler. The implication underlying this combined authority is that the ruler has received both the ecclesiastic and political rights directly from a divine, supernatural force. This system evidences a complete fusion between the nation's spiritual beliefs (religion), on the one hand, and the political process (government), on the other. Until recently, that is, for some time after World War II, Tibet represented a country with a Theocratic system of government.

The Royal Autocratic Stage is mainly characterized by the existence of a Monarch who, as a supreme ruler, governs the state and the people with responsibility to no one. The Royal Autocratic Stage may be divided into two different forms, or sub-stages of evolution. The boundary between these two sub-stages is represented by the range of the monarch's power. Royal rule during the Middle Ages may be viewed as a typical illustration of the first sub-stage. Later, France under Louis XIV exhibited the most sophisticated form of Royal Autocracy. The entire political system of the country was then very clearly encapsulated in his famous statement: "L'Etat, c'est moi" (I am the state).

Although being essentially a political system of the medieval era, this earlier form of Royal Autocracy has survived to quite modern times. For instance, the system of government of Imperial Russia, until 1906, clearly bears witness to this. The Czar had unlimited and arbitrary political power over the affairs of the state and of the people.

The second, somewhat more recent form of the Royal Autocratic system, is basically the same and is exemplified by Imperial Russia between the years 1906 and 1917. This form is characterized by the fact that although the Monarch still had the ultimate, unlimited, arbitrary political power in the decision-making process, he, in a way, gradually began to share a portion of this power with the upper echelons of the aristocracy. Whether in its first or second form, the final decision-making power in a Royal Autocratic regime was quite securely concentrated in the hands of the Monarch.

The Traditional Authoritarian Stage would demonstrate, if one agrees with the Aristotelian definition of Tyranny, that the Traditional Authoritarian systems are, in essence, simultaneously a derivation of both forms of the earlier Royal Autocratic Stage. They are, indeed, as typical of modern times as is Democracy, and may rightfully be regarded as a transition between the Royal Autocracy and the concept of the ModernTotalitarian Dictatorship.

Briefly, the most distinguishing characteristics of the Traditional Authoritarian systems are: (1) a number of privileged groups share political power; (2) one can always detect a general economic underdevelopment and a social backwardness; (3) a very essential element in the state administrative machinery is a large, sluggish bureaucracy.

The sociopolitical system of Traditional Authoritarianism may also be viewed as a product of a *compromise* reached through the long political evolution of both the strong conservative forces characterizing earlier eras of human organization, forces always attempting to preserve the status quo, and the emerging liberal ideas attempting to bring about changes leading to a democratic organization of society. Therefore, if one accepts these premises, one can further state that Traditional Authoritarianism also represents the last attempt made to preserve the old regime of Royal Autocracy. Precisely because of this, the fourth stage of the development of Absolute Autocracy may be regarded as a *transition* between the Royal Autocratic Stage and the Stage of Modern Totalitarian Dictatorship.

The most representative examples of such a transitional sociopolitical system are the kingdom of Prussia, the German Empire of 1871, the former Austro-Hungarian Empire, and a number of contemporary Arab states.

The Stage of Modern Totalitarian Dictatorship possesses some characteristics identical, or similar, to those of the Royal Autocratic Stage and the Traditional Authoritarian systems; they are similar to the third and fourth stages of the evolution of the idea of Absolute Autocracy. This fact again justifies the view that the Traditional Authoritarian systems are, in general, a transition between Royal Autocracy and Modern Totalitarian Dictatorship.

However, in spite of these similarities, the fifth stage features an entirely new, till then unknown within the authoritarian framework, phenomenon which has become one of its very fundamental characteristics, a distinction which can be found in none of the four preceding stages of development. This phenomenon does not originate with aristocratic or other privileged groups but is purely and simply a product of a fundamental change in the socioeconomic order. This dynamic characteristic is the massive rise of *Industry*. Of course, *Industrialization,* under the regimes of Modern Totalitarian Dictatorship, is planned, and through one form or another, always controlled by the government.

Thus, Industrialization makes the main difference between the Modern Totalitarian Dictatorship, on the one hand, and the political systems of Royal Autocracy and Traditional Authoritarianism, on the other. Therefore, one might rightfully argue that Modern Totalitarian Dictatorship represents one of various culminating forms in the contemporary evolution of society.

The above explanations make it possible to narrow down the comparison; indeed, one might narrow the study by systematizing it in a dichotomous form. First, it may be useful to propose a more detailed comparison between the fourth and the fifth stages of the evolution of the idea of Absolute Autocracy, that is, a comparison concentrating on the Traditional Authoritarian systems, on the one hand, and the Modern Totalitarian Dictatorship, on the other. Second, one could then take up the more accurately defined concept of Totalitarian Dictatorship and compare it with the known portions of the elements of Democracy.

In order to obtain clarity in this matter, the first proposed comparison may be carried out by illustrations of pertinent cases. One might take a country that has developed one of the more refined and sophisticated sociopolitical forms representing the Traditional Authoritarian Stage and compare it with a state reflecting in a similar fashion the stage of Modern Totalitarian Dictatorship. In other words, one may simply take the Austro-Hungarian Empire and compare some of its major features with their respective counterparts in National Socialist Germany.

Such fundamental characteristics of Austro-Hungarian absolutism and of the National Socialist Dictatorship may be ascertained in the following ways:

1. The next to last Emperor of Austria-Hungary, Franz Josef, was believed to rule by divine right. He was recognized and fully accepted by the empire's population as superior in every respect, invested with an unquestionable authority and above all a *right* to rule. These factors point out the transitional nature of the Traditional Authoritarian Stage. The Austro-Hungarian Empire clearly belong in the Fourth Stage, because it retained vestiges of the Royal Autocratic Stage (the *divine right of kings*), and at the same time developed innovations which lead to many of the pertinent characteristics of Modern Totalitarian Dictatorship.

The last Chancellor of the Weimar Republic, Adolf Hitler—the ruler-leader of National Socialist Germany—on the other hand was *not* regarded by his people as possessing a divine, or any other special kind of, right different from their own. On the contrary, he was recognized by the people as a typical product of the German "grass-roots" environment. Nevertheless, in spite of this association, he enjoyed the same type of unquestionable authority as the former head of the Empire. Therefore, his decisions were always regarded as in every respect superior to those of any other authority or political group.

2. The supreme ruler of the Austro-Hungarian Empire relied, while wielding power, on a series of traditional and legal concepts which made him a fully *legitimate* ruler. First of all, the system featured royal succession through heredity as a legal right. This feature alone provided the Emperor with total legitimacy.

In contrast to this aspect of the Empire, one may observe and conclude that the National Socialist form of Modern Totalitarian Dictatorship contained within itself a substantial *illegitimate* aspect. This illegitimacy may have stemmed from the fact that National Socialism was in reality nothing but the product of a revolution—peacefully conducted in obtaining office, but still a revolution and mainly so in respect to the abrupt, radical sociopolitical change the regime brought about regarding *past* concepts of legitimate government. Therefore, National Socialism could not and did not provide claims for the hereditary succession of the ruler. In this respect, the regime may be looked upon as basically different from Theocracy and Royal Autocracy, as well as the Traditional Authoritarian Stage.

3. The Austro-Hungarian political system was also characterized by the *sharing* of governmental power, or more precisely, by a combination of at least two factions within the supreme authority when it was a question of practical ruling functions; it was a combination of authority between the Emperor, on the one hand, and the dual Austrian and Hungarian aristocracies, on the other. By virtue of this combined authority, the concept of a *ruling elite* was fully developed, an elite regarded unquestionably by the masses as a ruling class simply *destined* to rule. Therefore, it seems obvious that the system featured a strict and distinct separation between the ruling class and the masses. The system also featured a distinct element of a *heavily inflated* bureaucracy. The size of this bureaucracy had a natural tendency toward ever-increasing numbers for reasons related to either opportunistic endeavors by innumerable professional climbers, or the determined desire of the still quite small upper-middle class to achieve governing status and prestige. The former always supplied a large number of people flowing from all classes as qualified candidates for state administrative positions, while the latter was naturally regulated by the sociological *Law of Imitation,* which then affected the traditional social class stratification in the country. This law, related to the interaction of social strata, assumes that all layers of society are divided and categorized in groups, or classes, whose socioeconomic status can be used to determine the differences among them. These differences are in turn measurable

(through an analysis of the groups' interaction) in the sense of ascertaining the groups' individual, social, and economic "power." Further,

. . .the law implies that each less powerful social class would have the instinctive drive to "imitate" both rationally and instinctively, but uniformly (through its particular mode of group behavior reflecting the limitations of their relative power), the attitudes of the immediately more powerful class in the hierarchy; thus, constantly having the subconsciously felt goal of achieving eventually the status of the most powerful class and in the process assimilating for itself that class' modes of attitude. However, while basing oneself on these premises, one could also observe that not all of the superior class actions are practically "imitable" by the inferior groups. . .[3]

The National Socialist regime in Germany featured no distinct social class separation between the ruling and the ruled. In fact, such class division was formally nonexistent. On the contrary, National Socialism continuously featured a *personification* and *identification* of the masses of the German people with their leader. For instance, while Hitler's actions were all taken formally in the name of the people, they were always made in a manner emphasizing a total union between masses and leader. However, this is not to imply that the National Socialist regime was not based on the concept of elite rule. It was, indeed, a rule of the elite, but an elite continuously identifying itself with the people. As a general rule, none of the men in authority (no matter how high or how low their office in the hierarchy) was selected and appointed to his administrative position because of considerations of hereditary, or aristocratic, or other special class origin. A well-established trend in the selection was, indeed, personal merit and qualifications.

4. In the Austro-Hungarian Empire hardly anyone objected to the right of both the Emperor and the aristocratic class to rule. While objections periodically did exist, they were motivated by the drive for *national* self-determination and self-government by the multiplicity of different national-ethnic groups of the Empire; the groups wanted to break away and live apart from Austria-Hungary, but did *not* question or doubt the right of the Emperor and the aristocratic class to rule. This acceptance of the ruler was brought about and was constantly maintained during the *early* phases of the Empire's life because of the solidifying role of legitimacy based on divine right to rule and hereditary succession.

Under National Socialism, however, the most important factual difference from the above was the existence and the functioning of an *opposition* to the

---

[3]J.-Lucien Radel, "A European Perspective on the Theory of American Racism," in *Conflict and Crisis in American Politics* (Wm. C. Spragens and R.W. Russell, eds.), Chapter V, Dubuque (1970).

regime. Regardless of people's criticism of the internal policy of the Third Reich—a criticism which today normally exists in any kind of sociopolitical organization—one may observe and rightfully conclude that under National Socialism the lack of legitimacy was in the final analysis one of the major causes of this opposition. One can also add, as a probable psychological reason, the fact that the leader of National Socialist Germany was regarded as and claimed to be one of the people with no special or privileged origin. Therefore, a certain degree of *insecurity* of the regime was easily observable. Consequently, in order to strengthen his position, the leader (once personified theoretically with the masses) constantly attempted, through his administrative organs and law-enforcement agencies, to penetrate into the people's mind and the individual man's soul. In these attempts, achieved through the creation of special laws and other regulations, the government punished the individuals *not* necessarily for what they had done, but rather for what they *might* have done if they had the opportunity to do it. This same tendency, quite a bit more strongly emphasized, could also be found in the functioning of Marxian Communism as illustrated by its application in the Soviet Union. This also explains quite clearly (in spite of some contrary conclusions reached and publicized by some Western governmental agencies and newspapers) the frequently occurring periods of relaxation promoted on various occasions by the party and state of the U.S.S.R. The deeds and tendencies of the masses are on such occasions carefully watched and evaluated. Punishment of individuals for unacceptable activities shown during such periods may be, in rare cases, imposed at that point; but as a general rule they follow at a later time, the pretext or the alleged offence often being quite different. This particular practice makes both the National Socialist and the Soviet Union's regimes *totalitarian* in the modern sense of this word.

5. Another major characteristic of Austro-Hungarian absolutism was the Empire's *pseudo-parliamentarism.* The parliamentary form *was* present in Austria-Hungary, but only in appearance. Factually, it had no real or practical significance.

Nothing of this kind was to any significant degree exhibited under the National Socialist form of Modern Totalitarian Dictatorship. One could safely say, though, that such a phenomenon appeared in a more practical level in its *Fascist* form in Italy (prior to 1938).[4]

6. In the Austro-Hungarian Empire, the Emperor and the dual aristocracy

---

[4]In 1943 Mussolini was stripped of his power through a decision at a meeting of the Grand Council of Fascism which he himself chaired. This action was taken on the basis of a simple majority vote following accusations and defense speeches on the proposed motion. Mussolini lost by a very narrow margin and submitted to the decision.

used the functions of the government to serve their own interests by attempting constantly to preserve the traditional political, social, and economic values and aims of the old established status quo.

In this regard, the National Socialist regime of Germany also appeared as quite different. It was indeed a very dynamic regime; it exhibited a dynamism aimed at a radical change in the old traditions, an abrupt departure from previous rulers' attempts to preserve or promote their own interests by tying them to the old sociopolitical and economic status quo. While ruling the country, the leader himself was not predominantly concerned with his own interests. Instead, in his own way, he desired to work for and serve the people as such, *not* selected individual interests, but *the nation* as a single *organic* unit.

7. Finally, one can generalize and rightfully state that the entire sociopolitical and economic system of the Austro-Hungarian Empire functioned on the basis of pure rationality. The political actions were all carefully measured and no political emotionalism was ever recorded as having influenced the ruling classes.

While comparing this last, but not necessarily least important, characteristic of the Austro-Hungarian system with the National Socialist regime of Germany, one can easily detect one of the most drastic differences between the two. National Socialist rule was characterized by a substantial lack of rationalism. Indeed, it was irrational, predominantly emotional, and very *sentimental* in relation to the affairs of what concerned the German nation. This condition was, however, perfectly in step with the fundamentals of the National Socialist ideology, totally Germanic in its essence, drawing upon the ideas of German Romanticists who reflected the eighteenth and nineteenth-century philosophic sentimentalism of the region.

In concluding this type of comparison, one may also add—in relation to the legitimate nature of the Austro-Hungarian system—that because of the National Socialist realization and fear of illegitimacy, leading as a consequence to the insecurity of the regime, the leaders of the Third Reich were constantly endeavoring to discover a formula and a theoretical explanation which could justify the regime's and their own "legitimacy."

Within the framework of the second proposed comparison, that is, the comparison between Democracy on the one hand and the totalitarian sociopolitical ideas and concepts on the other, one may proceed by looking at this comparison from a dual perspective. This dual categorization is needed in order to maintain the systematization of the work in the sense of avoiding possible intermixture of characteristics of different essence and values. Therefore, the proposed division will be the following:

First, a broad comparison related to the concepts reflecting their *general characteristics;* second, a comparison between the values related to their *legal and constitutional nature.*

In terms of the first comparison, one might begin by stating that Democracy is characterized by its relatively optimistic view of man's nature. On the other hand, it seems that Totalitarianism is characterized by a strong pessimistic attitude in relation to the nature of man. For instance, supporters of totalitarian ideas believe that man does not, in most cases, act on rational grounds. They maintain that, in general, due to factors of emotion and personality, he is not master of his own actions, thus he cannot control them. Therefore, he must be led or, in some way, have his course of action illuminated by what is conceived to be a group of "better" men. Therefore, this group of better men connotes a *minority* rule based on the premise of the alleged higher quality of the elite group.

Here one may pose a question in relation to the U.S.S.R. The Communist regime is now generally viewed as a component part of Modern Totalitarian Dictatorship; therefore, it must be pessimistic as far as man's nature is concerned. The Marxian theory, however, upon which rest the foundations of Communism, believes otherwise. Karl Marx, in his earlier writings, like Jean-Jacques Rousseau, made a substantial point in showing his conviction that man is good by nature. Therefore, just as Democracy expresses its strong faith in man's own ability to reason in directing his own destiny, Marx too relied on man's natural goodness. He was fully convinced that man is quite capable of directing his own future in a rational manner. As a result, one may argue that Marxian Communism would not fit within this characteristic of Modern Totalitarian Dictatorship.

A complete study of *contemporary* Communism, however, based on the application of the Marxian Theory (particularly in the U.S.S.R. and China), will definitely show that so far the *practice* has varied substantially from its basic theoretical directives. In brief, the actual functioning in that case—due to the indefinite extension of the duration of the first Marxist stage of Communism, with its pertinent characteristics—is quite different from the theoretical *ought* question ("what it ought to be"). This functioning openly exhibits several factors, enough in number—and sufficiently tangible in substance—to categorize contemporary, applied Communism as an inseparable part of Modern Totalitarian Dictatorship. Indeed, there is evidence of activities whose essence indicates that the present Communist regimes in the world are basically pessimistic concerning man's nature.

Democracy is also characterized, to a varying degree, as being *individualistic*. Idealistically it accords full respect to man as an individual, who is placed above society and above the state institution. In other words, he is regarded as more important than either. Totalitarianism, on the other hand, taken in whatever form, is always *collectivistic*. This collectivism can be expressed in various degrees from one regime to another, or even within one single sociopolitical order. Its variants are a function of the internal arrangement of the regime according to the extent to which collectivism is enforced. Totalitarianism finds one of its major expressions in this concept of collectivism because it looks upon the idea of individual freedom, the reliance on the individual and his decisions, as dangerous to the state institution. The individual is more efficiently controlled under a system of collectivism.

Democracy is based on the *Instrumental Theory of the State.* This theoretical concept, adopted by political scientists from sociology, regards the institution of the state—with all its subdivisions, such as complicated administrative apparatus and agencies—as nothing more than an instrument, an instrument whose sole "raison d'être" is service to the individual.

Totalitarianism, however, looks upon the institution of the state not as a servant, but as an *ultimate goal.* The individual and society are usually jointly identified with the state. In spite of this identification, however, the totalitarian concept maintains that the state has simultaneously an existence of its own, quite mystical in essence, especially so in the case of National Socialism—a separate existence which is not regarded as a derivation of the people living within the state. Therefore, it forces upon the individual the duty not only to cherish and glorify the state, but also to serve tangibly the interests of the state since these interests are looked upon as being identical to his own.

This reasoning is extremely close to an older (nineteenth-century) theory, known as the *Organic Theory of the State.* This theory maintained that the state institution not only has an existence separate from the people and the nation (if a nation does exist), but also that its life and existence are predetermined from beginning to end. This predetermination also indicates the state's major stages of development. The theory emphasized that, like a living biological organism, any state institution has its moment of *birth,* then proceeds through stages of *growth, development, maturity,* and *decay.* Finally, it arrives at *old age* and eventual *death.* As for the evidence justifying this theory, history has been called upon to help; the rise and fall of empires and civilizations have been advanced as proof.[5]

Democracy recognizes only certain limited means to implement political and social change. By definition, such means must always be of a democratic nature, and their primary concern must *not* be to violate the well-being of the individual. In Democracy this idea is carried out theoretically to the extent that not only anti-democratic but merely non-democratic means cannot be used even when the goal is to improve, to further, or even to secure Democracy.

---

[5]F. W. Coker provides an excellent analysis of the organic theory of the state in *Organistic Theories of the State, 19th Century Interpretations of the State as Organisms or Persons,* New York (1967).

Totalitarianism, on the other hand, recognizes (in an unrestricted fashion) all means which can be beneficial to the state institution—which can serve the state's interests and the state's goals. An emphasis on the *collective* good and welfare of the people is being used as a substitution for the "state institution" in the functioning of contemporary Communism. The individual's well-being is, in these cases, substantially disregarded, to the extent that if a need arises he simply has to be sacrificed for the well-being of the state.

Democracy claims that it permits and encourages all kinds of free discussion as a solution to problems, and also maintains that the people's consent must be secured in the solution of problems. This characteristic of Democracy emerges as crucial because, as was mentioned earlier, one cannot separate without free discussion the ideas which are appropriate for adoption from those which are not. The emergence of a majority and a minority are dependent upon an unrestricted airing of *all* relevant views, regardless of how peculiar these views may be.

Totalitarianism, on the other hand, requests nothing more than total obedience and discipline. The individual simply must obey the state. Discussions are either forbidden or only partly permitted, but when permitted they are led through channels especially prepared and controlled by the state. In a totalitarian sociopolitical and economic order, the leader claims that he himself has found the absolute truth needed for the solution of whatever the country's problems might be. Indeed, he always claims that he has found the best possible solution; and this solution happens to be geared to the best interests of the state and party authority. Any opposition in this respect is regarded as treason.[6]

The concept of private property cannot be looked upon as a finite line, or a separating factor, between Democracy and Totalitarianism. Private property and private initiative are always regarded as a constituent part of Democracy, but they can also exist and be preserved under totalitarian regimes. For instance, they existed in National Socialist Germany and also in Fascist Italy, but both are in principle abolished in the Soviet Union. On the other hand, a state owned or planned economy (on a given national level) is always regarded as a concept of Totalitarianism. However, it can also exist in a Democracy.

In regard to *legal and constitutional values,* Democracy is theoretically based on representative bodies freely elected by majority vote, at all administrative levels, from national to regional, local, and municipal. Totalitarianism also upholds the principle of general elections and elected representation, but it

---

[6]One can find a very illustrative example of this in Trotsky's case. He was charged with developing an opposition faction, a faction of dissent, within the Communist Party of the Soviet Union and was therefore proclaimed a "traitor" to the U.S.S.R

stresses the *institutional* aspect alone. In other words, like Democracy, it also ties itself to "what ought to be" democratically, but differs in that it professes to consider the wishes of the *people* taken as a societal "organic" unit with no mention of the individual. From a *functional* standpoint, the individual is not given the opportunity of proper, free, and secret suffrage. To begin with, the electorate is not confronted with a choice between candidates. They must vote only affirmatively or negatively, that is with a "yes" or a "no," on a single list of candidates contained in a uniform state-party sponsored ticket. To cast a negative vote would mean to assume a large personal risk. As a result, one always observes that a very high percentage of the votes cast are affirmative to the state-party ticket in totalitarian elections. For the same reason, that is, minimizing personal risks, the turnout at the polls is also very high (in the 95th percentage or higher).

Democracy is always based on a dual, or multiple, party system. Under this system, each political party freely competes for power and national office. Totalitarianism, however, allows the existence of only one political party, which is always identified with the state institution. This party does not compete politically for power; because it is in office it does not have to engage functionally in free competition. It possesses the power, and rules the state with an assumption of permanency.

Democracy is always based on a liberal document of some sort—in most known cases, a constitution—whose major theoretical aim is to curb effectively, in varying degree, the power of the state. Totalitarian regimes also have constitutions, but functionally their purpose is not to limit the power of the state but rather to insure that the people serve it better. Through interpretation, or other methods, what is known in Democracy as the individual's constitutional *rights* are transformed in a functional sense to the individual's constitutional *obligations* to the political regime. Therefore, totalitarian constitutions serve a dual purpose: as an effective instrument upon which to base internal and external "democratic" propaganda; and as a means of ensuring individual obligations and servitude to the regime. As an adequate illustration one may cite the constitutional right to vote which is transformed under totalitarianism into an obligation to vote. The high percentage of voter turnout and the high percentage of favorable votes cast for the government are both aimed at ensuring domestic and international popularity for the regime. A similar observation could be made in relation to the *right* to work. It is transformed into an obligation to work, which in the final analysis serves not the individual but the interests of the state. Democracy seems less pretentious and more realistic by not providing for such a right, but, as in the United States, it confines itself theoretically to the more limited concept of an *equal opportunity* to work.

In totalitarian regimes, the constitution is not regarded functionally as the supreme law of the land as it is in Democracy. For some time the constitution of the U.S.S.R. was used by the state authority as nothing more than a *general guide*. This view was even supported by a special theory stating that a constitution is something static in nature, something which does not develop once it has been codified and shelved. In other words, frequent amendment to a constitution involves a slow and arduous procedure before functional implementation can take place. This *static* phenomenon, which is, in essence, designed to regulate *dynamic* society is, it is maintained, nothing but a methodological contradiction. This is justified on the grounds that society is anything but static in nature. Indeed, it is extremely dynamic, changing from day to day and from hour to hour; changing at a much faster pace than the time needed for the adoption of any amendment or other orderly change in the constitution. Therefore, the theory maintains that if one attempts to regulate society by fencing dynamic, progressively evolving group behavior within the concrete meaning of the letter of a static constitution it would mean not only slowing down the process of progress but possibly preventing it. This is accepted as fact because dynamism is defined as denoting progress.

Democracy is always based on the *rule of law,* a theoretical procedure devised to serve primarily the individual; all individuals are considered to be equal under the law. This equality also encompasses the government as a state agency (institution) or in relation to individuals within these institutions and agencies. Totalitarianism, on the other hand, uses the law skillfully in order to serve the interests of the state institution. In this respect, the ruling elite and the leader are privileged to the point of standing practically above the law.

We may now narrow the study to the point of focusing it for the first time directly on the three major types of Modern Totalitarian Dictatorship. Still bearing in mind the above discussion (as a prerequisite to the major topic), one may now begin to broadly consider Fascism, National Socialism, and Marxian Communism—the focal point of this work. At this point they lend themselves gradually to a somewhat more precise treatment as opposed to the *broad* discussion just concluded.

The three major types of Modern Totalitarian Dictatorship may also be systematized comparatively. *First,* one may compare them relative to the concept of man's nature in a psychological, or probably philosophical, sense. *Second,* one may attempt a comparison between the factors reflecting their essentially political nature. *Finally,* their implications related to the economic and social aspects of society might be brought to the surface.

In relation to the Fascist, National Socialist, and Marxian Communist basic views on man's nature, one might in a way isolate the Communists' view. In dealing with society and societal group behavior, the Marxist-Communist understanding of the nature of man seems not only different from, but also contrary to, the views held by Fascism and National Socialism. Marxian Communism looks upon man's nature rather optimistically: man is in essence very good. This point of Marxian Communism basically, and theoretically, appears as quite similar to one very essential (previously mentioned) characteristic of Democracy. The belief in the goodness of man is furthered and somewhat modified by theoretical Marxism in assuming—as did Jean-Jacques Rousseau—that it is only the inadequacy of the current universal social order (offering nothing to man but an evil sociopolitical and economic environment) that is responsible for bringing about all the observable imperfections in society. Man as such bears no guilt. He is very good by nature, but has been at the same time, through generations, wrongly *conditioned* by the environment in which he is forced to live. This point in Marxian Communism strikingly resembles the pre-1789 thought of Jean-Jacques Rousseau (a concept which will become substantially relevant in Part IV). Also based on this reasoning, contemporary Communist regimes claim as most important the need for structural change within capitalist society. There is no need to attempt a direct change in the mentality of capitalist man. When the environment is changed—that is, when the institutional setup is improved according to Marx's prescriptions—then only the basic *goodness of man* will remain and his nature will gradually prevail during the conditioning period needed for man's entry into the second stage of Communism. This stage is characterized by a total societal harmony, complete fulfillment and happiness for the individuals with no state, government, or man-made law to guide them. The assumption is that man's natural goodness is of such a magnitude that once the noxious social order, the inadequate environment, has been removed, and after a suitable period of adjustment, man would need no more guidance or enforcement of any sort.

Fascism and National Socialism, on the other hand, held a contrary point of view. They looked upon man's nature quite pessimistically. Fascism and National Socialism were based on the premise that man possesses a nature characterized by an indefinite number of shortcomings. These basic shortcomings gradually developed evil tendencies in man's basic intentions. Consequently, when one has to deal with great masses of people—when one has to encounter problems stemming from group behavior—one will automatically face nothing but amplified forms of individual evil tendencies. Therefore, only a group of far superior quality—a selected elite among men—should be entrusted with the guidance of, and task to, control the rest of the populace, correcting and leading them toward a noble development.

Because of these two concepts and two opposite points of view (both related to man's nature), one is faced with problems related to two entirely different functional phenomena. The present stage of Communism considers itself (at least in theory) to be a temporary stage. It is only during the first stage of

Communism that it needs a strong party authority and a stable government in order to achieve the transformation of the inadequate social environment. Theoretically, its goal during this stage is limited, namely, to change man's institutional environment in such a way as to let the natural goodness of man prevail. Once man is cleansed of selfishness and human exploitation, characteristic of the capitalist order, he will embark on the road to the second stage of Communism. Then, there will be total individual freedom with no guidance or obstruction from the party or state authority. The transformation during the first stage should consist mainly of the destruction of the bourgeois-capitalistic institutional order which is based on the idea—and has forced the individual to engage in the practice—of exploitation of man by man. Once this is achieved, man, as an individual, will become solely responsible for his actions. He will bring about ideal environmental conditions because of his good nature and origin. Therefore, it is quite clear that theoretically the first stage of Communism serves the role of a correctional institution, a *deconditioning* process, having as its task to cure the ailment (the noxious social order) which makes man evil.

The Rousseauan influence on this portion of the theory of Marxian Communism is obvious. In that sense, one of the major criticisms of Jean-Jacques Rousseau—and of Auguste Blanqui, for that matter— may also be directed at Marxian Communism. This criticism is based on the Rousseauan, and Blanquist, assumption that the individual's perception and awareness of freedom can emerge from a development of dictatorship (characterized by the first stage in Marx and Blanqui), which is constantly stripping, through control by the ruling authority, the sense of freedom from the individual. How can such a sense be expected to develop in man, in a short span of time during the second stage, after his having been psychologically conditioned to feel the opposite?

While in the Communist view, the ruling authority—party and state— (according to the above reasoning) has only a temporary value, Fascism and National Socialism regarded the state institution as a permanent phenomenon. Since in their view man is evil by nature, since he cannot be trusted to strive on his own toward noble development, he must be placed under constant surveillance and total control. Both Fascism and National Socialism maintained that only through the skillful supervision provided by a very highly developed and centralized state institution can man be guided toward his own good and therefore toward his own happiness. Consequently, man should be permanently identified with the state, his own interests presented as identical to those of the latter, and by serving it to the best of his ability he will reach his total self-fulfillment.

The second proposed comparison, still directly related to Fascism, National Socialism, and Marxian Communism, is in reference to their political nature. One might begin by looking at the respective concepts of parliamentarism. Parliamentary institutions seem to appear to a certain degree in all three, with a substantially greater emphasis in contemporary Communism than in National Socialism. The Soviet Union, indeed, has featured elements of parliamentarianism, such as regular and frequent elections and apparent legislative practice, ever since its birth in 1917.

Fascism, on the other hand, although much less pretentious in its adherence to parliamentarism, preserved, at least in theory, the principles of parliamentary practice. As compared to Democracy, the Fascist legislative process was of a more superficial nature. Nevertheless, it remained more genuine in a functional sense than parliamentary practice in Communism. For instance, as noted earlier, Mussolini was stripped of his powers quite peacefully by a majority decision taken during a 1943 summer meeting of the Grand Council of Fascism.

National Socialism, therefore, remains in this respect, the only form of Modern Totalitarian Dictatorship which showed a total disregard for parliamentarism and parliamentary practices. Parliamentary rule was never functionally stressed in National Socialist Germany, and the few elections that took place were arranged primarily for external consumption.

As far as the other political aspects of the three major types of Modern Totalitarian Dictatorship are concerned, it seems that all were held in common.

1. All three maintained a one-party rule, that is, only a single political party was allowed to exist in the country; it served as the basis for the entire regime.

2. In all three, one could easily observe the evident lack of genuine free elections.

3. There is in Communism, and there was in Fascism and National Socialism as well, suppression of the fundamental liberties, that is, freedom of thought and of expression.

4. A special political police force was also a common phenomenon in Fascism and National Socialism, as it is at present in Communism. In practice, it was the state instrument for the suppression of the individual. Consequently, arbitrary arrests and executions with no trials as well as the emergence and constant growth of concentration camps ("communities for people's labor reeducation" in the U.S.S.R.) are evident in contemporary Communist states as they were in National Socialism. Again, Fascism is an exception. There was no evidence of concentration camp activities in Fascist Italy in the sense of activities beyond the occasional group detentions of foreigners of the type which was also in evidence in the Western democracies during World War II (particularly France and the U.S.A.).

The final general comparison that one can make in relation to Fascism, National Socialism, and Communism is one of an economic and social character. In that respect, one may observe the sharpest differences between Communism on the one hand, and National Socialism and Fascism on the other.

The first stage of Communism (as concretized by the regimes in the Soviet Union and China) is based on an almost total *socialist economy*. All means of production belong to the state institution; the state plans and engages directly in the process of production; the state guides and decides on the market distribution of all produced goods; and the state entirely absorbs all profits from production and sales. In spite of frequent periodical publicity given to changes in the Soviet economy, often interpreted by some Western observers to mean a partial introduction of capitalist tenets, it appears that basically the economic foundation of the U.S.S.R. remains the same.

On the other hand, Fascism and National Socialism have shown an entirely different economic emphasis. Fascism and National Socialism retained the capitalist economic structure and principles. The only difference could be found in a certain limitation on these principles, a limitation indicated by the application of broad state supervision over large private economic activities. This supervision, however, took more or less the shape of guidance and not of direct state operation of large private industries and agriculture. As far as the means of production, the planning and the execution of this production, the distribution of goods, and the absorbtion of profits are concerned, they always remained in the hands of private business. Therefore, one might say that these two regimes were based on the principle of a *directed economy*, not on the principle of a socialist economy. As pointed out earlier, a directed economy is *not* necessarily a non-democratic phenomenon.

The state ruling class in Communism is essentially supplied by the proletariat. Indeed, the percentage of participation in the Communist ruling class by descendants of the old bourgeoisie and nobility is extremely small. In general, the bourgeoisie and the nobility, with all of their descendants, were liquidated during, and immediately after, the October, 1917, Bolshevik Revolution. There are, however, a very few exceptions. One might mention in this respect the former commissar for foreign affairs of the U.S.S.R., also at one time the Soviet Union's delegate to the United Nations, Andrei Vishinski. The general attitude of Communism, however, in regard to those classes is essentially one of unlimited hostility.

If one looks upon Fascism and National Socialism from the viewpoint of social class, one is bound to discover not only different but contrary basic premises. In Germany and Italy the ruling class was essentially composed of the bourgeoisie, although not necessarily of the nobility. Indeed, only a few individuals of working-class origin succeeded in reaching important administrative levels. Such exceptions were due to the individual's exemplary efforts of support for each of the regimes in question, not only through slogans and formal adherence but through merit and loyalty. Basically, however, it was the bourgeoisie that occupied the vital administrative offices, and the state institutions were in turn aimed at preserving it as the elite group.

On the other hand, one should mention that, as James Burnham has implied in one of his major works, there was a certain ever-increasing tendency in Fascism and in National Socialism to provide important managerial and statecraft positions for people who had shown, above all, qualifications, ability, and merit. This tendency was, indeed, based not so much on party affiliation or on class distinction as on qualifications and ability. Had these two regimes survived, they probably would have brought about the emergence of a *separate* class of able, *expert directors* supervising state economic functions and managing administrative matters. As Burnham has pointed out, the same trend is observable in Communism and its regime in the U.S.S.R.[7] Thus, an entirely new class might have emerged in time, a class not only identical in each of the three forms of Modern Totalitarian Dictatorship, but also one which would have consequently enjoyed and provided the same, or at least similar professional interests. Its major characteristic would have been ability and expertise. However, while this observation may be true, the pace of the development of such a separate class under Communism appears to be much slower than the speed of this same trend under Fascism and National Socialism.

Prior to our individual analyses of the three major forms of Modern Totalitarian Dictatorship, one should recall a final set of characteristics related to general conditions in society, conditions which in some cases have proven most suitable for the emergence and growth of the various forms of Modern Totalitarian Dictatorship. One may group such basic characteristics in three different categories, namely: characteristics of economic, political, and social nature.

For the emergence and growth of Modern Totalitarian Dictatorship, pre-industrial as well as post-industrial societies (that is, societies evolved to a national economic stage where the industrial process of development has been completed, and the incertitude from the conflicts related to the *industrial revolution* eliminated) could provide the necessary conditions. However, in this respect, Modern Totalitarian Dictatorship manifests differences related to its three different forms. These differences could be, in fact, divided on *functional* grounds into two groups. The first group is related to the emergence and growth of Modern Totalitarian Dictatorship in a pre-industrial society while the second group seems to indicate a suitability for the emergence and growth of Modern Totalitarian Dictatorship in a post-industrial society.

The first group (pertaining to pre-industrial societies) is clearly illustrated—contrary to Marx's prescriptions—by the present Communist states. One should be aware, however, that this pre-industrial suitability of Communism is true only in regard to those countries where Communism emerged and grew as a result of

---

[7]J. Burnham, *The Managerial Revolution*, New York (1941).

natural, spontaneous people's revolutions; those countries are basically two, the Soviet Union and the People's Republic of China. North Vietnam might plausibly be regarded in a similar light, but the situation in Cuba seems much less valid, since the anti-Batistan revolution there appears to have been more of an agrarian-reformist character rather than having a direct ideological goal based on a political theory, or even a doctrine. In any case, this pre-industrial suitability does not apply to the countries of East-Central Europe where most (as a matter of fact, all except Albania) prior to World War II were engaged in a *post-industrial* stage of development. Indeed, Communism was introduced into the East European area not through internal revolutions, but by outside forces; thus, the emergence of Communism was not related to any social and industrial conditions (whether pre- or post-industrial) and had no regard for popular consensus as to acceptance or rejection of a Communist regime.

As mentioned earlier, industrialization is one of the basic features of Modern Totalitarian Dictatorship. Therefore, the primary task, during the initial development of Communist regimes, is to begin bringing about industrialization. As a general rule, all naturally developed Communist revolutions of the above mentioned Soviet, Chinese, and North Vietnamese type have taken place in pre-industrial societies, contrary to the Marxist prescription in regard to the *post-industrial* prerequisite for Communism. Because of this pre-industrial status, the government possessing investment and labor forces superior to the pre-industrial underdeveloped business enterprises, bases the beginning of the industrialization process on a combined state and collective ownership. This seems quite logical because in a pre-industrial society adhering to Modern Totalitarian Dictatorship it is necessary to *bring about* industrialization from scratch. A planned economy is one of the foundations of totalitarian regimes, and in Communism it takes the form of direct *state intervention* through carefully projected short and long-range economic planning for the entire country, including state investment, ownership, and allocation of labor.

The second characteristic grouping, in fact relevant to post-industrial societies, is illustrated not as Marx has predicted, but by the other two forms of Modern Totalitarian Dictatorship: Fascism and National Socialism. Not only the two states which reflected most conspicuously these respective forms (Italy and Germany) but also a number of other regimes of the post-industrial stage of development may be included in that group. In other words, other countries, in addition to Italy and Germany, were inclined, particularly during the 1930s and the 1940s, to adhere to Fascist or National Socialist forms of government in a *spontaneous* fashion. For instance, it was clearly observable in Vichy France that without much German coercion a major part of the French youth organized itself quite enthusiastically along Fascist although not National Socialist, ideas. In addition, one might also consider East-Central Europe, where Czechoslovakia (the most industrially developed country in that area) offered practically no resistance—as other countries of her size and smaller capabilities did after their fall to Germany—against the National Socialist occupation and form of government. Rumania not only emerged spontaneously during the interwar period and throughout World War II as a Fascist-oriented country (attempting to model itself after Mussolini's Italy) but the stronghold of Rumanian Fascism could actually be found in the factories, among the working class.[8]

Industrialization was mentioned earlier as one of the basic economic innovations of the stage of Modern Totalitarian Dictatorship. Thus, industrialization was also strongly emphasized by both Fascism and National Socialism. Both regimes, however, contrary to Communism, have found the *post*-industrial stage of development as the most suitable grounds for their emergence and growth. Therefore, their task was *not* to bring about but to channel and further this already existing development. This task was undertaken with an eye toward serving the interests of the nation generally, and of the state institution in particular. Finding industry already in existence, with substantial private capital investment and an abundant supply of labor, the Fascist and National Socialist governments did not need to expand state investments for a state-owned or collective industrialization. However, because they too shared firmly the totalitarian belief in collectivistic economic development, they felt the need to plan, channel, and guide this development through skilled supervision, although essentially, through preservation of private initiative and capitalistic economic principles.

From a political standpoint, the Modern Totalitarian Dictatorship has demonstrated that it can emerge and grow in pre-democratic and post-democratic societal conditions—post-democratic in the sense of a national political stage where the process toward accepting Democracy as a form of government has been completed, and the political incertitude from people's struggle against the earlier established authocratic ruling tradition, eliminated. Either of these conditions *appears to be a suitable soil for its emergence and growth.* This means that it can gain a stronghold in countries which have not yet reached the stage of democratic-bourgeois regimes as well as in countries which already have achieved this stage of political development.

Again a distinction may be made between the three major forms of Modern Totalitarian Dictatorship as to their suitability or applicability in pre- or post-democratic societies. In this respect, they may again be divided into two separate groups: Communism; and Fascism and National Socialism.

---

[8]As an example one may cite the Malaxa Ammunition Factory from where the workers exported Fascist ideas to other parts and social classes of the country.

It appears that Communism could go well with and develop naturally in societies in the *pre*-democratic political stage of development. Although Marxian theory predicts Communist revolutions only among established democratic sociopolitical societies (that is, only amidst post-democratic conditions—conditions where the socioprofessional division between the industrial proletariat on the one hand and the bourgeoisie on the other has been pronounced for some time), experience has shown that, contrary to Marx's predictions and prerequisites, Communist revolutions could *naturally* occur with enthusiastic *popular* support only in pre-democratic societies. Those countries which Marx envisaged as his most suitable models for Communist revolutions (because of their advanced *post*-democratic stage of political development) displayed instead a much stronger tendency toward Fascism and National Socialism. While Germany and Italy are countries which would fit the model of Marx's predictions, they are good illustrations to the contrary.

Contrary again to Marxian predictions, countries which were in the pre-democratic stage of political development provoked violent revolutions that led to the implementation of Communism in a quite natural fashion, that is, with a substantial and enthusiastic popular support. Neither 1917 Imperial Russia, pre-World War II China, nor postwar Vietnam, had an industrial proletariat and a democratic bourgeoisie as distinctive classes in their respective socioeconomic, political, and professional stratification. Therefore, they were in a pre-democratic stage of development. So far no other countries appear to have adopted the Communist form of government internally, by themselves with popular support and an eye toward the use of Marx's theory for their further political development.

Thus, in spite of Marx's predictions regarding the inevitable two prerequisites for Communist revolutions in post-industrial and post-democratic societies, the actual experience has manifestly shown that instead of Communism, the Fascist and the National Socialist forms of Modern Totalitarian Dictatorship are more likely to occur in such relatively advanced societies. The most typical models which support this line of argument would be Italy and Germany between the end of World War I and 1943–45. In contrast to Marxism, it appears quite improbable for a Fascist or a National Socialist form of government to emerge *enthusiastically,* with a substantial popular support, in a country with no preliminary experience in Democracy. Inasmuch as Marx thought of Communism as a theoretical alternative to Democracy (an alternative naturally motivated as a reaction to democratic inefficiency and shortcomings), it seems in fact that Fascism and National Socialism sustained that alternative in a much more realistic and natural fashion. An important distinction should be made here, a distinction between Fascism and National Socialism, on the one hand, and the other kinds of merely (in most cases secondary in terms of their international importance and impact) dictatorial forms of government, on the other. Reference is made to regimes based exclusively on the personal force of a dictator who enjoys very little popular support. This characteristic is blended, in such regimes, with no ideological justifications for the dictator's power. The dictatorship in such a case is neither Fascist nor National Socialist because, if any popular support does exist, it is extremely limited and usually within the country's armed forces alone; on their raw power rests the entire state authority. Such dictatorships could, of course, easily occur under pre-democratic societal conditions, but they are neither Fascist nor National Socialist. There are two basic factors which provide the finite line separating Fascism and National Socialism from ordinary dictatorships. Ordinary dictatorships lack the element of *mass enthusiasm* in support of a leader and they are not identified with a *programmatic ideology*. These two aspects are functionally operative and observable in Fascism and National Socialism. While one might eventually accept the unproven but frequently advanced argument that the Fascist and National Socialist governments had no majority support, nevertheless, it is very difficult to deny that to a substantial degree enthusiastic mass support played an important role in originating and maintaining Fascism and National Socialism. Such support was definitely present among the middle class and those societal groups which considered themselves to be the country's actual, or potential, elite. Thus, the sociopolitical regime in Portugal until 1974, for instance, or the different regimes in South America (with the possible exception of Peron's Argentina) cannot rightfully be regarded either as Fascist or National Socialist, but simply as forms of the ordinary dictatorship model based on raw military force. Classification of Franco's Spain and Peron's first administration in Argentina is quite open to debate because, while attempts were made to follow the Fascist ideological blueprint, neither of them ever developed to the point of sophistication observable in Italy.

In discussing the question of mass enthusiasm characterizing Fascism and National Socialism, one must not neglect to emphasize a generally observable sub-pattern. From past experience it appears that the more radical and violent the Fascist and/or the National Socialist regime becomes, the more popular support it seems to attract. This serves partly to explain why National Socialism in Germany enjoyed much wider popular support than did Fascism in Italy. This sub-pattern of modern Totalitarianism can be explained only on the grounds of an existing effective and operative *charismatic ideology* with a suitable leader strongly contaminating people's emotions. The sub-pattern, however, seems to work in a reverse fashion in the cases of the above-mentioned ordinary secondary dictatorships; that is, the more radical and violent the given dictatorship becomes, the more it loses popular support. This reversal is most likely due to a lack of significant and effective ideology justifying on an emotional basis radicalism and violence. Such dictatorships, compared to Fascism and National Socialism, appear unstable, with frequent changes in leadership. The sociopolitical development in the various republics of South America clearly illustrates this point.

Returning to the relationship between post-democratic societal conditions of life and their suitability for the emergence and growth of Fascism and National Socialism, one should stress one major limitation: long democratic experience and democratic traditions are a natural obstacle to the acceptance of Fascist and/or National Socialist ideologies. In such cases democratic *traditions* have already shaped the processes through which the people are used to solving national problems, even the problems connected with a national emergency. Thus, it seems that countries like Switzerland, Sweden, Norway, Denmark, the Netherlands, and England are simply immune to these two totalitarian ideologies.

Modern Totalitarian Dictatorship may indeed find substantial mass support across the entire spectrum of social stratification: among the poor working class; the middle class and the intelligentsia; and among the wealthy class of industrialists and landowners. Not all of these classes, however, are likely to lend their support to all the three major forms of Modern Totalitarian Dictatorship. In fact, one can also divide these three classes into the same two distinct groups, one of which would most likely support the form of Communism, while the other would more naturally favor Fascism and National Socialism.

It appears that in a given pre-industrial and pre-democratic society, one large portion of the intelligentsia and almost the entire poor working class would offer the least amount of resistance to the emergence of a Communist regime. The October, 1917, Bolshevik Revolution clearly illustrated that amidst the above-mentioned economic and political conditions, even the peasantry (which Marx refused to view as a potential revolutionary force) is likely to support Communism. In this case, however, it is difficult to establish similarity in the behavior (as is usually done by some sources) between the Russian peasantry and the reaction to Communism by the peasant class of East-Central Europe at the close of World War II. The different attitudes taken by the Russian and the East-European peasantry may be accounted for by the fact that the societal conditions in East-Central Europe were then quite different from those of pre-revolutionary Imperial Russia. Indeed, almost all of the East-Central European countries (the only exception being Albania) at the end of World War II were in their post-industrial and post-democratic stages of development, although it is true that in some of the countries neither industry nor especially Democracy was greatly developed. Nevertheless, all of them had some experience with Democracy and had already attained a sufficiently high degree of tradition of private initiative among the peasantry and a desire for preservation of their private property. An additional factor contributing to this difference in attitude may have been East-Central Europe's closer contact with Western European affairs and development, a contrast which succeeded in creating a sociopolitical trend contrary to the traditions in Imperial Russia. As a result, the peasant class of East-Central Europe resisted the introduction of Communism.

On the other hand, Fascism and National Socialism appear both as a post-industrial and post-democratic phenomenon. Therefore, one may expect that they would naturally draw support from different social classes than those which would favor Communism. Indeed, the middle class of the gainfully employed, a small portion of the intelligentsia, many industrialists and landowners, and almost all leading military circles recruited from the last two classes, are likely to present least objections to the emergence of Fascist and/or National Socialist regimes. As mentioned earlier, in a predominantly militaristic atmosphere even a substantial part of the poor working class would support Fascism. In Rumania, for instance, with her particular pre-World War II uncertain attitude toward the U.S.S.R., Fascism was supported by what may have been a majority of industrial workers. As mentioned in a footnote above (p. 30), the workers on the assembly lines of the Malaxa Ammunition Factory were a popular breeding ground for Fascism in that country during the 1930s and throughout the war.

Normally, the gainfully employed in the middle class and a portion of the intelligentsia feel constantly threatened by a certain job insecurity which might endanger their economic status; indeed, they fear that they might be compelled to join, or in some cases, rejoin, the working proletariat. Within unstable democratic regimes any small economic crisis may easily convert this fear into reality. At this point, Fascism and National Socialism may both appear as a remedial alternative to the middle class, as a remedy guaranteeing the preservation of the latter's social and professional status. Both seem to offer to the *non-political* fragment of the middle class more security and protection than does the competitive (in many cases, unchecked) economic-professional struggle characterizing democratic forms of government. In addition, the middle class in Democracy feels in a sense unprivileged vis-à-vis the power of established big business and the industrial magnates. On the other hand, Fascism and National Socialism, through their supervised economy, openly propose to control big business and the activities of the captains of industry. One should, indeed, keep in mind that the actual, face-to-face, supervision of the economy under Fascism and National Socialism is usually done through the services provided by recruited employees, auditors, and administrators, from the middle class; hence, the middle class feels that its importance has been enhanced. Finally, while Communism also opposes private big business and industry, it simultaneously works for the fulfillment of short-range goals ruinous to the status of the middle class: theoretically this is done by increasing the importance of the working proletariat.

The gainfully-employed portions of the middle class are somewhat hesitant to create or join labor unions in the manner of the socially "inferior" class of factory workers. The drive for prestige and status may be one of the reasons for it. The existence of such unions, however, provides the proletariat with group bargaining for minimum wage levels, various fringe benefits, and suitable working conditions. In this case again, Fascism and National Socialism may be quite appealing to the middle class because both propose to control the expansion not only of big business but of the workers' labor unions as well. The enforcement of this double control is again likely to fall functionally into the hands of the middle class, which has always been the chief element in state agencies and governmental bureaucracies in modern times.

In countries with a weak democratic tradition, Fascism and National Socialism could also be very attractive to big business and captains of industry. This stems from the fact that both regimes refuse to abolish private initiative, private property, private business, and private profits, while they at the same time propose to check and control the activities of the workers' trade unions. Indeed, Fascism nationalized these unions by placing them under the control of the special Ministry of Corporations. Fascism and National Socialism aimed at the control of big business and industrial production through the principle of a directed economy (a control functionally exercised by the middle class), but such control may also take place in Democracy; but Democracy is not likely to restrict the activity of the labor unions, and these in turn might change profitable business stability into favoritism toward the working proletariat.

All programs of control within the Fascist and National Socialist states conferred on the middle class central importance; however, much of that class draws its subsistence not only from the governmental institutions of the regime but also from employment provided by big business and industry. Thus, the upper business and industrial class, by virtue of being the employer of a good portion of all salaried personnel, could hope to use its power to exercise its influence and prestige over the middle class, hence, to decrease the severity of the controlling activities of the state.[9]

In conclusion, a few words may also be said regarding the appeal of Fascism and National Socialism to the military class. One of the basic features of both regimes was their strongly expressed favoritism vis-à-vis the armed forces. The

---

[9]F. Thyssen, in *I Paid Hitler,* New York (1941), provides an excellent illustration of the complexity of interests of the industrial class in National Socialist Germany.

major task of these regimes was always to build and maintain strong military establishments on a permanent basis, in time of war as well as in time of peace. The actual experience revealed that the respective regimes achieved substantial success in fulfilling this task. When the armed forces are strengthened and given added prestige, it is quite natural for the military to greatly increase its influence over state matters. The National Socialist principle of permanent mobilization for war even in time of undisturbed peace[10] would, in fact, be very appealing to the nation's top military circles. Such a policy would enormously increase the prestige and influence of the military since everyone would automatically realize that the state and the regime depended on them. This overemphasis on the armed forces in Fascism and National Socialism, however, has one substantial functional drawback. As illustrated by the National Socialist regime in Germany, political disagreements between the top officers' corps and the political leaders of the country constantly poisoned the political decision-making process.[11] Also, the attempts on Hitler's life were decided on and carried out by his own top-ranking military leaders.

---

[10]H. Picker, *Tischgespräche im Führerhauptquartier, 1941–42,* Bonn (1951).
[11]Gen. H. Guderian, *Panzer Leader,* New York (1952).

Part II
Fascism

The only fully developed and sophisticated expression of the doctrine of Fascism involving a popular Fascist movement, a political party, a Fascist state organization—in brief a total Fascist socioeconomic and political structure—was found in Italy beginning with the very radical political change that took place shortly after World War I. This regime lasted from 1922 until late in 1943.

It was Benito Mussolini who first planned, organized, applied, and directed the Fascist movement, later to be transformed into a Fascist state and a Fascist system of government. However, to state that he was at the same time the creator or the inventor of the Fascist ideas would be to grant him more credit than he deserves. At least two other men, Giovanni Gentile and Alfredo Rocco, were regarded by the Fascists themselves as contributors to the ideological foundations of the doctrine. Gentile was claimed to be the theoretician of Fascism—the man who elaborated the Fascist theory in a systematic way. Rocco was in turn regarded as the philosopher of Fascism.

Even though Gentile and Rocco are accepted as respectively, the theoretician and the philosopher of Fascism, and Mussolini as the man who applied the doctrine, the group of ideological contributors is still substantially larger. It includes various partial influences from a number of sources. For instance, Giuseppe Mazzini is one who Mussolini himself claimed to have been the initial and direct influence on which the Italian Fascist movement was based. Another source very often cited by Mussolini was Georges Sorel.

In spite of the impact of the aforementioned sources (whether claimed legitimately, or not), there is no doubt that Mussolini is the central figure of Fascism; this is to say that he was regarded as being more important to the Fascist doctrine than the theoretician Gentile or the philosopher Rocco. Acceptance of this statement, however, implies that one is reversing the actual technique of investigation regarding the process of implementation of political theory; that is, one considers the practice—the functioning of Fascism (as expressed by Mussolini)—before the theory, before its fundamentals. In the traditional realm of political theory this arrangement would not only be unusual but it would appear to be paradoxical. According to the conventional political development of ideas and doctrines, the usual order of three elementary factors must be preserved, their evolving interdependence creating clearly detectable stages leading from a loose theoretical proposition to a practical political achievement:

1. The emergence of similar but unconnected ideas which, through time, gradually begin to establish loose connections among themselves.

2. The consolidation of these same ideas and connections within one single framework—their common theoretical and ideological bound. This bound will represent only the developed stage of the formerly loose connections between the ideas, connections formed because of the similarity of the ideas.

3. The application of this whole set by the ruling body of a political party, coalition of parties, or state, in the form of a given system of government.

In other words, the application and the practical functioning of ideas usually come as a result of previous *theoretical* development leading to a substantial acceptance of these ideas. In Fascism, however, it would appear at first glance that the functioning of this movement and even the establishment of the Fascist state were already well on their way before the theory was produced. Giovanni Gentile's theory was prepared only after the Fascist regime had been born and had already been for some time in existence. Therefore, its theory is based on what was observed of the regime's functioning. The same would hold true for the philosophy of Fascism as elaborated by Alfredo Rocco. Therefore, one may put forth the hypothesis that the roots of Fascism and its spontaneous emergence in Italy were based less on rationality than on emotional outburst. Thus, we may assume that Fascism was not a rational but an emotional phenomenon.

By the same token, since Fascism is alleged to lack a theory or ideology preceding its application (and on which it would be based), traditionally oriented scholars of different shades of opinion have often maintained that Fascism cannot be regarded as an ideology, whether political or otherwise. They have mostly concluded that Fascism must be looked upon merely as a political doctrine, or probably more appropriately, in a psychological context, as a *frame of mind.*

It was only after its spontaneous emergence and application that efforts appear to have been made to place Fascism within an ideological framework. Nevertheless, this, too, did not come about through a natural process of emergence and development of ideas but through a strong appeal, probably ordered by Mussolini himself. In deciding to create a philosophy and theory of Fascism, he apparently had in mind not only the desire to strengthen his regime but also to provide it with a logical justification through a form of political ideology. Thus, it appears to have been Mussolini's prime concern to legitimatize the regime he had created by supporting it with a theory and a doctrine, both of which were said to have been lacking at the beginning.

Giovanni Gentile as well as Alfredo Rocco were both asked by Mussolini to provide an ideological background for Fascism. While developing the theory and the philosophy of the doctrine, they relied for the most part on two major sources:

1. Observation for about two years of the functioning of the regime—more precisely getting acquainted with its basic practical features.

2. What Mussolini himself had to say about Fascism; thus Mussolini's views were included in their investigation of the massive and enthusiastic application of Fascism in Italy.

Mussolini constantly referred to what he called the *Mazzinian concept* as being the regime's foundation, that is, the concept of *Thought and Action.*

He also stressed that the establishment of strong unity among the conflicting social classes was the chief social goal of Fascism. One may interject at this point and say that this goal is a derivation from the Marxian recommendation for a "classless society," arrived at through a "class struggle." Mussolini stressed that the societal unity which the classless society would symbolize can be established, instead, through the strong intermediary services of the state institution. This institution can provide the meeting ground in which the two socioeconomic and political extremes may achieve unity, thus avoiding the painful process of the "class struggle."

One might also propose to look at Fascism for Hegelian overtones in terms of the process involved in the formulation of Hegel's *synthesis;* if one finds such overtones, then the proximity of this particular idea to the Marxian writings would seem to have been strengthened, but the similarity between the two would go only that far. After the proposed initial social and political union is completed within the state of Italy, there is no more provision for such a union to continue and generate again another *thesis* which in turn would bring about a new synthesis; thus the Hegelian triadic principle of development (the "Dialectical Determinism") would be interrupted. As far as the state institution is concerned, it will be eternally preserved within the national culture as an ultimate factor in order to maintain this union with no further dialectic evolution.

The question would then be: Is Fascism Hegelian, since it looks upon the institution of the state as the ultimate goal, the Hegelian "universal absolute," or is it just the beginning of one Hegelian principle which Fascism will abandon as soon as the first major synthesis has been accomplished; that is, does it freeze the process of further evolution and progress—the process of the Hegelian "becoming?"

Neither Mussolini nor Gentile and Rocco ever developed the idea that Fascism is the implementation of Hegelianism. They appear to have been not the least interested in this, never even mentioning it in their writings or public speeches. On the contrary, they tended to present that part of Fascism that looks Hegelian under a different heading, namely the so-called concept of *Thought and Action.*

The preaching of this concept was done by Mazzini, not by Hegel. In Mazzinian views (as well as in Mussolini's), the concept of *Thought and Action* is based on the creation of a union between a given newly born idea and its immediate implementation. It is, in fact, a sort of synthesis consisting of these two elements, but not of a Hegelian type because it stops abruptly as soon as the first union, or to use the Hegelian term, "the first synthesis," is accomplished; that is, it is a synthesis with a limited goal. One might say that in Mazzinian views this concept can be analyzed as follows:

Thought is an institutional concept; it is the idea conceived by the human mind in a rather static fashion.

Action is the heart, the impulse, the putting into practice, the execution and functioning of the idea in a dynamic fashion.

According to Mazzini (and Mussolini), *ideas* are worthless, no matter how good they might be, if they are left to remain ideas. On the other hand, *action* alone is something immature, something childish and adventurous based on emotional impulses rather than on a refined idea. Therefore, according to Giovanni Gentile's theory of Fascism, and also according to Rocco's philosophy, the essence of Fascism can be found precisely in this concept—the concept of *Thought and Action.* Because of Mussolini's and Gentile's claim that Mazzini was the forerunner of Fascism, we must take a closer look at Mazzini's life with an eye toward understanding the environment that conditioned him and shaped his sociopolitical ideas. Some writers on Fascism, who have undertaken such an analysis, are probably right in concluding that Mazzini is in reality not a forerunner of Fascism. The opposite could be difficult to prove—according to some scholars—because it was merely a coincidental fact that certain of his ideas happened to support Mussolini's political goals for Italy at a time when Fascism was allegedly searching for its theoretical justification. A certain number of Italian academicians have called Mazzini a national prophet, not because of the advent of Fascism after World War I (as it has been sometimes interpreted), but because Mazzini's domain of ideas was extremely diverse, embracing such a sphere of sociopolitical activities that any peculiar, unconventional political platform was bound to contain certain Mazzinian principles.

Giuseppe Mazzini (1805–1872) was one of the most active revolutionists during the time of the Italian unification. His thought was optimistic and emotional; his actions, diversified, but both—thought as well as action—were aimed at the heightening of Italian prestige in Europe and at the recognition of the Italian contributions to civilization.

Mazzini's father, Dr. Giacomo Mazzini, had a revolutionary background although his profession was that of a physician. When General Bonaparte, leading the French revolutionary army, invaded Northern Italy and seized Genoa in 1797, Dr. Mazzini feverishly supported the revolution there. The succeeding Ligurian Republic, coming as a result of the revolution in Genoa, offered

Dr. Mazzini a series of responsible positions. In 1816 he was awarded a professorship at the University of Genoa.

Dr. Mazzini was in favor of the total unification of Italy; but at the same time he felt somewhat unhappy about the actual procedure of the unification process. The reason for this discontent was based on regional chauvinistic considerations, namely, that Genoa was not allowed to play a bigger role in the kingdom of Piedmont-Sardinia. He was in agreement with the useful role which this kingdom was playing in the process of Italian unification, but he was also of the opinion that Piedmont-Sardinia was nothing more than an artificial kingdom.

Dr. Mazzini was a firm republican and decidedly anti-clerical, and in this respect he exerted a strong influence on his son, Giuseppe. While maintaining his anti-clericalism throughout most of his life, toward the end he became disappointed with the role of the revolutionaries. Turning his back on them, he found consolation with the Filippini Fathers of a nearby monastic church.

Whether in his role as revolutionary, or later, following his disillusionment with the revolution, Dr. Mazzini was always in favor of helping the lower classes. Throughout his life he sincerely tried to develop some tangible means for a solution to their problems. As a physician he always exhibited charity toward the poor. All of this clearly seems to have made a tangible impact upon the development of his son.

Giuseppe's boyhood was predominantly spent under his mother's supervision; she, in turn, was guided by the advice of her friends. This was especially true in relation to his education. The variety of advice received and accepted by his mother and her attempt to be strict with her son resulted in a tremendous amount of work on Giuseppe's part in relation to his studies. During this period of his life, Giuseppe discovered his father's old collection of newspapers dealing with the eruption and course of the French Revolution of 1789. He read them with great enthusiasm. There for the first time he read of the deeds of men he considered heroes, men such as Lafayette, Mirabeau, Danton, Robespierre, and many others. All this played a significant role in the formation of his character.

Mazzini studied for a while at the Royal College of Genoa. There he learned of, and accepted with vivid enthusiasm, the formation and functioning of secret societies. He was fascinated by the role and the goals of such societies and tried to utilize this new knowledge in his association with other college boys. Things like secret gestures, secret passwords, and various meanings expressed through secrecy and mysticism simply fascinated him. In 1819, at the age of fifteen, he secured admission to the University of Genoa; but a year later, on June 21, 1820, he was arrested for participating in an offensive act against the University Church. Due to his lack of understanding of the then complex dilemma of State-Church relations he was amazed the next day when, upon his release, the University authorities protested to the police against his arrest!

At the tender age of sixteen, during March of 1821, he had his first opportunity to associate with "real" revolutionaries. At that time he demonstrated in Genoa in support of the revolt led by Piedmont through the Carbonari Secret Society. In spite of his being attracted to revolutionary activity, an attraction which was due primarily to his father's influence and organic hatred of any kind of authority, Mazzini possessed in fact an extremely sensitive and emotional character; indeed, he was by nature a very affectionate man, hating the sight of suffering around him and doing everything in his power to relieve it. Having supported the Carbonari revolt of March, 1821, Mazzini managed to secure formal admission into this society, and by 1827 he was already one of its full-fledged members. As such, his first assignment was to recruit new members among the university students in Genoa. While busy with this task, Mazzini also devoted his time to extensive and very diversified reading focusing on two unrelated areas: the French romantic *poetry* and the works of German *philosophers* such as Lessing, Herder, and Kant. This hardly compatible duality in reading interests gave Mazzini the psychological buildup, the stepping-stone for the further diversified development of his thought. Simultaneously, Mazzini had a very dynamic nature: he remained at heart an insurgent, deeply affected by his reading about the French Revolution. Thus, his task of recruiting members was not in harmony with his natural drives and interests. His spontaneous and vigorous realism combined with the mystical and romantic aspects of his personality, the result being his rather unique character.

Mazzini gained much satisfaction from his romantic and philosophical readings. However, his own inactivity and the continuous lack of implementation of the progressive ideas in Italy began to create in him a feeling of frustration and a drive toward violence. Indeed, he often found himself quietly meditating on violence, and suddenly one day he shouted to his friends that *thought* without *action* is useless, especially in the sleepy state in which Italy finds itself. He also added that they must now act, they must sacrifice themselves, suffer martyrdom if need be; but at all costs, start the Revolution.

But the Italian center of the Carbonari was reluctant to act before their chapter in Paris assumed the initiative. This attitude, as promulgated in Carbonari policy, infuriated Mazzini, who argued that it was Italy that had given the Carbonari movement to France and not France to Italy. Therefore, the Italians need not wait for French initiative, but must act soon, and violently, on their own.

Except for a very few short missions assigned to him outside Genoa, Mazzini spent three years in that same chapter of Carbonari; but at the same time, due to the chapter's inactivity, he started to group an inner circle of Carbonari around himself—men who were more inclined toward radicalism and violence. It amounted to a secret elite organization *within* the Carbonari society.

On October 21, 1830, when Mazzini was coming home from a secret meeting with his friends, he was followed (upon a betrayal) by the police and apprehended. Three months and a week later, that is, on January 28, Mazzini was acquitted and released. The release decree, however, was conditional; it contained a provision prohibiting him from living on the seacoast. The rationale of this provision was based on the police discovery that Mazzini's secret meetings were all organized on docked ships. In order to eliminate such meetings, he was ordered to live inland. Mazzini preferred, however, to go into exile than be reduced to inactivity. Thus, his ban and the increased police surveillance of his movements, made him depart for France and establish himself at Marseilles. There he immediately resumed his conspiratory revolutionary activities. During the fall of 1831 he already had in his hands a well-organized, consolidated, and working secret group called *La Giovane Italia* (The Young Italy).

"La Giovane Italia's" task was not to preach the already popular idea of unification of Italy with Rome as its capital, nor was it to preach the Republic. The chief Mazzinian idea was to raise the Italian *national spirit*, and from this, he thought, it would logically follow that the Italians would become aware of their duty and mission to work toward a united Italian Republic. Therefore, the idea was to reform the Italian *mentality* and the essence of the Italian Carbonari character, rather than to aim directly at a conclusive final and clearly defined *political* goal. The idea was to make the Italians fanatic—fanatic to the point of being ready for personal sacrifices and to "suffer martyrdom" for their ideas, as Mazzini had often demanded.

The "Giovane Italia" held that its mission was one which Italy owed to the world; it meant the creation of a state of mind among the Italians—a psychological buildup geared toward an awareness of the importance of that Italian mission to the world. The chief overtone of this idea was that such a mission executed by free Italians was of much greater value than that of the French mission as expressed by the ideas of the French Revolution of 1789.

The membership of the "Giovane Italia" was at first restricted to loyal, young men. Later on Mazzini liberalized this policy by stating that older men could also be admitted providing they were loyal to the cause and still *young in spirit*. During the buildup of Mazzini's organization, the French government expelled the leading Italian exiles from Marseilles as a result of Austrian and Sardinian pressure. Mazzini too was served with an expulsion notice. He accepted it, but merely changed his address and remained a resident of the city of Marseilles.

During this period, the "Giovane Italia" organization published large quantities of clandestine literature. It also published a newspaper, *La Giovane Italia.* However, only six issues of this paper were published during the three years of its existence: three issues in 1832, two issues in 1833, and one issue in 1834. In addition to spreading revolutionary literature, Mazzini worked on a master plan for a general revolution in Italy. According to his plan, the revolution, which was to be led by his beloved secret society, was scheduled for May or June of 1833. In fact, he had by then organized a whole underground army in Italy. Various reports indicated that the time was right for an uprising. In order to ensure the success of this master plan, Mazzini decided to associate himself again with the old Carbonari of Italy and also with the leader of the chapter in Paris, Buonarroti. Probably due to the expansion of the secret activities related to this plan, many of them carried out outside the "Giovane Italia" organization, Mazzini's plans were discovered by the police of Turin, and an extensive investigation followed. Mazzini realized that his revolution had been betrayed. Most of Mazzini's chief commanders in higher revolutionary positions throughout Italy, motivated by the Mazzinian call for *martyrdom,* began to commit suicide instead of surrendering to the police. These acts angered Mazzini; he thought it was better to be arrested than dead. His affectionate nature was stunned by the sight of bloodshed. While proceeding with its investigation, the government discovered not only the preparations made by the "Giovane Italia" and the Carbonari, but also found the entire army was widely infected with Mazzinianism. This was also a major setback for Mazzini; overshadowing the arrest and suicide of his important aides, the discovery of the Mazzinian infiltration of the armed forces enormously increased the significance of the disaster. He had, indeed, worked very hard to accomplish these results. Finally, with a death sentence pending, Mazzini left Marseilles for Geneva, Switzerland. Many of his surviving friends joined him there. From Geneva, Mazzini immediately started to conceive a new plan. He again began to recruit large groups of revolutionaries, but in Geneva he found them to be of mixed national origin. Indeed, there were Italians, Swiss, Poles, Germans, and French. The new plan called for a large-scale invasion of Savoy. This time Mazzini was much more careful in choosing his confidants; moreover, he decided to create a more accomplished, highly secret revolutionary organization. He chose Ramorino to assume the post of commanding general of the entire invasion. Ramorino had an excellent military background, in addition to having graduated from the French Military Academy of St. Cyr. However, the general failed to show up on the day when he was supposed to launch his invasion. Evidence has shown that while he was on a secret mission to Paris he began to spend the organization's finances on the good life, offered by that city, forgetting that it was time to come back and lead his army. Instead of replacing him with someone else, Mazzini decided to postpone the invasion and await Ramorino's return, against the advice of his closest associates. Finally, Ramorino showed up, but the revolutionary momentum was lost and a mass desertion had begun among the soldier-revolutionaries. This was fatal, because the entire plan for the invasion of Savoy was based on the calculation that a general revolution would follow in Genoa. Mazzini had a secret hope that the revolution in Genoa would be aided by the government army which he still thought was infiltrated with the undiscovered remnants of Mazzinian supporters. Nothing like that happened. The actual invasion of Savoy, when it took place, collapsed.

With the failure of this expedition, the "Giovane Italia" ceased to exist. Mazzinian views on the collapse of the enterprise and of his most cherished secret society were summarized in his statement to the effect that, "Only the first period of 'Giovane Italia' is over. In fact, nothing has changed 'La Giovane Italia.' " In order to prove this statement, he formed a new association on the basis of "Giovane Italia" principles but with expanded goals; as a matter of fact, it was to cover the entire continent. This society he called the *Pact of Young Europe.* However, it wasn't as broad a European structure as it claimed to be. Its revolutionary leadership consisted only of Italians. It also had a constitution with very humanitarian goals of the type expressed in Rousseauism (Part IV, pp. 144–151). "The Pact of Young Europe" was in reality not intended to be a center of dynamic activities. It was, rather, an instrument meant to transfer the revolutionary initiative from French into Italian hands; the society was created to compete with French revolutionists, being based on Mazzini's mystical idea about the superiority of the Italian world mission.

In order to continue activities similar to those of the "Giovane Italia," Mazzini founded still another society, *Young Switzerland.* It was meant to be the revolutionary spearhead. However, here he encountered a number of organizational troubles, and this made him join hands in his planning with a German society which was about to launch a militant action. This society, named in the Mazzinian tradition, was called *Young Germany.* However, in this case, too, everything collapsed.

Besides its alleged Mazzinian content, there is another basic feature of Fascism so basic that it sets this doctrine apart from any other sociopolitical program known today. This is the doctrine based on the famous *Corporate Theory* or *Corporate Structure* of the state. As a matter of fact, this does not seem either Mazzinian or Hegelian. However, like the Mazzinian concept of "Thought and Action," the Corporate Theory does not carry any philosophic or abstract overtones; it merely makes very good practical sense for achieving sociopolitical unity, a unity which Mussolini claimed to be the basic goal of Fascism. Such unity, however, can also help to achieve an undisturbed domestic political climate, thus allowing the state to concentrate its efforts on foreign affairs. It tends to eliminate, in a rather efficient manner, internal sociopolitical and economic contradictions so that a full-scale concentration on foreign affairs may be possible.

If one does not care to label the Corporate Theory of Fascism a totalitarian concept, one should nevertheless be aware of one of its two aspects aimed at centralization and efficient, strict government supervision of labor-management relationships. It might be looked upon as an extreme form of a directed economy, similar to those often prevalent within Democracy. However, the form appears to be so extreme that it may be justified in a democracy only when it is in a state of national emergency.

One aspect of the Corporate Theory of Fascism presupposes the total elimination of the small, inefficiently operated and privately organized labor unions. Instead, the institution of the state is called upon to assume the sponsorship of a small number of major nationwide labor unions—one union for each type of occupation or trade. On the other hand, the institution of the state also assumes the sponsorship of a number of management associations, one for each kind of production or trade; thus, one management association is to correspond to each of the workers' labor unions. An executive governmental agency, the Ministry of Corporations, is charged with this dual sponsorship and supervision. In practice, this supervision was expected to work as follows:

1. Through regularly scheduled meetings between organized labor and management, constant contact and exchange of ideas on production and the state of economic affairs in Italy were to take place.

2. In case of dissatisfaction, problems, or friction between one or more branches of labor and the respective organized branch or branches of management, the state institution was to observe carefully the bargaining procedures and the eventual agreement reached on the dispute, but in the case of failure in solving the issue the state was to intervene either as a mediator or as an arbitrator imposing a compulsory settlement.

Efficiency through this arrangement may be obvious, but when the state is by definition continuously present with the threat to intervene through arbitrary measures, it seems that the chances for a freely agreed-to labor-management settlement would not be great. Such a decision will be regarded as an order from the state and might favor, at the state's will, either one of the parties involved. In fact, this arrangement could be useful in a state of national emergency and, particularly, in wartime because it eliminates the causes for disruption of the national economy. For instance, through this arrangement strikes become virtually impossible. However, the Corporate Theory is rather inconceivable for peaceful and normal economic development in a democratic regime.

Some political observers have maintained that the Corporate Theory, along with the rest of the official Fascist ideological claims, has no ideological roots other than a good sense of efficiency as reflected in Mussolini's own thinking. To support such a contention, however, would mean to oversimplify matters. In order to trace and discover the true motivation and background for the Corporate Theory, one should, among other sources, concentrate on the immediate post-1789 revolutionary era in France, a time known for the emergence and the development of *Early French Socialism*. While this development, so important to Europe, will be referred to later in greater detail (see Part IV, the discussion on

Marxian Communism), one fragment may, at this point, be extracted from it—a fragment from the pro-Rousseauist evolutionary branch of Early French Social-ism—because it appears that there lies the beginnings of the Fascist Corporate Theory.

Claude-Henri de Rouvroy, Comte de Saint-Simon, (1760–1825) may be regarded as the originator of the first French syndicalist labor movement. Although fully dealt with by scholars on *Marxism* (in their efforts to trace the origins of the Marxian School of Thought), the doctrine of Saint-Simon also contains an important, although currently quite neglected, line of thought which seems to link the actual structure of *Fascism* directly to the Saint-Simonian propositions, thus providing the contours for the possible ideological connection between Socialism and Fascism. Saint-Simon was a French nobleman, his father being the chronicler of the court of Louis XIV. He even claimed direct descent from Charlemagne; but whatever the validity of this claim, one thing was certain—although an aristocrat by blood, Saint-Simon was a freedom-loving aristocrat. During the American Revolution he fought with General Lafayette against the English and subsequently, upon his return to France, resigned from the army with a high rank. Only then did he undertake his social work. Saint-Simon's ideas were founded on his concern for mankind and his desire to help man increase his power to shape and control his own environment. This broad approach was, however, limited by his obsession with an uncompromising *striving for unity.* At first it was only unity in a physical sense, but it gradually reached the point of making Saint-Simon advocate a social and ideological and in some sense political unity. For instance, while still in America, he began to press the ruler of Mexico to give his consent to a project linking the Atlantic Ocean with the Pacific by a canal. Later on, when Saint-Simon was in Spain, he proposed the building of a canal between the capital city, Madrid, and the sea. These two early proposals throw much light on his frame of mind, i.e., his obsession with unity in a physical sense. Saint-Simon set for himself a quite difficult and complicated program of study. He never completed this program, however, because at the time of his most serious work, the French Revolution broke out. The need to finance further learning prompted him to use the Revolution for his own goals. As a result, in a few years Saint-Simon amassed a small fortune to enable him to "help mankind." Up to that point in his life, Saint-Simon had studied, at the Paris *Ecole Polytechnique,* science, mathe-matics, religion, and philosophy. His general goal for man was to make him powerful enough to master and influence his own environment, and sub-sequently public events; and to do so successfully, man had to undergo a wide variety of personal experiences which would represent an accumulation of knowledge *relevant* to his time and circumstances. This alone would enable him to understand the trend of public events. Thus, his obsession with physical unity had by then transformed itself into a drive for *unity of knowledge.* Indeed, he was thinking vaguely of discovering a principle which would enable mankind to unify all sciences into one; only through such a unified science could man acquire a clear view, and working knowledge, of the future. Primarily, Saint-Simon thought of a *science of morals,* but subsequently he developed the idea that a *science of fine arts* and *natural sciences* could be useful as well. This kind of reasoning made Saint-Simon propose an eventual unification of these three sciences which together would bring about *universal knowledge.* At this point of development, Saint-Simon began to dream of a "New Encyclopedia" with which to express the spirit of the new age.

Fully aware of his aristocratic origin and his advanced education, Saint-Simon suddenly realized that he had been called by destiny to fulfill a new "mission" in the world. In fact, he became convinced that he was one of those great men predestined to set the world on a new course. He believed that humanity stood on the doorstep of a tremendous evolutionary change, the greatest change since the birth of Christ. A firm believer in human progress, Saint-Simon engaged more intensively in the study of philosophy and gradually worked out the idea of a *universal philosophy of history.* Already quite critical of the achievements of the French Revolution, he began to think of progress as a continuing human process involving a *construction* of a civilization (an organic period); a *destruction* of a civilization (a critical period); and a *new construction* (a new organic period), the last-named representing a definite advance over the preceding organic periods.

Saint-Simon focused his work on the Western world because he regarded the East as unworthy of attention due to its lack of progress. In Saint-Simon's view the world had developed through two great historic organic periods: the classical antiquity of Greece and Rome; and Christianity. The latter he viewed as a great advancement over the total achievements of classical antiquity. According to Saint-Simon, a third era of significance was about to open, an area characterized by the advancement of science. Personally, Saint-Simon loved the terms *universal law* and *universal order,* both symbolizing the idea of unity, while simultaneously he despised disorder, civil wars, revolutions, and bloodshed—an attitude quite astonishing in a top-ranking army officer who had earlier volunteered to serve in the French forces in the American Revolution. While Saint-Simon admired Napoleon I for establishing unity and order in Europe, he found occasion to tell him that he must not establish a dynasty through the means of force and conquest.

In Saint-Simon's mind, the proposed universal unity were to be initiated with the creation of a union between France and England—the two most advanced nations in the world. He preached the enormous usefulness of such a federation—France represented the ultimate in ideas and philosophical development, while England offered an unsurpassable talent for industrial organization, to be used toward the material betterment of mankind. Industrial organization would control society because industry creates progress, the means for the subsistence of the masses, and eventually would bring about abundance in everything. The key point in Saint-Simon's advocacy of industry was not based on what theoretical Communism would term "capitalistic oppression of the proletariat," but on the *union* between the industry-owning class and the industry-working class. These two, the factory owners and the factory workers, together represented in Saint-Simon's mind the *producers' class,* a class destined to lead the world toward an advanced state. Thus, contrary to advocating the Marxian idea of a class struggle—which Marx (some time later) stated would bring progress in societal life by implementing Communism—Saint-Simon saw during his time nothing but a unity of interests between capitalist employers and their workers. He directed his energy toward convincing both of these groups of their identical interests. Intending to establish a system which could be adopted and put into practice, he proposed a division of society into a producers' class and a non-producers' (leisure) class. Saint-Simon named the first a *national-industrious* class; the second he referred to as the *anti-national* class. In order to illustrate his point, he insisted that France as a nation would suffer a much greater loss if only three thousand members of the producers' class (the industrious class: industry-owners and industrial workers) would suddenly perish, than if the country were to lose thirty thousand of its leisure-loving nobility, often referred to by him as "legalists-militarists." In the latter case, he supposed that no irreparable harm or political evil would come to the country.

As a further illustration we may point out Saint-Simon's references to the idea and practice of man's political affiliations. He clearly implied the uselessness of the conventional types of political parties and organizations as they were then and are known today. Saint-Simon refused to affiliate himself with either a Conservative or a Liberal party; he would be, though, a very active member of the *parti industriel.* The term "parti industriel" cannot be translated into English as "industrial party." The precise meaning of this term is quite different. By *industriel* Saint-Simon meant something contrary to *political* and *leisure.* Therefore, when one excludes from society the political and the leisure classes, only two major socioprofessional units remain: the active *entrepreneurs* of business whose activity, in turn, receives its full value through labor performed by the proletarian *workers.* Logically then, while bearing in mind the French meaning of the term ("industriel" could also be translated as "industrious") and Saint-Simon's attachment to his concept of unity, one may rightfully state that *industriel* means and is most appropriately translated as the "producers' class," or party, a class consisting jointly of *producer-capitalists* and *producer-factory workers.*

In order to legitimize his plan, Saint-Simon proposed the imposition of taxes on the producers' class. Since at that time only taxpayers enjoyed suffrage, the non-producers' class would automatically find itself excluded from state and legislative matters.

At this point we will revert to the Corporate Theory of Fascism; not only did one aspect of that theory advocate that the trade organizations be a union of interests between the industrial capitalist class and the working proletariat (both representing the producers' class of Italy), but, with some exceptions its second aspect allows only such trade organizations to prepare election slates from among the ranks of their members. Thus, borrowing Saint-Simon's leading idea, Fascism proposed to place in the hands of the producers the legislative function of the nation.[12]

Unlike the egalitarian labor principle of Marxian Communism, Saint-Simon insisted that man's labor should be remunerated not necessarily according to man's needs but according to the labor contribution each man made to the community. Thus, in his envisaged new order, a man would be respected only in proportion to the labor given to his community. This non-Marxian formula automatically provided the conditions for measuring human prestige: since the privilege to perform labor would be vested only in the producers' class, this class would gradually emerge as superior to others because of its unity, competitive efforts, and loyalty to the community. In Fascism all of these elements were encouraged and made to work for the party and the state.

As envisaged by Saint-Simon, this unity within the producers' class (the capitalists plus their workers) seems to evoke quite clearly the idea of labor syndicalism, a syndicalism extended to the point of influencing the governmental decision-making process. Indeed, Saint-Simon advocated the establishment of an administration consisting of three chambers:

1. *A Chamber of Inventions* composed of engineers and artists. Its proposed function was to draw up plans for the benefit of society.

2. *A Chamber of Examination* consisting of scientists. Their task was to examine and approve the plans of the preceding chamber and also to control education.

3. *A Chamber of Deputies* representing the industrialists, the leaders of the producers' class. Their proposed function was to approve and enforce passed legislation.

It seems that the Saint-Simonian type of labor syndicalism was firmly embodied in the Fascist corporate state. Attempts were made to organize the nation's economy on the basis of state-supervised corporations (trade unions)

---

[12]See pp. 89–90 and charts on pp. 92–95.

representing capital and labor. They were to develop jointly, in harmony, and bring only good to the community. Therefore, exactly as Saint-Simon had proposed, under Fascism men had no value unless they contributed through their labor as members of a *professional* group. This again meant that such men of honor must be a part of the producers' class, regardless of whether the individual was a capitalist or a worker.

Being a modern phenomenon, Fascism did update the raw Saint-Simonian ideas. It placed them, for one thing, on a more realistic foundation necessitated by their practical implementation. However, Fascism applied the Corporate Theory in a pessimistic manner. Unlike Saint-Simon, the Fascists proceeded on the premise that the capitalists could not be expected to look upon unity with labor as being in their best interest. In their view the industrial owners would not voluntarily help to promote the interests of their workers, that is, they would not freely form a joint producers' class with the industrial proletariat. They would not willingly create an economic structure diametrically opposed to the current model, one based on a rigid class distinction between capital and labor. Consequently, under the Corporate Theory the Fascist state intervened by sponsoring the creation of nationwide employers' unions (one per trade) with their counterparts (again one per trade), the workers' unions. Their chief economic goal was to control management-labor relations by promoting friendship, a feeling of professional unity, and a general harmony between employers and workers. In fact, this arrangement virtually eliminated strikes, and helped substantially to spark industrial production in Italy in the years between 1925 and 1938.

If one reverses the order of the administrative chambers proposed by Saint-Simon, and then compares his proposition to the actual functioning of the Fascist regime in Italy, one discovers the following similarity:

1. The *Grand Council of Fascism,* the supreme decision-making body of the Fascist Party, may be looked upon as analogous in function to Saint-Simon's third chamber, the Chamber of Deputies. The Grand Council of Fascism had the function of approving passed legislation and enforcing it.

2. The *Monarch's role* could be compared to the function bestowed by Saint-Simon on the Chamber of Examination. With no real power under Fascism, the Italian Monarch watched, examined, and expressed opinions, but always accepted the legislation passed by parliament and approved by the Grand Council of Fascism.

3. The *Senate's* role was marked by its weak ties with the Grand Council of Fascism; just as in Saint-Simon's proposal the Chamber of Inventions would have had no real effect on the functioning of the Chamber of Deputies.

All of Saint-Simon's ideas may be found in his seven major works produced between 1803 and 1824. None of them contains the sum total of his proposals because he often modified his ideas and constantly invented new propositions expressing his drive for unity. The *Lettres d'un habitant de Genève à ses contemporains* was his first work, published in 1803 when he was 43; the *Réorganisation de la société europénne* followed in 1814; *L'industrie* in 1817; *L'organisateur* in 1819; *Du système industriel* was published in 1821–22; *Catéchisme des industriels* in 1824, as was his last work, *Nouveau christianisme.*

Whether on theoretical grounds due to certain similarities of Fascism to Marxian theory, placing these two in a state of ideological antagonism, or on account of practical political competition between Fascism and Communism, the latter assumed a totally negative attitude toward the Fascist doctrine. In relation to its aspect of Thought and Action, and in relation to the Corporate Theory, the Communist attitude is so negative that Mussolini himself and the regime he implemented in Italy were both regarded by the Communist International as a betrayal of the working class, and Mussolini was very frequently referred to as a "traitor to the working people."

It would not be difficult to discover some of the major reasons for this attitude:

1. Until 1914 Mussolini himself was not only a part but a leading member of the leftist revolutionary faction of the Italian Socialist Party. He provoked his own expulsion from the party and formed his own Fascist movement. Thus, from the Communist point of view, he betrayed his party.

2. The Fascist regime as implemented by Mussolini was in fact looked upon by the Communist International as an effective attempt to reconcile the struggle and solve the problems within the *bourgeoisie* itself as well as to accomplish this through the Fascist concept of unity. This was felt to be detrimental to the interests of Communism. Also, it is contradictory to the predictions made by Karl Marx, because if Fascism succeeds, the bourgeoisie would in effect be removing disruptive tendencies and working toward class unity. The bourgeoisie would become united and strong and better able to concentrate on its struggle against Communism.

It is precisely this point which makes the Communists regard Mussolini as a vile traitor. On this point he deviates from, and betrays the most fundamental principle of Karl Marx: the encouragement of the class struggle in order to bring about the Revolution. He negates this fundamental prediction by Marx by healing the class split which would inevitably bring about the all important proletarian "Revolution" which is, in fact, the motor and the means of achieving Communism.

3. According to the Communist International, the emergence of the Fascist regime in Italy prevented a possible Bolshevik Revolution there, for it seems that the social, political, and economic conditions in Italy were quite ripe for such an event, especially shortly after World War I.

The most significant political events, frictions, and conflicts relevant to the modern development of Italy, belong to the period beginning before the unification of the country and lasting until almost the end of World War II. While each event occurred in a somewhat isolated fashion, each contributed to the political, economic, and/or social ambitions of certain groups in Italian society. While the Mazzinian legacy, a strange combination of romantic idealism and violent action, did not, in fact, dominate the Italian atmosphere, it was very often used as a convenient tool for the achievement of many political and social ambitions. When one analyzes these events individually, one may conclude that they all occurred in a sort of quiet, but disorderly fashion. Nevertheless, they were the basic elements of Italian political and social evolution. One may group them as follows:

1. The group of events belonging to the *Risorgimento-Transformismo* era. (*Risorgimento* means upsurge after awakening, triggering a transition.) These events occurred in the period immediately prior to the unification of Italy.

2. The group of events related to the emergence of *Socialism.* Initially one can detect a strong French influence, identical to early French Socialism stemming from Rousseauan loose and quasi-idealistic reasoning; but this kind of Socialism later seemed to have switched under German influence into the Marxian type.

3. The group of events related to the emergence of *Fascism.* If we look at the sociopolitical development of Italy, it seems that the first two groups of events were the necessary prerequisites for the two basic conditions which, in turn, aided the rise of Fascism. The first condition was the gradual transformation of Italian society from being backward and romantic, consisting of pastoral "noonday dreamers," to the economic and political state of post-industrial and post-democratic dynamism. The second condition was the eruption of strong socioeconomic conflicts forming, on the one hand, a powerful group of industrial capitalists, and on the other, a true industrial proletarian class in the Marxian sense.

Risorgimento. Although Mazzini claimed that Italy and not France had a mission in the world, and for that reason wanted to compete vigorously with France, the fact is that the revolution of the French middle class and the invasion of Italy by Napoleon were two events that left a tremendous impact on the development of Italian society. French ideas of nationalism and liberalism (the latter expressed by the revolution, and both brought to Italy by the Napoleonic invasion) spread and took root all over Italy, but in a somewhat restricted manner, affecting only a minority. This launched a string of developments which can best be categorized as a mere repetition in Italy of the French sociopolitical scene. In other words, the result was a series of conspiracies, secret societies, insurrections and revolts, topped off by the emergence of a very shrewd diplomacy—a sophisticated domestic diplomacy which invented the means necessary for skillful upper-class manipulation amidst these upheavals. In fact, the Risorgimento succeeded in Italy for two basic reasons:

1. It was supported effectively by the intellectuals who propagated the new ideas through their writings. These intellectuals were hidden in key positions, pulling vital strings and directing revolts in order to implement, to force, or, better said, to experiment with their written ideas. The masses were unknowingly becoming submissive subjects for the experiments and activities of the intellectuals.

2. The ideas of the Risorgimento proved to be very well suited to the interests of the business and semi-industrial classes of Northern Italy. The implementation of the Risorgimento's ideas was regarded by these classes not only as a guarantee of free local trade and competition on a *laissez-faire* basis, but also called for the abolition of internal Italian tariffs, duties, and sales taxes.

Therefore, the first important conclusion is that large masses of people were in general not at all affected by the waves of the Risorgimento. Without giving their conscious support, and unwittingly becoming psychologically conditioned to and indoctrinated by the new ideas, people at large became little more than an amorphous mass merely serving to further the limited causes of the various uprisings and, above all, to sustain the interests of business and the emerging semi-industrial class in the North. The crux of this indoctrination may be stated as follows: "What is good for the new rulers of unified Italy is necessarily good for the people at large." The state institution was thusly transformed from its previous role of serving the Prince, of the pre-unification era, into serving the new class of business and the interests of the emerging private industries. Consequently, the leaders of business and industry automatically became the Italian elite, while the people at large consisted mainly of peasants. At first, the split between these two classes was not consolidated, nor was it in a process of consolidation; it was, rather, in a state of a potential but sharp distinction. Then another very significant class emerged in between these two, a class whose appearance on the Italian sociopolitical and economic scene could be looked upon as an important force as well as a spontaneous attempt to establish a unifying link between the elite and the people at large. The importance of this class may be traced throughout the sociopolitical development of Italy, including the Fascist regime of Mussolini. This was the class consisting mainly of *Catholic ecclesiastical figures;* it was composed mainly of the aristocracy but due to its religious affiliation it was a class which found numerous followers among the peasantry of Italy. This class would later play an all-important role in connection with the emergence of Marxian Socialism in Italy.

With such a general background in mind, we can now turn to an analysis of class stratification in Italy. Beginning with the period of the Risorgimento, there were four distinct classes which dominated Italian society.

1. *The class of the nobles and the upper bourgeoisie.* These were the owners of large tracts of land, banks, trade enterprises, and emerging small-scale industries. This class was geographically located primarily in the *northern* part of Italy, and liked to look upon the state institution as their own private tool for preserving and promoting their professional interests.

2. *The middle class (in Italy placed somewhat below the bourgeoisie) and the Intelligentsia.* This class consisted of owners of small tracts of land and trade enterprises (no banks); it encompassed state officials and clerks, the bureaucracy, and the free professions. Geographically, this class was spread all over Italy, but again with a higher concentration in the *North.*

3. *The majoritarian class of Italy.* This class was powerful in number but quite ineffective in defending its own interests. It consisted of the large masses of peasants and the workers in the newly emerging small industries. Geographically, it was spread all over Italy, but with higher concentration in the *South.*

4. *The class of Catholic ecclesiastical strata.* These usually kept themselves apart from the government, felt some reluctance vis-à-vis most of its policies and its actions, but were not in opposition to the *social system* which the government was in the process of helping to establish and consolidate. In other words, they did not go along politically with the national government but approved of its social activities, provided that the government did not obstruct their recruitment of followers from among the peasant class.

The industrialization process was a new phenomenon in Italy, the focus being on the development of small-scale industries. Thus, the industries in Italy did not then amount to anything of importance, nor did the industrial workers compose the majoritarian class of Italy. The peasantry represented some 3/4 of the entire majoritarian class—and the majoritarian class composed more than 3/4 of the population. These data clearly show that the Italians were predominantly an agrarian people, and because of this Italy had all the problems that are usually faced by predominantly agrarian societies. Two of those problems deserve special mention because of their importance in the Italian setting. They were:

a. The prevailing existence of the *Latifundia.*
b. Extensive *overpopulation* (especially in the South) followed by severe underemployment in the countryside.

The major reason for the existence of the Latifundia in Italy was the extremely disproportionate ownership of the land. In fact, approximately 2/3 of the arable land belonged to about 250,000 landowners, constituting the nobles and the bourgeoisie. Only 1/3 of the land was then left to the remaining five million owners. One could add other millions of peasants who were totally landless and who were either unemployed or were working as agricultural hired hands, doing seasonal work on the large estates. If it is true that there was not at that time in Italy an industrial proletariat in the Marxian sense (because of the existence of small-scale industries with a relatively small number of workers) it is also true that there was a large *agricultural proletariat.*[13]

The extensive overpopulation in the Italian countryside, with its consequent underemployment, was attributable to the fact that Italian industry at that time (being not sufficiently developed) was unable to absorb the hordes who were not needed on the farms. Their productivity on the farms was, indeed, equal to zero. With or without them the full production capacity of the farms would have been reached; but their non-contributory labor, given to the family farm enterprise, nonetheless entitled them to an equal share of the yield of agriculture. They became a burden on the Italian agricultural economy.

The above-mentioned disproportionate and inadequate social class structure prior to the emergence of Fascism was reflected in the political scene. Even the unification of the country, as a major political achievement, was not accomplished by Italy herself. The unification of the northern and central parts of the peninsula was a direct result of the political and military activity of France. This may be quite clearly illustrated by the fact that when France, distracted by other matters, interrupted the push for Italian unification (as in the cases of Venetia and Rome), Italy did nothing to continue the unification process by herself. In such instances, the process was simply abandoned. When, on the other hand, France resumed the work for further unification at the point where she has left off, the whole of Italy joined in.

The year 1848 was a time of political chaos all across Europe. It was characterized by numerous revolts and varieties of conspiracies which, however, were nothing more than the result of the diffusion of the new idea of political freedom. This phenomenon, which one might have regarded as the ailment of Europe, was about to touch the Italian region, and Prince Charles Albert of Piedmont-Sardinia conceived the idea of sparing his kingdom from a similar fate. Accordingly, he convened a special conference of notables, asking them to help prepare a plan which would save Italy from becoming part of the general revolutionary upheaval. After several sessions, Charles Albert was advised to grant the people a constitution, the rationale being that if *he* granted it, the people, being relatively easy to manipulate, might find themselves momentarily appeased, and then he could work to increase his popularity as a ruler. The general rationale was that if he refused to defer at least partially to the people's fundamental rights, the people might take advantage of the general revolutionary development and take matters into their own hands; as a result, they would *impose* a constitution with far fewer curbs on the masses than those which they would be ready, at the moment, to accept. Finally, as a compromise between the

---

[13]In addition, a significant number of small farmers were compelled regularly to leave their own lands to work as hired hands for the large landowners.

council's advice and his own views, a limited fundamental law was approved—a sort of constitution, which received the name of *Statuto*. The discussions had begun in 1848, and the Statuto came into effect in 1861. Previously the people's participation in national politics had been almost nil in terms of suffrage and eligibility for elections. The Statuto, however, firmly established the right of 2 percent of the people to vote and become eligible for elective office. This limited suffrage was only granted to the male population. The inadequacy and limitations of this provision naturally brought about a series of disturbances, but they fell far short of mass revolts. In 1882 an amendment was passed and referred to as the *Great Electoral Reform.* This reform still denied the vote to the majority of the population, but it raised the eligibility percentage from 2 percent to 9.4 percent. This situation lasted until 1912, when universal suffrage was granted to the Italian people, albeit still restricted to the male population.

Non-participation in the political activities of the nation over a long period seems to have made out of the Italian peasantry a totally passive political element. While individualistic by nature, the peasants became political followers rather than political leaders. The Statuto of Charles Albert, with all its limitations, was in force until 1925. In that year, Mussolini, without formally repealing it, merely changed the fundamentals of the Italian political structure.

This in brief is the gist of political conditions in pre-World War I Italy to which, however, a major factor of an economic nature was added, namely, the stress on, or the drive toward industrialization. This new economic phenomenon was later to make a very strong impact on Italian society. However, the impact of the industrialization was mainly confined to Northern Italy.

As a rule, in most countries industrialization would mean the following:

1. The strengthening of investment capital.
2. The concentration of business proprietorship and services.
3. The emergence of a proletarian class of factory workers.

Thus, industrialization processes are closely related to social changes. Italian industrialization was at first slow in comparison to then-contemporary industrial standards in Northern and Northwestern Europe. One of the reasons for this slow start was that industrial know-how as well as technical and organizational knowledge was lacking in Italy. There was no accumulated private capital available, and there were no industrial raw materials nor ready-made tools of production. Because of this, it was the state institution which stepped in and helped to promote the industrialization of Italy. As time passed, the state became more and more active in this respect. The main flow of assistance accorded by the state to the emerging Italian industry took place in the following areas:

1. The creation of a rigid codified legislation entirely geared to protect Italian industry. This system gave rise to a solid wall of protective tariffs.
2. Low-interest state credit generously provided for investment in new indus-

tries or for the expansion of old ones. Of course, in spite of this generosity, the state distributed this help only to industries that would be useful to it. The sharp increase in the building of railroads, merchant ships, military fortifications, production of weapons, as well as the swift creation of a strong navy, is concrete evidence of priorities in the selection and use of state help to Italian industry. In general, one might say that all industrial sectors that could be useful to the state institution developed first and with great rapidity.

3. The arrangement, the negotiation, and the conclusion of a series of treaties and state-sponsored contracts with foreign countries concerning foreign investment of capital in the emerging Italian industries. Consequently, in addition to state assistance, investments from Germany, France, England, Belgium, and Switzerland, to name only a few, began to pour in to benefit the country's industries.

The year 1878 marked the beginning of the end of the free trade system in Italy. This system, based on free competition with foreign industry, had long kept Italian industry in a substantially disadvantageous position. Approximately one decade later, that is after 1887, state industrial protectionism in Italy became a fact.

There was an important element of contradiction in this policy, a contradiction which, nevertheless, over the long term was successfully solved, thus avoiding substantial damage to Italian industrial development. This contradiction may be described as follows: having few industrial raw materials (the Italian economy almost totally lacked iron ore and coking coal with which to refine the ore into steel), the new Italian industrialists depended very much on the importation of these materials. On the other hand, the state policy of high tariffs, the attempt to keep out of the Italian market competitive foreign industrial products, antagonized the major countries from which Italy was seeking investment capital. As a reaction to that policy, a number of foreign states began to retaliate by interrupting (or at least substantially decreasing) the export of raw material and other essentials to Italy. Some even refused to accept Italian farm products. In this respect, the period around 1887 was quite crucial for the future of Italian agriculture, as major foreign markets came closed to it.

In the long run, however, Italian industry was able to overcome the extreme hardships involved, by skillful diplomacy and persistent governmental action. In a relatively short time a first-class heavy industry emerged with its big corporations, and impressive brand names of world significance—all of which, though, developed in *Northern* Italy.

In spite of this remarkable success, the long period of state protectionism had conditioned the industrial leaders to accept governmental guidance instead of relying on their own initiative. The entire process of industrialization in Italy brought not only very significant socioeconomic changes but also very important political modifications. The ever-increasing number of factories resulted in the emergence of a strong, urban proletariat. This group was composed primarily of migrants from the farms. Protective tariffs, aiming at the elimination of foreign competition, created cheap labor for Italian industry in terms of low wages and long working hours. Finally, as an immediate reaction to the above, the industrial proletariat of Italy began to strike in protest. The government reacted with open hostility to most of the workers' demands for improvement. Finally, facing such an attitude on the part of the government, the workers began to consider various forms of violent action.

As with most of the factors contributing to Italian development, *anarchistic* and *socialistic* ideas also came from abroad. They settled deeply in the soul of the working proletariat. The whole working class, a large part of the peasantry, and even some government employees joined in support of an insurgent labor movement which displayed a real potential for the successful achievement of its goal. The proletarian movement became progressively penetrated by Socialist ideas, these again coming from abroad (mainly France and then Germany), and being, for the most part, promoted by the Italian intelligentsia.

The stand of the Italian government and of the Italian industrial and business classes, being opposed to improvements in working conditions, provoked radicalism among the proletariat. The latter began to organize in various groups and prepare for a lengthy struggle, e.g., the creation of a workers' *league of resistance* and the various *labor councils.* These served not only to excite to a fever pitch the Italian population, but also to aid striking workers in the factories. The first success of Italian labor was due in large measure to these workers' associations. Primarily because of them, the government was compelled, by the end of the nineteenth century, to recognize the legality of the existence of the labor unions.

This official recognition brought about a tremendous increase in union membership. By 1909, approximately 320,000 workers were united for action in the *General Confederation of Labor.* This confederation was not only infiltrated but effectively led by Socialists. However, they declined, for tactical and political reasons, to identify themselves at first with any political group. This was done in order for them to serve as a unifying labor link among *all* workers instead of creating a precedent for political division within the working class. In reality, however, the second most important goal (in addition to improvements of the working conditions) was to obtain from the government a series of parliamentary concessions in favor of labor. This was, indeed, a political goal *par excellence* which, however, the Socialist leaders of the Confederation tried to conceal in the phraseology of nonpartisanship.

Because of the character of the second goal, that is, obtaining parliamentary concessions, the Socialist movement in Italy became at first geared toward reformism rather than toward revolution—toward evolution, not revolution in the Marxian sense. This trend was of great importance. It was assisted by the writings and public expressions of the Italian intelligentsia, who in turn were deeply influenced by the vague and evolutionary character of early French Socialists such as Saint-Simon and Fourier (see Part IV, pp. 151–157), and also by French anarchistic ideas stemming from Proudhon (pp. 157–161). Quite surprisingly, however, these were exactly the ideas which brought about much disturbance inside the Italian labor movement. The result was a Socialist split within the General Confederation of Labor. It came quite suddenly, brought on by a radical-minded group of workers who believed in a different kind of Socialism, one strongly influenced by the ideas of German rather than French Socialists. German Socialism, however, meant the adoption of Marxian violent, revolutionary ideas. This group at first split from the Confederation and later created the so-called *Syndicalist Union.* Through it, these workers began to preach not reforms and calls for concessions from the parliament and the government (concessions to be achieved in quiet negotiations), but demanded more direct and more violent unilateral action to be taken by the workers. What all this amounted to was preaching and working toward Marxian revolution.

Following the Socialist example, and in spite of the Christian reformism of Pope Leo XIII, Catholics, too, began to form their own labor unions. An important phenomenon was the fact that all these activities, including those of the General Confederation of Labor, the Syndicalist Union, and a number of emerging Catholic unions as well, were concentrated, mainly, in the northern part of Italy. This area represented the only efficiently industrialized region of the country.

By contrast, in the South, the large peasant masses were rather unresponsive to the workers' labor union activities. In spite of this, they had to find a solution to their problems, which mainly stemmed from agrarian misery. The solution they found was one of a quite different nature—a nonviolent solution. The peasant classes in the South did not form agricultural unions of any importance. Indeed, they continued to refrain from any moves toward even the loosest kind of organization. However, on an individual basis, a mass emigration from Southern Italy took place toward the end of the nineteenth century. The bulk of this emigration was directed toward the Americas. Emigration reached such a magnitude that in a relatively short time a very considerable reduction of the labor surplus in the countryside had come about. Thus, the diminution of the labor force in the South and the savings sent back home from immigrants in the New World contributed very much to the raising of economic and social living standards in that part of the country. The labor union activities in the North, on the other hand, gradually attained their goals and greatly improved the situation. A gradual improvement in living conditions began to be felt all over Italy mainly for these two reasons. As a direct result of this development, one decade prior to the outbreak of World War I, the daily wages of the farm laborers in Italy were approximately 40 percent above those of a generation earlier.

This considerably improved political, economic, and social situation gave birth to another important movement. The new *Nationalist* movement became popular in Italy about the year 1910. It too originated with the intellectual elite. An immense quantity of literature began to call for a renovation of Italy through imperialistic means. Industrial achievement was probably one part of the reason for the birth of these ideas, since it gave the Italian people a national awareness of and self-confidence in their industrial strength. The Nationalist movement called on Italy to break completely with her old traditions, which it called "inefficient," the final goal being to transform the basic character of the Italian people. This call was in its essence quite similar to that of Mazzini in the nineteenth century.

This must surely have been one of the points that Mussolini had in mind when he referred to Fascist indebtedness to the Mazzinian system of thought. Through "La Giovane Italia," Mazzini had called for a transformation of the Italian character. He wanted the "noonday dreamers" to become aware of their greatness, wanted them to compete efficiently with the liberalism of France and pointed out the importance of the Italian mission to the world, a world which was, nevertheless, gradually shaping itself on the French model of 1789.

The philosophy of the Nationalist movement was based also on a vague conception of national glory. Quite Mazzini-like, one of the philosophical cornerstones of this movement was that only the *young* and the *renovated* person would possess the future. Mazzini had, indeed, stressed youth and renovation as primary factors in the change of the Italian character. One might claim that Mazzini also called for glory, more specifically in his call for competition with France in influencing Europe. One should keep in mind, though, the difficulties faced by Mazzini: he did not start out with a unified Italian state. For him, that was still something to be achieved, and yet he called for a competition with a sociopolitically sophisticated though at that time, revolutionary, France.

Another important feature of the Nationalist movement was the concept that only through war could a nation become conscious of its national creed and of its national goals. Thus, the Nationalist movement of 1910 firmly opposed the parliamentary regime of Italy. The movement also opposed the Socialist labor movement in either of its shades, reformatory or violent, that is, evolutionary Socialism, as expressed by the programs of the General Confederation of Labor, and the revolutionary Socialism of the Syndicalist union. This same nationalistic stand was also taken vis-à-vis the Catholic branch of Socialism which had formed its own labor unions.

Still another point that one should not fail to mention in relation to the political attitude of the Nationalist movement of 1910 was its leaning toward a concept quite similar to the German "Lebensraum." Indeed, the Nationalist movement placed a high priority on the eradication of the proletarian character of the Italian nation by means of foreign conquest. It preached the idea that spreading the Italian population over newly annexed territories would eliminate overpopulation in the peninsula. One point is of interest in this connection, namely, that this movement, while aiming at national glory, simultaneously recognized the *proletarian* character of the Italian nation, a fact which does not particularly evoke a sense of glory.

Although one cannot be certain as to what would have been the fate of this movement under normal conditions, the Italian-Turkish War of 1911 (over Tripoli) led to a rapid consolidation of its strength. The war not only excited to the utmost the movement's followers, but also brought them a substantial number of new sympathizers and supporters. The war and its successful conclusion created a significant widespread feeling among the populace that the Nationalists had embarked on the only true road toward a solution of Italy's problems.

The very slow rate of social development, on the one hand, and the quite inadequate state of the suffrage, on the other, can best be illustrated by statistics taken from three consecutive election years.

In 1870, there were only 530,018 eligible voters in the total population. This number represented the 2 percent given the right to vote nine years earlier through the enactment of the Statuto of 1861. In reality, however, only 240,974 persons voted in the election of that year, that is, only about 1 percent—less than one half of the eligible voters had exercised their right.

By the time of the national election held in 1892—ten years after the implementation of the Great Electoral Reform amendment—the number of eligible voters in Italy had increased to 2,934,445, the percentage having been raised to 9.4. In reality, though, only 1,639,298 voters participated—about 4 percent of the entire population or about one half of the voters.

In the election year of 1921, nine years after the granting of male universal suffrage, with the Fascist movement of Mussolini very active although still not in office, 11,447,210 persons in Italy were eligible to vote. This figure represented 28.7 percent of the population. Again, in actuality, only 6,701,496 people voted, which approximated 13 percent of the population; that is, once again only one half of the eligible voters went to the polls.

These data would indicate that about 50 percent of the eligible voters participated in every election of Italy during those years. Many suggestions have been advanced as to whether this reflected a meager interest by the people in national affairs. This question is especially significant when related to the elections of

1870 and 1892—at a political conjuncture with the recent granting of a limited suffrage. One would normally expect that at that time, more so than in 1921, there would be a strong popular desire for a voice in governmental affairs because of the then newly acquired right of suffrage after the long suppression of self-governance. Many studies have been made to discover the reasons for the political apathy of those years. Some have suggested that the State-Church relationship in Italy was the chief cause among several. This indeed, seems to be the most important reason. Therefore, it would be useful to look into this question before we analyze the Italian political parties and their interrelations. It has been suggested by some scholars that Church influence should be held responsible for the mediocre turnout in Italian elections during the period of *Transformismo.*

Indeed, State-Church relations triggered one of the most serious political problems facing the country. This whole complex of animosities is usually referred to as the *Roman Question.*

When the unification of Italy was in its beginning stages, and indeed throughout the entire process, the papal attitude remained at best passive and, at times, even hostile to the idea of unification. Unification, however, became a fact, and the Italian state initially interpreted the Vatican's passive hostility as one of the major factors that prevented the emergence of political parties of national significance. The State also implied that the attitude of the Pope affected unfavorably the development of the new Italian socioeconomic order. Viewing the State-Church relation from this angle, the new Italian state made in September, 1870, an attempt to arrive at a mutual agreement. It prepared a broad proposal as a basis for discussion and submitted it to Pope Pius IX. This attempt, however, turned out to be unsuccessful because of the immediate negative reaction from the Pope. He simply refused to negotiate.

Believing that an agreement with the Church would result in more active political participation by the Italian people in State affairs, and also that it could contribute to an improved socioeconomic order in Italy, the State persisted in its endeavors. The government wanted to discuss matters of substance, not just vague proposals, with the hope that the Pope would realize the State's sincerity. Therefore, while the Church apparently remained disinterested in negotiations, the State attempted to stimulate Church interest. These attempts began with the introduction in parliament of a special State-sponsored bill pertaining to State-Church relations. The Italian parliament in 1871 adopted that bill under the title *Law of Papal Guarantee.* Among its provisions five may be considered of special importance:

1. It contained a promise to the Pope guaranteeing him unrestricted freedom within the jurisdiction of the State for the exercise of papal spiritual authority.

2. It promised the Pope inviolability of person and communications.

3. It recognized as papal possessions the *Vatican*, the *Lateran Palace*, and the *Castle Gandolfo* (naming the major ones only) and emphasized the State's disinterest in these properties.

4. The bill rescinded the State's right to nominate bishops.

5. It provided for a State annual subsidy to the Pope of approximately $600,000.

The Vatican did not react at once to this package, which was universally regarded as a generous State offer to the Church. Retaining his noncommittal attitude, the Pope probably waited to see how the State's apparent good will would be implemented in practice. In fact, when the time for implementation came, the practical application seemed quite disappointing. In reality, the action did not correspond to the generous spirit with which the Law of Papal Guarantee was adopted by the Italian parliament. The State continued under various pretexts and legal interpretations to seize papal territory and proceeded to dissolve several monasteries as well as other ecclesiastical foundations.

It thus became quite evident that the Pope did not believe in the promise of independence for the Catholic Church in Italy. Thus, both Pope Pius IX and, from 1878, Pope Leo XIII, definitely refused to be reconciled with the unified Italian state. They not only refused to negotiate on the basis of the Law of Papal Guarantee (including the provision regarding the $600,000 annual subsidy to the Church), but they also looked for and found ways to retaliate. This retaliation ultimately took the form of Italian Catholics being debarred from voting in parliamentary elections. At this point it appeared that the State's aims had received a severe setback. Through these proposed arrangements with the Church, the government of Italy had intended to achieve a higher level of popular participation in the nation's affairs. The result, however, was that all Catholics were enjoined not to participate in such affairs. This prohibition lasted until 1909, and is supposed to have resulted in the above-mentioned decrease in voter participation. The emergence, at least, of a strong *Catholic political party*, able to influence the political and social development of the country, became virtually impossible.

In 1909 after approximately one decade of increased Socialist ideological activity in Italy, Pope Pius X repealed unilaterally this prohibition, but not with an eye toward rapprochement with the State. It was argued at the time that he did it primarily because of the influx of Socialist thought which was affecting, or at least disturbing, the stability of the Catholic Church. Thus, the repeal of the prohibition to vote could be regarded as a step taken to combat Socialism, and not mainly an effort to encourage popular participation in the conduct of State affairs.

Amidst these controversies a number of political movements gradually appeared and eventually coagulated into political parties. For the purpose of this study, however, we might focus our attention on only *four* of them and limit our discussion to only those parties that played a major role in the events leading to the rise of Fascism. First of all, we must consider the *Italian Liberal Party,* if for no other reason than that it was the major Italian political party prior to the emergence of Socialism as a strong political force in the country immediately preceding the rise of Fascism. The importance of the Italian Liberal Party was enhanced by the fact that it held power during both the period of *Transformismo* and the time the Roman Question was debated. The domestic policy of the Liberal Party, when in office, was clearly evidenced by the following actions taken:

In the first place, we must mention the *discontinuation* of the strong *tariff protection* for small handicraft industries. Such industries were beginning to blossom in the southern part of Italy, following (naturally) the northern industrial pattern of development. Through this policy, the Italian Liberal Party interrupted the possible industrial development of the South; such development, of course, had been accelerated in the North precisely because of this type of tariff protection.

In the second place, the party *authorized* the *sale of Church property* and of public lands which were appropriated following the annexation of formerly independent or semi-independent principalities and regions in the peninsula.

Finally, the Liberal Party *imposed* new and *severe fiscal policies.* The party leaders sincerely believed that such stringent policies were the only practical means of bringing the State budget into balance. This policy also brought with it heavy taxation. As might be expected, owing to their controversial nature, hot debates occurred on all these issues within the Liberal Party. Disputes took place not only among the party leaders but also involved the party membership at large and the affected population of the country. Finally, the debates resulted in splitting the party into two factions, the *Left* and the *Right.*

In 1878 the Right faction was finally defeated in the parliamentary elections. According to the constitution, the King then approved a cabinet representing the Left faction. The leading political figure of the Left faction was Agostino Deptetis (a mild Left liberal), who subsequently became prime minister. With the exception of a few intervals of limited duration, he remained in that position for eleven years.

The main features of this eleven-year regime in Italy turned out to be political careerism and opportunism. Personal interests and glory for the ruling elite seemed to have become far more important than all the socioeconomic reforms that were included in the platform of the Italian Liberal Party. These conditions eventually provided the backdrop for the emergence of another man, who, however, was not a politician. He was a pragmatic socioeconomic writer who viewed with regret the shortcomings of the regime.

Vilfredo Pareto (1848–1923) was born in France and ended his life in Switzerland. Since boyhood he, like his family, had taken a vivid interest in the socioeconomic and political affairs of Italy. A nonconformist in regard to the accepted societal values and norms of his time, and also somewhat affected by Mazzini's ideas, he emerged as a devoted republican determined to work for Italian independence.

Unlike most of the European ideological leaders in his time, Pareto did not take part in the activities of revolutionary and secret political societies that groped for radical solutions to the various burning sociopolitical issues of the day. His early life and development were free of such endeavors. Instead, he took great interest in the study of economics, this interest later crystallizing into a constant search for solutions to the complicated practical problems inasmuch as they were related to that discipline. On the other hand, Pareto also achieved extraordinary success in the study of mathematics. Indeed, it proved to be a very convenient and necessary tool for his future analysis of economic issues.

Establishing himself at first as an engineer in the city of Rome, he later became, for six years (1874–1880), the manager of iron mines in the valley of the Arno. This particular experience prompted him to voice some theories of his own related to the role of the manager in economic affairs. Shortly afterwards, he became gradually aware of the continuous social implications of economics. Thus, one may say that Pareto's mind came to encompass both the socioeconomic and political aspects of human activity while attempting to provide concrete solutions on a mathematically precise scientific basis.

After having accepted in 1893 a chair in political economy at the University of Lausanne in Switzerland, Vilfredo Pareto began to write his major works. They were all characterized by a determined effort to discover, through applied mathematical analysis, new scientific theories applicable to the solution of social and economic problems.

His most important work, *Trattato di soziologia generale,* was published in 1916 in Florence in two volumes. It was later (in 1935) translated into English and published in four volumes under the title, *The Mind and Society.* In addition to many articles, he also published in Paris the two volumes of his *Le système socialiste* (1902–1903) and the one-volume *Le myth vertuiste et la littérature immorale* (1911). In Milan he issued in 1906 *Manuele d'economia politica,* published in French in 1909, and *Transformazione de la democrazia* in 1921. *Fatti i teorie* was published in Florence in 1920, and posthumously, in 1952, appeared his *Soritti teorici* in Milan.

All of these works, but mainly *Trattato di soziologia generale,* later attracted the attention of the leadership of the Italian Fascist Party; they were to claim Pareto as one of the theoretical forerunners of Fascism. In *Trattato,* Pareto seems to give vent to his disenchantment with governmental practices in Italy.

He also condemns in general terms all kinds of democratic methods of government, including, of course, the phenomenon of parliamentarism. This attitude
appears to be the result of Pareto's own observations of the inadequacy,
inefficiency, and sluggishness of Italian democracy. Most of these characteristics
were then openly displayed in Italy. According to Pareto, these shortcomings
were caused mainly by a blind, "at-any-price" adherence to democracy.

In spite of several Fascist claims to the contrary, nowhere does Pareto espouse
a sociopolitical system reflecting, in its entirety, or in most parts, Fascist
doctrine. One can observe only *some* similarity between the ideas expressed by
Pareto and Mazzini, on the one hand, and the tenets propounded by Fascist
leaders, on the other. While Pareto neither prepared nor endorsed a theory
elaborate enough to fit the entirety of Fascist doctrine, he nevertheless did
assume an anti-democratic stance—and made very clear his preference for the
idea of *ruling elites*. This sentiment, however, was not Pareto's alone; it has been
a popular one (for quite a long time) in many politically organized societies. All
that Pareto actually did was to present in a more sophisticated form a reaffirma-
tion of some of the already developed ideas of such thinkers as Saint-Simon and
Sorel in France, and Mosca in Italy.[14]

Gaetano Mosca (1858–1941) viewed the primary role of ruling elites as being
unattached to political causes. While favoring strongly the workers' class in a
true Marxian sense, he interpreted the workers' dilemma in a non-Marxist
fashion and proposed a solution based on an already observable and known
practice of elite rule.

Mosca was born on the island of Sicily. Throughout his life he was a severe
critic of democracy and parliamentarism. More so than in Pareto's case, it was
the Italian political scene which seems to have been Mosca's major object of
observation. Hence, his conclusions attacking democratic parliamentarism were
based on close scrutiny of the Italian type of democratic parliamentary rule
rather than on practical application of the parliamentary idea in its broad sense.

Mosca was simultaneously a political scientist, a journalist, and a scholar of
some eminence. Grounded in his expertise in constitutional law, his particular
method of analysis placed him among the most accomplished political scientists
of his time. He advocated scientific systematization of political research and
launched an entirely new development: empiricism in political science. Since he
was one of the pioneers in that endeavor, his contribution consisted mainly of
determined *attempts* at truly modern empirical research, and his total accom-

---

[14]See pp. 73–76 for a discussion of Sorel's ideas emphasizing the syndicalist view of
professional (producers' class) significance in the leadership of society, rather than the
traditional political planning and action.

plishment was in actuality little more than a presentation of *rudimentary* empirical forms. Probably on account of this rudimentary quality most contemporary political behavioralists have ignored Mosca's contribution to their own area of work, even in cases when they attempt to trace the history of this domain of political science. Attempting to discover valid general laws and concrete rules applicable to the political process and thus making possible the prediction of political events, Gaetano Mosca belonged to the Deterministic School. Indeed, it is on that particular methodological foundation of determinism that he could be most easily associated with the approach of Karl Marx and even with that of Georg Hegel. Mosca differed from both, however, through his rather *inductive* application of their determinism. The most unusual, but nonetheless valuable, aspect of Mosca's intellect was the fact that most of his concepts and ideas were already firmly crystallized in his mind at the age of twenty-five.

A parallel can be easily drawn between Mosca and Niccolo Machiavelli, an analogy related not to their advocated sociopolitical solutions but to the type of problem both were attacking: Machiavelli was preoccupied with the question, "what made princes succeed in gaining power, what qualities did they need to maintain such power once it was gained, and, what were the societal forces which made them lose it?" Mosca looked basically into the same problem, although through a much more advanced and modern conceptualization, reflecting his own time and the world's stage of political development. Mosca's basic objective was "to identify the modern rulers, to determine the manner in which they gain political power, and how they are able to maintain or lose it."

Beginning his career in the most underdeveloped area of Southern Italy, the island of Sicily, Mosca's first important step was his appointment to an unpaid lectureship at the University of Rome, and in 1869 to a professorship at the University of Turin. Later, he was also given the editorship of the Italian *Chamber of Deputies' Journal,* the proceedings of that legislative body. Between the years 1914 and 1916 Mosca served as an undersecretary in the Italian cabinet; in 1919 he was offered a seat in the Italian Senate; and in 1923 he received a full professorial chair at the University of Rome.

Mosca's first published work appeared when he was twenty-six: *Sulla teorica dei governi e sul governo parlamentare* was published in Turin in 1884. A second edition of this book was printed in Milan in 1925, under a modified title, *Teorica dei governi e sul governo parlamentare.* Next came Mosca's second major work, *Elementi di scienza politica,* which was published in Turin in 1896. In 1923 it was republished as in two volumes; a third edition appeared in 1938, and a fourth in 1947. It was translated into English and published in New York in 1939, under the title *The Ruling Class.* A German translation of the fourth edition, *Die herrschende Klasse: Grundlagen der politischen Wissenschaft,* was published in Berne in 1950. Another work, *Il principio aristocratico e il demo-*

cratico nel passato e nell'avvenire, was published in Turin in 1903. Mosca also published *Lezioni di storia delle instituzioni e delle dottrine politiche* in Rome in 1932, a second edition of which, *Storia delle dottrine politiche,* was translated into French under the title *Histoire des doctrines politiques depuis l'antiquité jusqu'à nos jours* and published in Paris in 1936. In 1933, in Bari, appeared Mosca's *Cenni storici sulle dottrine razziste,* and in 1949, also in Bari, *Partiti e sindicati nella crise dil regime parlamentare.*

Although frequently attempting to relate the Fascist regime to Pareto, Mussolini neither in his writings nor speeches ever mentioned Mosca as a forerunner of Fascism. In reality, however, such an association is quite obvious not only by the close similarity—and in some cases identification—of Mosca's propositions with those of the Fascist doctrine, but also by their ideological motivating factors.

Gaetano Mosca did not create a new sociopolitical theory. He only made a substantial re-evaluation of original Marxism. In fact, he re-interpreted the Marxist school of thought by transforming its class-struggle theory of historic determinism into a determinism unrelated to any struggle between the social classes as such. While Mosca was convinced of the relevancy of determinism to struggle, he advocated a struggle which affected and acted solely upon fragments within each of the social classes, fragments of different (and even opposing) classes, but fragments which were constantly guided by natural deterministic forces toward identical desires and goals regardless of the class to which they belong.

The early sociopolitical and economic beliefs of the leader of the Fascist movement, Benito Mussolini, were indeed identical to Mosca's. Like Mosca's, they were all deeply immersed in Karl Marx's thought and proposed solutions. In this respect, though, both Mussolini and Mosca had a problem. Mussolini's dilemma was of a dual character: in his understanding of Marxism he thought he had discovered a series of inconsistencies in the official interpretation of that doctrine as given by the Italian Socialist Party of which he was a member. At the same time, he was doubtful that the proposed method to apply Marxism was suitable to the particular sociopolitical and economic conditions of life as he was observing them in Italy.

Mosca's reinterpretation of Marxism definitely lent a firm helping hand to Mussolini's dilemma. In short, Mussolini needed an ideological framework for Fascism, a new doctrine which had crystallized in his mind but which could easily trace its origins to Marx's philosophic determinism, and which—prior to its final crystallization—had gone through only one modification, that of Anarchism, equally Socialist in nature and origin.

The ultimate stage of Marxian society is a "classless" society, a society characterized by an enormous degree of cooperation and good will between individuals belonging to no class. The problem created by conflict of interests between the classes, as envisaged by Marx, was to be eliminated through the Revolution of the industrial proletarian class. It seems, however, that such ideal cooperation appeared to Mosca to be quite utopian. Although apparently unopposed to the Marxian suggestion of historic determinism, Mosca stressed a different aspect of that same determinism. He removed it from its broad social-class foundation (a foundation introduced by Marx) and proceeded to reduce it to an activity related only to the level of small fragments *within each class,* fragments which are predetermined to struggle with one another and use various means to impose their respective political authority on the remaining nonpolitical portions of *all classes.* Such a predetermined course of action appeared to Mosca as much more realistic and scientific than the broad Marxian conception of an extremely high degree of cooperation between social classes in their entirety.

Extracting basic historical data from the past (as Marx had done, or more precisely, like the modern empiricists in political science), Mosca attempted to develop mutually linked predictive *patterns* not on a broad, speculative, and a vague general foundation (the method of historic "trends"), but psychologically, through the influence and power of the vital, functional nuclei of human society. These nuclei were the small but power-attracted, enthusiastic political groups within each of the social classes. Thus, he brushed aside the Marxian idea of struggle between social classes, a struggle culminating in the "classless" society. Instead, he related that same predetermined struggle to small political groups only, regardless of their class affiliation. In order to make his analysis even more realistic, Mosca proposed that whatever group happened to retain State power during a given time should not pretend, demagogically, to apply the principle of democracy to all classes (or speak of "classless" interests) but should set itself the task of arranging for a rule frankly favoring the broad interests of that class to which the ruling group happened to belong.

Mosca saw the wave of the future in Socialism; but so did Mussolini, whether as a radical leftist and revolutionary Socialist at one time, or as an Anarchist at another, or finally (probably subconsciously) as a Fascist. Indeed, Mussolini did carry within himself the Socialist tradition, and adhered to it for a long time as a loyal Marxist. Therefore, the question may arise as to whether Fascism is merely a peculiar form or perhaps a *degeneration* of Socialism (see pp. 90–91).

Very much like Pareto, Mosca predicted the end of the parliamentary-democratic systems because of their inefficiency and lack of merit, shortcomings which the people were bound to become aware of at some future date.

In the second edition of his first book (the *Teoretica dei governi e sul governo parlamentari*) Gaetano Mosca proposed two remedies for the evils of democratic parliamentarism; he entertained the idea that national lawmakers should be independent of political considerations; he also favored the establishment of a system of mutual control among the prime political movers in a given regime: the groups exercising power. Thus, he advocated the introduction of means to avoid the chaos caused by arbitrariness in the decision-making process, as well as by the arbitrariness of radical impulses in the small groups in power. We can easily see that both of these remedies were applied by Fascism inasmuch as they were reflected in the Corporate State Structure (see pp. 45–47).

We may also conclude that (regardless of the unconfirmed but frequently emphasized allusions related to some ideological transformation of Mosca, during the last years of his life, toward greater tolerance of parliamentarism, as some Western scholars are saying in an attempt to "absolve" Mosca) Mosca's basic stand may rightfully be regarded as having influenced to a high degree both Fascism and its leader, Mussolini.

With these contributions in mind (Pareto's and Mosca's) we can return to the discussion of the Italian Liberal Party. In that context, one should make mention of another leader and prime minister, a man very active in the years immediately preceding the outbreak of World War I: the liberal Giovanni Giolitti. Giolitti first assumed leadership of Italy in 1892, then went out of office to return in 1903, 1906, 1911, and finally, in 1921, after World War I and prior to Mussolini's rise to power. He was known as an extremely shrewd politician, always capable of balancing all political groups within parliament in support of his Liberal Party's policies. He attracted these groups with generous promises, but always kept them only in part. These tactics proved very successful because the frequency of promises, followed by their being partially kept, made the opposing parliamentary groups modify their political stands and make concessions to the government of the Liberal Party in the hopes that eventually they would see their electorate's demands met, at least to some extent. The same tactics succeeded in bitterly disappointing the electorate of the opposition parties because of the always unfinished work and the unclear, constantly shifting stands taken by their representatives. One may say that the opposing parliamentary groups cooperated with the government; at the same time, by doing so, they were losing their constituent's support.

One may accept to a certain extent the argument that the papal prohibition for Italian Catholics to engage in voting and other State-sponsored activities prevented the emergence of a strong Catholic political party. Such an argument might be supported by the fact that once the prohibition was repealed in 1909, only a decade later (that is in 1919) a number of priests and Catholic laymen founded the Italian Catholic Populist Party. Like the Socialist Party, this political group had attracting mass support as one of its goals. In retrospect, however, one may detect a definite contradiction between the policy goals and the leadership composition of this new political party. On the one hand, it was geared toward a mass appeal, that is, it was trying to capture the support of the proletariat and/or the lower middle class; on the other hand, it was a highly conservative party if we are to judge by the ideas of its leading members. It was founded in 1919 (immediately after World War I), and the first political "baptism of fire" for the new party was scheduled to take place the following November, when general elections for the national parliament were to be held. Indeed, all political observers were amazed by the success this new party registered during the elections. As a matter of fact, it captured a very large percentage of the vote, electing 99 representatives to the Italian parliament. The profile of this vote clearly showed that it was largely proletarian and somewhat middle-class, just as projected by the party leaders. The vote came at the expense of the Socialist Party. The surprise was due not only to the sudden success of the young party, but also to the precision of the electoral calculations made by its leadership. The major planks of the party's platform in that campaign were as follows:

1. Mild reforms in favor of the poverty-stricken class, not calling, however, for a change in or modification of the existing spiritual conditions and social structure of the country. The mild reforms were mainly economic in nature.

2. Local political autonomy for the Italian provinces and regions.

3. A series of legislative measures making it possible for small proprietors to enlarge their holdings.

4. Creation of opportunities for close cooperation between the main opposing social classes represented by *employers* and *workers*. This feature, as well as its success, became quite important in the later development of Italy, especially for the ensuing corporate structure as an essential basis for the future Fascist State.

5. Inauguration of a peaceful foreign policy based on the spirit of the Covenant of the League of Nations.

Following the election, attempts at implementation of this platform caused a split within the Catholic Populist Party. The split could largely be attributed to the basic reason for the emergence of the party: to counteract the disturbingly strong waves of rising Socialism. The fulfillment of this goal, indeed, made it necessary to repeal in 1909 the debarment of Italian Catholics from the polls. The split was also due to the following reasons: the party rank-and-file membership had embraced the above platform to the letter, and, like the Socialists, they sincerely expected the implementation of anything which would favor the individual's well-being. Some of the activities by Catholic party members, in fact, outdid the Socialists in this respect. But the party leaders, who ran on this platform, were essentially very conservative; attraction of votes from the Socialists was, to their mind, the sole aim of the platform. Thus, the structural division within the party, on the one hand, and the political dispute regarding the platform, on the other, created the split. Although obvious, this conflict was not formally expressed. On the contrary, prior to the emergence of Fascism, the party succeeded in splitting the forces of discontent opposing the existing regime. In this manner it contributed to the strengthening of the government by weakening its opposition. This action was, indeed, timely, because the political forces of the opposition were then showing a clear tendency to coalesce within the ranks of the Socialist Party.

Another Italian political party, which at the time of the rise of Fascism was also prominent on the sociopolitical scene, was the Socialist Party. As mentioned earlier, the labor unions of Italy emerged in the North parallel to the advent and growth of industries. Although the unions' leadership carefully avoided identifying themselves with any particular political group, ideology, or doctrine, the Italian Socialist Party began gradually to take the shape of an organized body which was in fact rooted in the unions. To be more precise, we should mention that the Socialist Party of Italy emerged from those unions that presented the most radical and most determined demands in their defense of the interests of the working class; those unions stemmed from the local *Leagues of Resistance,* which had been quite active in the 1880s and 1890s. In fact, the Italian Socialist Party came into being at a time when the drive for improvement in the conditions of the industrial working class was being strongly penetrated by Marxism. Thus, it was German Marxism, not French Socialism, that colored the political outlook of the Italian trade union movement. Following the recognition of the legality of the unions by the State (toward the end of the nineteenth century), a strong Socialist drive for unification of the local unions with the larger provincial labor federations took place. This move finally climaxed in the formation of the *National League of Unions.* And the stronger this league became, the more pronounced appeared to be its radical political aspects of Marxian Socialism. In fact, the striking success of the Italian Socialist Party was due to a great extent to the party's excellent coordination of its activities with the demands of the labor unions; basically, the mass support for the party came from factory workers, farm laborers, and from small peasants.

Georges Sorel's influence (also attributed to have had an effect on Mussolini) may in this case have had an indirect impact on the Italian Socialist Party. Sorel had emphasized the paramount status of the *professional class* in government; in his eyes it was paramount to such an extent that by comparison all "political" groupings and parties were viewed by him as a useless absurdity. Sorel's stress on the power of the professional class may have contributed substantially to the overemphasis on "coordination" between trade-union activity and the actual emergence of the Italian Socialist Party. This would be, of course, a deviation from genuine Sorelianism.

Georges Sorel (1847–1922) was born in the French Atlantic port-city of Cherbourg. For most of his life he was strictly a professional man, a construction engineer. It was not until 1892, that he lost interest in his profession and devoted himself fully to the problems and the controversies of Socialism. Gradually he specialized to the extent of becoming one of the leading theoreticians of its Syndicalist brand. Deeply immersed in the Marxian school of thought, Sorel did not question the goals of that school, save for some theoretical dilemmas regarding a systematic and practical approach to the application of the Marxian provisions. However, the writings of the German philosopher Nietzsche influenced Sorel to such a degree that he found what appeared to him a satisfactory solution to this problem.

In addition to numerous articles in the French Socialist press, Sorel published at least seven important works beginning with *Le procès du Socrate,* published in 1889, followed by *La ruine du monde antique.* In 1900 he published *L'avenir socialiste des syndicats,* and in 1903 a work in Italian, *Saggi di critica del Marxismo.* In 1909 Sorel published two books, *L'illusion du progrès* and, what later became his most impressive work, *Réflexions sur la violence.* The latter was translated into English (by T. E. Hulme) in 1912—*Reflections on Violence*—and a second major edition appeared in 1915.

Sorel's last book, *De l'utilité du pragmatisme,* was published in France in 1921.

Sorel was strongly preoccupied with the idea of decadence amidst the bourgeois socioeconomic structure of society. He viewed the bourgeoisie as a group dedicated to leisure; it is unproductive and unnecessary to society, though dominating it. As a matter of fact, one may rightfully say that Sorel looked on them in as negative a manner as Saint-Simon did the "legalist-militarist" class in post-revolutionary France of the 1800s.

Believing in and adhering to Marxian determinism, Sorel interpreted it not in pragmatic terms, but through the image of an irrational force; that is, while he accepted the Marxian philosophic line of reasoning he was doubtful of the practicability of Marx's proposed economic solutions to the problems of the proletarian class. In other words, according to Sorel, the material conditions of the proletarian class needed improvement and they were improvable; but they were *not* improvable through rationally planned and pragmatic activity, since he maintained that the entire issue of dissatisfaction among the proletarian class is in its essence neither material nor rational. Therefore, it is of a different fabric, or denominator, thus it could be solved only through means identical to its essence. He viewed that class's frustrations as a reflection of something which, although not clearly defined, remains to be discovered in the realm of the *natural forces* of a mystical character. Natural forces enhance the proletarian class by creating among them a strong, determined, but essentially *emotional* drive which redounds to their benefit during the entire process of development of the modern world. But *force,* whether emotional, or material, always connotes *power;* therefore, when one uses power in the solution of controversies, one deals with an entity which is *violent* in its essence.

Sorel viewed the proletarian dilemma above all as a *professional* dilemma. Professional frustrations among the working class would find their most natural remedies *not* in a *political* but in a strictly professional cause. Thus, the use of a professional strike, or trade union movements, (as the expression of their natural and emotional drives) should be the most appropriate means for the proletariat. Precisely at this point one can observe Sorel's basic modification of, or departure from, original Marxism; one can observe Sorel's rejection of political action as a means for the workers' class, and consequently, his disregard of the political parties as useful to the proletariat and society. Logically and systematically then, professional problems could only generate their *natural* solutions in the form of a vaguely identified naturally corrective force, which could emerge only as a reaction to particular problems. Thus, solutions are to be based on an essential foundation identical to the essence of the problems; then, if the problems are professional in nature, all aspects of the solution should be also. Sorel observed, instead, attempts to place a natural impulse on rational grounds (on the platforms of workers' political parties, for instance) and characterized such attempts as an absurdity because one cannot make rational something which by definition is irrational—something which in its essence is a *myth.* Sorel's viewpoints may be also illustrated by religious teachings. Being mystical, religions are not disseminated and analyzed rationally, in fact, they are based on faith. As a result, if a political action should be needed to assure the fulfillment of a professional cause, then such an action *must not* be based on political rationality but only on guidance supplied by the impulse, the enthusiasm, the instinctive drives of the given professional group for such professional goals. It must be a *vision,* not a blueprint for human relationships. Therefore, political action is available, but should only serve as a tool controlled by professional emotional directives, and should work exclusively for reaching goals reflected in those directives. Thus, the myth—the professional, not the political, ideology—must form the foundation of all political expressions of the working class. Sorel saw such a professional ideology expressed in a dual framework: (a) *Socialism* in a broad, purely ideological sense; and (b) trade union *Syndicalism* in a narrow, concrete, or one may say, functional sense.

Drawing upon the Marxian concept of conflict between the socio-professional morality of the *bourgeoisie,* on the one hand, and that of the industrial *proletarian* class, on the other, Sorel seems to have synthesized the fundamental, most useful parts of each. This synthesis led to the introduction of his idea of a *producers' class morality.* As in the Saint-Simonian proposition, the leisure elements of society—the intellectuals and the non-service (non-tangibly constructive) portions of the bourgeoisie—are excluded in Sorel's system. Thus, he became a strong advocate of a new socioeconomic phenomenon—the unified producers' class—and, again resembling Saint-Simonian propositions, a class consisting of the productive bourgeoisie (the capital investors) and the productive industrial workers (the factory proletariat). This in Sorel's eyes was the essence of trade union Syndicalism, an arrangement which became the cornerstone of Fascism—the essence of the *Corporate Structure* of the Fascist State of Mussolini.

Considering himself an "interpreter" rather than a socioeconomic innovator, Sorel remained essentially a Marxist. He claimed, however, that through his definition of Syndicalism he had viewed and explained in its correct perspective the true meaning of Marxism. Mussolini, too, was a loyal Marxist during most of his political career, and one can now even begin to speculate that probably in his subconscious he was a Marxist throughout his life. This may be demonstrated by the type and substance of his legislative activity during the last months of the war in his *Fascist Republic* in Northern Italy shortly before he was seized and executed by Italian partisans.[15]

Thus, when placed within the Marxian context, Sorel's Syndicalism emerges as nothing but an integral part of Socialism—a quite refined and sophisticated part, indeed. It is stripped of all political rationalism, relying only on the natural impulses of the professional groups, on their incentives and instincts for the arrival at spontaneous and enthusiastic group actions; in other words: relying on a myth.

Following the October, 1917, Revolution in Russia, Sorel and Mussolini alike were rejected by Lenin as Socialists. Nevertheless, both remained at that time loyal Marxists, Sorel contributing substantially to the clarification of the meaning of the message left by Marx, while Mussolini searched for practical ways to implement the original Marxian doctrine in Italy.

Reverting to the emergence and development of the Italian Socialist Party, we may observe in it an inherent contradiction; it was very much like the contradiction in the Catholic Populist Party. A similar structural division within the party arose between the rank and file membership on the one hand, and the party leaders on the other. While the membership at large was homogeneous and limited to party supporters from the blue-collar working classes, the party leaders were in essence an *intellectual elite* consisting almost exclusively of lawyers and professors. So composed, the leading elite of the Italian Socialist Party kept itself aloof from the lower-class rank and file. When the Italian Socialist Party gained seats in parliament (a gain achieved because of the pronounced radicalism of the electoral platform), this elitist group of leaders and prominent political strategists gradually turned their backs on revolutionary Marxism and embraced a mild Socialist reformism. However, this policy gained

---

15A. James Gregor, *Ideology of Fascism: The Rationale of Totalitarianism*, New York (1969).

some support from the radical party membership at large. This condition soon created a virtual political split within the Italian Socialist Party. This split became painfully evident in the course of interparty strategy debates: should the party become one of *revolution* or *evolution?* The leader of the more restrained faction, advocating evolutionary Socialism through parliamentary reforms, was Leonida Bissolati. He was first elected to parliament in 1897.

Almost simultaneously the Socialist Party members, sympathizing with the radical syndicalist labor unions rather than with the other reform-minded workers' professional organizations, chose for their political leader a violent, radical man of action favoring open revolution, Arturo Labriola. During this period, Bissolati struggled to keep Italian Socialism within parliamentary bounds by constantly attempting to obtain a series of reforms for the Italian working class. Some of the major attempts at reform to be gained through parliamentary action were:

1. Improvement of workers' sickness compensation.
2. Extensive old-age insurance.
3. Improvement of working conditions in factories.
4. Reduction of the span of military service.
5. Establishment of a progressive income tax.

While Bissolati was preoccupied in obtaining all these innovations for the lower classes of Italy, the radical-minded Labriola, together with his group, was preaching the need for revolution. Their first step in that direction was to prepare and organize the populace for a large-scale general workers' strike, aimed at "terrifying the bourgeoisie."

While this contest between Bissolati and Labriola was taking place, the 1911 war against Turkey broke out. The ensuing victory for the Italian State, whose armed forces seized Tripoli, did not strengthen the appeal of mild reformism. On the contrary, the national spirit of the Italian people soared; it appeared that any kind of radicalism would gain ground faster among the people than would the preaching of evolutionary, slow-moving reformism. Suddenly, it seemed that Mazzinian early *"Risorgimento"* hopes for the "renovation" of the Italian people were near fulfillment. This situation created the *first major shake-up* within the Italian Socialist Party.

It was obvious that Italy's war against Turkey had strongly imperialistic aims. Such aims were, however, contrary to Socialist principles. As a result, Bissolati's policy of evolution and his willingness to work through the parliament, began to appear in the eyes of the workers as inefficient. First of all, he did not succeed in gaining parliamentary approval of Socialist principles; above all, he did not succeed in securing the most fundamental Socialist principle, that is, the *prevention* of imperialist war.

In such an atmosphere two consecutive congresses of the Italian Socialist Party were held. They proved very important for its future. The first took place in 1911, and the other in 1912. At the first congress, Bissolati was harshly criticized for the above-mentioned inefficiency by a number of congress delegates. At the congress of 1912, this same type of criticism of the evolutionary Socialist ideas continued and even increased in fervor. In fact, it proved to be the most crucial congress of the Italian Socialist Party during that era. During its sessions, a new figure appeared on the speaker's platform, a man who left a tremendous impact on the delegates. He belonged wholeheartedly to the radical revolutionary wing of Arturo Labriola. That individual was Benito Mussolini, from Predappio (Forli), then only 29. He gave an ardent and blistering speech vigorously attacking all reformist tendencies and methods of Socialism in general. He then introduced a series of wild political jokes which ended by ridiculing the bourgeois parliaments. He closed by calling for the expulsion of the reformist leader, Bissolati, from the ranks of the Italian Socialist Party. Mussolini's call was adopted, and Bissolati was expelled.

Mussolini's impact on the Socialist Party congress of 1912 was so overwhelming that soon after the close of the proceedings the party appointed him to the position of editor-in-chief of its leading newspaper, *Avanti.*

Benito Mussolini (1883–1945) was of simple peasant origin. Already during his earlier years he began to preach against poverty, misery, and tyranny. He firmly embraced the principles of revolutionary Socialism in the Marxian sense. Mussolini was an excellent speaker; he had the ability to play with the emotions of his audiences, and he also was unsurpassed as a journalist. He loved to read, hence he learned a great deal from the works of Machiavelli, Saint-Simon, Proudhon, Nietzsche, Pareto, Sorel, Mosca, and many others. He was also thoroughly acquainted with the ideas of Giuseppe Mazzini. Within the Italian Socialist Party he played the role of a very radical proletarian revolutionary.

As such, Mussolini had firmly embraced all the principles of revolutionary Socialism, principles which would be differently expressed following the formation of the Italian Communist Party. Toward the fulfillment of these principles, Mussolini used his excellent speaking and journalistic gifts. The almost continuous reading to which he devoted much of his spare time not only broadened his knowledge but also provided him with a great deal of theoretical ammunition in political disputes. By skillfully presenting his ideas to the Italian people he very often convinced them of the correctness of his position. During Italy's war with Turkey he appeared as a strong internationalist and a firm anti-militarist. In implementation of these two positions he successfully organized and led a number of workers' strikes in protest against the war. During the strikes Mussolini frequently countered the soaring nationalist spirit of the Italian people by teaching that there was nothing wrong with being a nationalist but that true nationalism cannot be expressed by war, especially not by an imperialistic war like the one Italy was waging against Turkey. Instead, true nationalism—love of the fatherland—can only be demonstrated through domestic struggle and, if necessary, through open hostilities, not to conquer foreign lands but to secure the best interests of the Italian proletarian working class.

Because of these speeches Mussolini was soon arrested. However, his imprisonment lasted only a matter of months. Upon his release, Mussolini continued to bitterly denounce the war, and, moreover, he now spoke against any colonial adventure, against any suppression of economic, and political democracy; he also preached against the absolutism of the State institution. He was equally opposed to arrests, deportations, and jail sentences, and above all, he remained a very strong believer in the proletarian revolution as the only means to remedy the deplorable conditions in Italy.

The second *major shake-up* of the Italian Socialist Party came only three years later (in 1915); it related to the burning issue of whether Italy should participate in World War I. At that time the country was bound by the Triple Alliance to support Austria-Hungary and Germany. Even though the country was bound by treaty, the Italian Prime Minister, Antonio Salandra, had secretly negotiated with the Western allies. He had proposed to France and England that Italy join their side on the condition that she receive a portion of Austrian territory after the final victory. He wanted an allied promise allowing Italy to incorporate the following provinces to be taken from Austria: *Trentino, Tyrol, Trieste,* and *Istria,* and the coast of the *Dalmatia,* and also a few less prominent areas, all remnants of the formerly strong but now dismembered Turkish empire in Africa.

In the meantime, however, Mussolini had introduced a change (probably a tactical change as a result of Socialist intra-party politics) in his anti-militaristic policy. While the main body and most of the leadership of the Italian Socialist Party were preaching neutrality for Italy in World War I, Mussolini, at the end of 1914, suddenly became a strong interventionist on the side of France and England. His speaking ability and journalistic gifts helped him gain immediate support from a highly radical wing of the Socialist Party. For taking this stance, interpreted by the Socialist Party leadership as a betrayal of their principles of nonintervention, Mussolini was relieved of the position as editor of *Avanti.* A second, more strongly retaliatory action followed: he was summarily expelled from the party.

Mussolini's reaction was immediate and forceful. First, with the support of Elias Jona, a Jewish adherent of Mussolini while organizing the first Fascist groups, he began the publication of his own newspaper, *Il Popolo d'Italia.* There are some indications that substantial financial help was granted to this newly-formed paper by the French government because of Mussolini's interventionist attitude favoring the Western allies. At any rate, clear proof of this has not been found in spite of the very careful and intensive research done in this work on that particular matter.

Mussolini's second reaction to his expulsion from the Party was the making of merely contact at first but later a virtual alliance with Filippo Corridoni, the uncontested leader of a substantial number of the Socialist party members, professionally organized within the radical Syndicalist Labor Union. Mussolini's alliance with Corridoni gave him Socialist support within the Party—a support given by the same membership from which he was expelled and whose leaders he was now engaged in fighting.

It was with these members led by Corridoni (and also with some smaller but equally radical nationalistic groups) that early in 1915 Mussolini organized the so-called *Fasci di Combattimento* in the northern part of the country, and the *Fasci di Azione Revoluzionaria,* centered in Milan. Mussolini became the leader of the latter organization. Literally translated, the term *Fasci* means "bundles," and the term was not new to Italy nor, in particular, to the Italian Socialist Party. On the contrary, it was strictly in line with Socialist tradition. As early as 1891 the Socialists had founded among the peasant communities in the South an organization known as the *Fasci Siciliani.* Thus, one can see that the term *Fascism* in its modern sense is a legacy from the older *Socialist* vocabulary, in spite of its popular attribution to the Roman Empire, to which even the leading Fascists later subscribed in view of the new domestic and international developments. However, the *Fasci Siciliani* of 1891 had quite different goals from the two new Fascist organizations. The aims of the former group were to further education, to encourage the building of public libraries, to promote land reform, and to establish agricultural cooperatives. Nevertheless, in spite of their humanitarian nonviolent goals, they were very bitterly suppressed by the government.

Mussolini continued to retaliate for his expulsion from the Italian Socialist Party. He prepared and delivered one of his finest speeches focusing entirely on the Socialist Party leadership. He stated, in reference to the Socialists who had voted for his expulsion, that in a few years the Italian masses would follow and applaud *him,* while the *Socialists* would no longer be allowed to speak, or even have followers. This could, indeed, be looked upon as a prophecy.

In spite of his break with the Party, Mussolini continued throughout the war to act as the champion of the underprivileged proletariat. This was not only his general attitude but he also used the *Fasci di Combattimento* in a radical Socialist tradition to compete with the Socialist and the Catholic Populist parties in upholding the interests of the lower working class. Both of these parties continued to call for gradual social reforms. These moderate demands, however, began more and more to acquire, even within their respective parties, radical and violent overtones. Finally, the radicalism which emerged during the war years (and which was freely encouraged by Mussolini) culminated toward the end of hostilities with the rise of another violently ultranationalistic leader, Gabriele d'Annunzio.

While the Versailles Peace Conference was debating the peace treaties, d'Annunzio learned from reports that Italy was about to be cheated in respect to the prewar promises made by France and England—those promises which had made Italy decide on an intervention in favor of the Western allies. As a result, fulfilling what he thought was his duty to the Italian nation, d'Annunzio decided to act in his country's best interests. Politically a nationalist and a radical, d'Annunzio was also a sentimental poet, a daredevil pilot, and above all, an extremely courageous soldier.

In September, 1919, d'Annunzio, leading a small, well-organized group of nationalist radicals, without advance notice or knowledge of the Italian government, and in defiance of decisions already made by the Versailles Peace Conference, used force to enter the Adriatic port city of Fiume. The city had belonged to the dismembered Austro-Hungarian Empire and had been included in the pre-intervention Anglo-French territorial promise to Italy. D'Annunzio's aggressive action was taken on the grounds that all indications pointed to the port of Fiume becoming part of the territory of newly created Yugoslavia. D'Annunzio and his men occupied the city and chased the Yugoslavs away, proclaiming Fiume a free city under their rule.

The coup was well organized and for many months the Italian government was unable to clear the city of d'Annunzio and his men. In fact, Italian governmental weakness was vividly displayed. One reason was the fact that a large part of the state's armed forces, seeing their wartime patriotism through d'Annunzio's rather than their government's eyes, were already aiding d'Annunzio. This circumstance prevented the implementation of governmental orders in regard to Fiume. Even the generals did not remain loyal to the government relative to this highly inflammatory issue.

One may say that the occupation of the city of Fiume illustrated the great weakness of the Italian government. As a matter of fact, the Prime Minister, Francesco Nitti, and his cabinet proved completely unable to clear Fiume of d'Annunzio's forces. Credit for the final achievement of this goal (after a few months of d'Annunzio's rule) must be given to the skillful political maneuverings of the former Prime Minister of the Liberal Party, Giolitti. Through direct negotiations with d'Annunzio he finally succeeded in clearing the city and establishing the new Italian boundary with newly created Yugoslavia.

This incident obviously constituted a very hard blow to the authority of the Italian government. Further troubles followed, all of which were caused by the Italian Socialist Party.

In spite of its popularity, the total membership in the Socialist Party was estimated immediately prior to World War I in the neighborhood of 50,000. However, in 1919, after the war years and just before new parliamentary elections were scheduled to take place, the number of card-carrying members had increased to 200,000. In the elections of 1919 the candidates of the

Socialist Party received 1,840,000 votes. All the other political parties and groups combined received no more than 3,500,000 votes. Thus, the Italian Socialist Party emerged as the strongest single political party in the country. The number of Socialist seats in parliament tripled to a total of 156.

The second strongest party in Italy, on the basis of these elections, was the Catholic Populist Party with 99, or as has sometimes been reported by Italian sources, 101, elected members of parliament.

For both parties, these were spectacular results, corresponding closely to respective developments within their specific spheres, namely, the trade unions under their control. The General Confederation of Labor, controlled by the Italian Socialist Party, had in 1914 a membership of about 300,000 organized workers. In 1919, however, just prior to the elections, its membership reached almost 1,375,000 workers. It continued to increase sharply after the elections so that one year later, in 1920, it totalled 2,300,000 members.

The Catholic trade unions controlled by the Catholic Populist Party had a much less spectacular membership total. However, in 1919 the number exceeded 700,000.

The results of the 1919 elections in Italy demonstrated very clearly that the end of the conventional bourgeois-democratic type of regime in Italy was clearly in sight. Something new was coming, and this new governmental arrangement, in order to be popular and acceptable to the Italian people, had to be very different from the prevailing political traditions. The spectacular Socialist success had excited—but as one may now conclude, quite prematurely—Socialist Party adherents to the extent that they publicly announced the birth of revolutionary and proletarian Italy.

Aside from the Socialist and the Catholic Populist parties and the Fascist movement, the other parties were all conventional bourgeois-democratic ones, and from that moment on ceased to play an important role in the sociopolitical development of Italy. Like the Socialists and Catholic Populists, Mussolini's Fascist movement was by no means a conventional one. It presented itself with vigor in the electoral campaign, a vigor which denoted a strong determination to win the elections. However, for the Fascist movement to win the elections at that time meant to compete successfully against both the Italian Socialist and the Catholic Populist parties, to defeat the two strongest political forces in the country. The electoral platform and campaign slogans of the Fascist movement were both revolutionary and proletarian in nature; its political strategy attempted to attract the very same societal layers to whom the Italian Socialist and Catholic Populist parties appealed.

But the results, in spite of a vigorous and dynamic campaign, were very disappointing. Not a single Fascist member managed to get elected to the parliament. In the Fascist stronghold of Milan, the headquarters of the *Fasci di*

Azione Revoluzionaria, Mussolini himself received only 5,000 votes out of the 268,000 cast in that city.

This setback, a veritable shock to the Fascists, may be regarded as the reason for the *first modification* of the Fascist doctrine in a broad sense and for the future Fascist platform in a narrow sense. Maintaining until then a Socialist-Marxian revolutionary stance—leading to a direct political confrontation with the Socialists and the Catholic Populists—Fascist doctrine now shifted its grounds. It would appear that as a result of this modification Fascism embraced the doctrine of Anarchism in order to appear more attractive and humanely individualistic to the Italian populace. In 1920 Mussolini announced this shift by using the usual slogans in carefully prepared speeches. He maintained that from then on the supporters of Fascism were the last survivors of individualism. Therefore, they should embrace the consoling faith of Anarchism.

The smashing 1919 electoral success of the Italian Socialist Party was not the only reason for the increasing governmental troubles in Italy; further troubles ensued. The newly elected Socialists continuously disturbed and obstructed the legislative function of the parliament. For instance, during the first post-electoral meeting of the new legislature the Socialists refused en bloc to meet the King in parliament. It was clear that the Italian Socialist Party was growing more and more revolutionary. Its representatives increasingly propagated disruption, and the party as a whole initiated a series of powerful anti-government strikes, all marked by brutal violence. Indeed, there occurred in succession strikes by post office workers, railroad workers, workers on the waterfront and in the textile factories, and by many others. As a result of this activity—after the proletarian spirit and revolutionary enthusiasm had reached a peak—a real Socialist "occupation" took place in 1919 and 1920. It limited itself to the northern half of the country. The industrial workers, as a part of organized revolutionary marches, purely and simply entered and occupied by force their places of work and refused to leave the premises. Once inside, they did not interrupt production; on the contrary, they attempted to continue it on their own through the aid of hurriedly-formed workers' councils (*soviets*). For a while, this original idea was to even speed up production. As had been the case in the Fiume situation, the government found itself completely helpless. This indicated the incipient end of the traditional bourgeois-democratic parties of the country.

Mussolini seemed to have readjusted the Fascist stand in order to increase the movement's influence over the people. In *Il Popolo d'Italia* and in numerous statements made on various occasions he complimented the Italian industrial proletariat. He praised the workers for having not only met their Socialist obligation (by seizing the capitalist-owned factories), but also for having been aware of the political and economic interests of the great Italian nation as well. This awareness of the nation's interests was, according to Mussolini, demonstrated by their attempt to better and speed up production, that is, they were fulfilling a *national* obligation. On this occasion, Mussolini again introduced a *new*, but this time, *final modification* of the doctrine of Fascism. At this point he apparently shifted from Anarchism toward a significant degree of nationalism. This shift was appropriately inaugurated with the unification of all the independent Fascist organizations into one single organization, *Fascio Nazionale dei Combattimenti.* Several accounts, some of them contradicting the others, are now available relative to the emergence and the strength of this endeavor. One pre-Nazi German source, which appears to agree most closely with the *real conditions* of the time, states that the constituent delegates met in the city of Milan, during the month of March, 1919. The attendance probably totalled about 145 persons, almost all of them members of the Italian workers' *Syndicalist* Union.[16]

Although our source does not especially emphasize this aspect, it is reported that the meeting was also attended by a delegation of Italian intellectuals: artists, mostly middle-class painters, and writers. All available evidence indicates that the meeting's primary objective, the proposed unification of the Fascist organizations, was achieved smoothly and with no apparent difficulties. It would appear that it was nothing more than a public formality since for quite a long time (since 1915) all the independent Fascist organizations had been acting in harmony, supporting and promoting the same cause. In reality, the major outcome of this meeting was of a different nature and had significant sociopolitical consequences. It was to formally reaffirm Mussolini's attitude toward the Italian workers in general, and their occupation of the industrial plants in particular. Indeed, the meeting did formally approve and send a message of encouragement and sympathy to all workers participating in the occupation, although the actual phrasing related primarily to the action undertaken in one particular factory, namely, that at Dalmine.

Obviously, all this was intended to increase Fascist membership by attracting larger numbers of the working class initially, and later, the middle and intellectual classes as well. This tactic aimed at preaching *class unity* in the Saint-Simonian sense rather than complying with the Marxian prediction on the inevitability of *class struggle.* Indeed, the attendance at the meeting of middle-class poets, writers, and artists, sitting alongside workers-syndicalists and manual workers, could only indicate that the idea had already worked quite well.

The maneuver of praising the workers' occupation of the Italian factories seemed to have paid off. Indeed, this play on the nationalistic feelings of the proletarian class had had its effect on a large number of workers. Gradually they

---

16E. V. Beckerath, *Wesen und Werden des faschistischen Staates;* Berlin (1927).

began to gather around the Fascist movement at the expense of the Socialist Party. However, the maneuver also gave the signal for a sharp and vigorous reaction on the part of the Socialist Party. Nevertheless, it backfired and brought about the party's *third major shake-up:* during a meeting of Socialist groups in January, 1921, as a response to Mussolini's gathering strength, one group vigorously praised Lenin for his work. The meeting ended with this group forming the *Italian Communist Party,* independent from the Socialists. Thus, the Socialist split became final.

Throughout these developments the Italian parliament remained packed with representatives of the Socialist Party who were radical enough to openly support the workers' occupation of the factories. The government completely lacked the authority, the power, and above all, the needed respect to deal smoothly and effectively with this Socialist threat. Finally, the government resolved to take action. But even this tardy move reflected the ultimate helplessness of the Italian central authority; the government made a desperate appeal to the former prime minister of the Liberal Party, Giovanni Giolitti. In its desperation, the government simply asked him to take over and do his best to restore normality. So desperate was this action that it was comparable only to the hesitant steps taken to counter d'Annunzio's occupation of Fiume.

Giolitti had already reached his 78th birthday. His physical and mental energies could no longer be compared to those the shrewd Italian diplomat had displayed in former days. For the first time, he failed in his attempts at political maneuvering on the domestic scene. He was not aware of the shift having taken place in political conditions and in the new state of affairs in general. Giolitti, taking advantage of a constitutional provision related to national crises dissolved the parliament and called for new elections, scheduling them for the spring of 1921. This was the simplest move he could have chosen. The Fascist movement under Mussolini, the Nationalist movement, and a few organized agrarians were invited to join the Liberal Party in appearing on a common ticket for these new elections. Giolitti's main purpose was to defeat the Socialists with a winning coalition. He had, in fact, no precise plans as to what to do with his three partners after the election. He knew only that it was essential to defeat the Socialists and Catholic Populists, and hoped to deal with the coalition at a later, less pressing date, by utilizing his former tactics.

Giolitti's plan, however, did not work as originally designed. The election of 1921 did not greatly modify the composition of the Italian parliament; more especially, it did not serve to diminish the strength of the Socialists and Catholic Populists. They again emerged as the strongest political parties in Italy, the Socialist Party alone receiving 138 seats in the parliament. An entirely new political phenomenon, however, appeared in the national legislature. As a result of Giolitti's alliance with the Fascists and the Nationalists, and Mussolini's recent maneuvers with the radical workers, the Fascist forces emerged for the first time as a power in the parliament; the Fascists won 35 seats.

The electoral campaign demonstrated quite clearly that Mussolini had succeeded in increasing substantially the popularity of the Fascists. A profile illustrating the pro-Fascist vote by professions clearly indicates that the Fascist movement had not attracted the bulk of the workers, but mostly the upper industry-owning class and the large and medium proprietors. In addition, the Fascists also received the support of the more prosperous peasants and farmers as well as small craftsmen. When one compares this profile with the type of campaign conducted by the Fascists, one can understand that Mussolini's electoral expectations were for the first time completely fulfilled. His campaign had called for a government supporting a full-scale laissez faire economy with due respect for private property, private business profits, and private initiative; the campaign insisted on limited governmental interference in the affairs of big business. This particular pro-Fascist vote was probably symptomatic of a fear of sweeping welfare legislation (which would naturally jeopardize high profit margins) if the Socialists were to remain in power. These categories of voters felt that they were already on the road to prosperity and consequently voted for Fascism.

Once in parliament, Mussolini began to accommodate his movement to that of the Nationalists. He then effected a rapprochement with the Church, and finally with the King. Through its accommodation with the Church, the Fascist movement gained some support from the parliamentary group of the Catholic Populist Party. The intent behind the rapprochement with the King was an increase in the prestige of the Fascist movement. Finally, during August of 1921 Mussolini even reached a temporary agreement for united action with the Socialist Party in an attempt to weaken Giolitti's coalition.

Curiously enough one may say that all this maneuvering on the part of Mussolini resembled closely the tactics of Giolitti; but Mussolini was to succeed while Giolitti was no longer able to make any progress.

Taking full advantage of the new situation, Mussolini launched a vast propaganda campaign explaining the *meaning* of Fascism. This campaign was aimed at a population which was totally disaffected by the state of affairs in the country. Its result was a smashing success.

Quickly, Fascism began to transform itself into a mass movement distinct and separate from other political groups. Mussolini's campaign was constantly expanding; the campaign not only emphasized the meaning of Fascism—that is, its ideology—but it also made use of psychological findings to create an appearance of spectacular achievement. Special signs and dress were used in order to distinguish the members of the movement from other groups. Thus, black shirt uniforms (purposely or coincidentally, the symbolic color of Anarchism) were to be worn by the members of the Fascist movement. This was coupled with the old *Roman* raised-arm salute which was used as a greeting.

It has been estimated that prior to 1920 there were only about 17,000 members of the Fascist movement. In 1920, however, total Fascist membership was estimated to have reached 100,000; a year later there were already 320,000 card-carrying Fascist members in black-shirt uniforms. In 1922, the units of the "Fascio Nazionale dei Combattimenti" officially formed a *separate political party* namely, the Fascist Party of Italy. It counted 477,000 members.

Toward the end of 1922 the chaotic sociopolitical and economic situation in Italy finally reached a climax. Members of the newly created Fascist Party, while continuing their propaganda campaign (now based on claims that they were the only ones that could save Italy from ruin), began in addition to organize violent action in the streets. As had the supporters of Mazzini, Fascist sympathizers succeeded in infiltrating the armed forces. This was relatively easy to achieve because the draft system was not interested in screening the new recruits. But the more important success of the Fascist Party infiltration policy was the infiltration of the police force. Once this was achieved, the Fascists began to model their endeavors on the Socialist Party. Starting in the North, they began a gradual but massive occupation of selected points throughout the country. The difference between the actions of the Fascists and that of the Socialists was that instead of occupying industrial plants (which would be primarily an occupation of a *professional* and economic nature) the Fascist Party ordered the occupation of local operative administrative agencies of the State, that is, an occupation of a purely *political* nature. In line with this action, the police force and the local administrative officers in northern Italy (already penetrated by Fascist thinking) allowed the Blackshirts to occupy police headquarters, State-owned railway stations, wireless facilities, and post offices. In general, the Blackshirts gradually began to occupy all types of public buildings in the North. Once again following the Socialist Party's example, the Fascist activists continued to maintain the existing organization of the administration, preventing any interruption in the functioning of the occupied offices. In this particular sense, one may say that the Fascist occupation in northern Italy was orderly and disciplined, and as far as the organizers were concerned, it never got out of hand. At this point the occupation began to expand gradually toward central Italy, and then toward the South. Estimated data on the number of participating Blackshirts in this action vary and are, indeed, in some cases quite contradictory. Very few of the available sources are in agreement in this respect; however, the minimum number seems to be around 50,000. On the other hand, the highest number reported in relation to Blackshirt participation in the occupation is 300,000. The movement toward the South was solemnly given the name the *March on Rome*.

Due to the successful Fascist infiltration of the armed forces and of the police, the March on Rome was essentially unopposed by the provincial administrations. Finally, on October 28, 1922, the occupation of the first public building in the suburbs of Rome took place.

For a second time on the sociopolitical scene in Italy, the model of d'Annunzio's occupation was acted out; at first such an occupation had been carried out by the Socialist-syndicalist workers, and now by the Fascists. The government leaders of Italy faced this action in a chaotic and panicky state of mind; they exhibited nothing but weakness. After a series of ministerial conferences, the government reached a decision for the King to proclaim martial law and a state of national emergency. An estimate made by General Badoglio, however, seemed to suggest that Fascist strength was more a façade than a reality, and that even slight military resistance would have crushed the assault on Rome. The Commander-in-Chief is quoted as having said on that occasion that if he had been allowed to direct a mere five minutes of gunfire against the marchers, the march on Rome would have disintegrated.

When the hesitant government presented the King with its desire for a proclamation of martial law and a state of national emergency, the Monarch refused to sign the document. He argued that his duty was to avoid, not to provoke a civil war. The King was indeed fearful of the possible results from such a proclamation; confidential reports reaching him had revealed that a large number of his high-ranking officers were already strong supporters of Fascism. Contrary to what Badoglio thought, the King felt that he could no longer trust his armed forces against the Blackshirts.

Although refusing to endorse the government-proposed action, the King came up with a decision of his own, a decision which—given the particular situation—he thought would be most beneficial for the country. On October 29, 1922, one day after the occupation of the first public building in Rome, the King dispatched a call to Mussolini who was directing the occupation from his headquarters at Milan. The dispatch asked Mussolini to come to Rome and form a new government; he was to become prime minister. Mussolini accepted without hesitation. He traveled by train to the capital, passing on the way crowds of cheering Blackshirts who had occupied every railroad station.

Initial support for the newly formed Fascist government came from big industry. On November 2, 1922, the General Confederation of Industries (the organization of employers) congratulated the new regime and expressed its great faith in Mussolini and in his domestic and foreign policy.

The hierarchy of the Italian Fascist Party at first comprised an unofficial assembly of leading members who gathered occasionally on a purely voluntary basis. This assembly was given the name *Grand Council of Fascism*. Its function was to advise the party leader of various social, economic, and State matters. Later, the Grand Council was formally incorporated into the Party. Thus, by virtue of the political seniority of its members, it became the Party's nerve center, quite similar by its role to the central committees of the various Communist parties. Finally, the Council became Italy's chief governing body— the general staff of Fascism.

The Grand Council of Fascism contained three different kinds of members: (a) members for life; (b) ex-officio members; and (c) extra-ordinary members.

Members for life included the prime minister; the "Quadrumvirate" (the four leading Fascists who, under Mussolini's direction, had led the March on Rome); former members of the Fascist cabinets on the condition that they had served in that capacity for at least five years; and all secretaries-general of the Fascist Party since the March on Rome.

Ex-officio members consisted of the president of the Senate; the speaker of the corporate legislative chamber; the cabinet ministers currently in office; the under-secretaries of the prime minister's office, the Ministry of Foreign Affairs, the Ministry of the Interior, and the Ministry of Labor; the members of the Central Executive Committee of the Fascist Party; the president of the National Organization for Industry and Agriculture; the president of the workers' trade unions; and five other leading party men with no administrative titles, directly chosen by the prime minister.

The group entitled *extra-ordinary members* was composed of people specially designated for two reasons: (a) having served well the national cause of Italy and of the Fascist Revolution; and (b) being experts on national issues when such were under discussion by the Council.

The composition of the last-named group was not permanent; it frequently changed according to the Grand Council's agenda. For instance, the group would have a majority of economists if economic issues were the main consideration of the Council; it would have, at another time, a majority of experts on social conditions if the Council were discussing national social problems, etc.

The first two groups (members for life and ex-officio members) totalled thirty-five persons. In view of the flexible nature of the third group (that of extra-ordinary members), the Council did not have a definite size; its size varied according to the Grand Council's agenda.

One of the chief functions of the Grand Council of Fascism was to approve candidates for the legislative chamber. The selection of candidates for the ticket was done according to the following procedure, based on the Saint-Simonian principle of enhancement of the "producers' class": During a special meeting in Rome, the members of the national councils of the existing National Confederation of Employers and the National Confederation of Employees, along with the representatives of the National Confederation of Professional Classes, were to submit lists of names of locally selected members from their own respective organizations. The total number of names was limited to eight hundred, four hundred each from the "employers" and "employees" organizations. To this original selection, two hundred additional candidates were added by various public organizations of cultural, educational, and charitable significance. However, those organizations, in order to be eligible to present their own candidates, had to have special governmental accreditation. Accreditation was granted only when recommended by five members of the Italian Senate and five members of the Chamber. Out of this total (one thousand candidates) the Grand Council of Fascism was to eliminate through a screening process six hundred names while retaining (in the above proportions) the most appropriate candidates, thus, reducing the number to four hundred. These, then, constituted the election ticket which was then presented to the Italian people for their vote; they were either to approve or disapprove the entire list in toto.[17]

Determined at first (in 1914) to influence the Socialist Party from within by inspiring radicalism and working for revolution, then attempting to appeal directly and almost exclusively to the lower working class in direct confrontation with the interests of the Socialist and the Catholic Populist parties, followed by overtures to Socialist Anarchism, the Fascist leader finally received (in 1922) the full support of Italian industry and big business.

During the early months of 1923, the Fascist Party endeavored through another action to increase its support and popularity. It merged with the Nationalist movement and formally *in theory* got rid of the last vestiges of Marxism in its ideology. This is, in fact, the usually recited evolution of Fascism, thus attributing to its leader the above series of simple political maneuvers all of apparently demagogic character, aimed at personal opportunistic goals. However, one might also attempt to advance another line of argument which may eventually have more substance.

First: Mussolini developed his political career as an intellectual adherent of Marxism, having read substantially all the French revolutionary and world syndicalist literature.

Second: he had embraced the radical revolutionary interpretation of Marx's school of thought. This made him reject Socialist *legal* attempts to reform society and the workers' conditions through peaceful, evolutionary, primarily parliamentary means. Thus, he automatically took his place among the leaders of Communist philosophy, that is, the violent, revolutionary wing of Marxism. Mussolini's continued adherence to the Italian Socialist Party may be accounted for by the fact that Italy at that time had no formal Communist Party.

---

[17]See *Chart I* (referring to the period 1925–1938) and *Chart II* (1938–1943), pp. 92–93. Table on pp. 94–95 reflects the result of the Grand Council's screening of the corporations' nominees for the 1929 legislature.

Third: before switching to the ranks of Nationalism, the Fascist leader, while deeply involved in disputes with the Socialists, made desperate and very serious efforts to remain within the framework of Socialism. These attempts are most clearly reflected in Mussolini's momentary acceptance of the Anarchist creed. He called it the "absurd faith in Anarchism"; but nevertheless, it appeared to be his last resort, the least compromising of any effort to remain close to Socialism. Indeed, Marxism and Anarchism share an almost identical long-range goal, namely, disposing of the institution of the State.

When one attempts, on the one hand, to view Mussolini from the above perspective, and, on the other, when one keeps in mind the *theoretical limitations* of Marxism (limitations which quite clearly state that Communism can only emerge in a post-democratic and post-industrial society), one may, indeed, formulate a very interesting conclusion. One may say that all attempts at adapting Marxism loyally and to the letter to Italian post-democratic and post-industrial conditions, in spite of all of Mussolini's efforts, degenerated. They degenerated to the extent of revealing an entirely new form of dictatorship, *Fascism,* a sociopolitical phenomenon completely unforeseen by Marx; it was a phenomenon based on local *national* conditions offering a suitable terrain for bridging the socioeconomic and political contradictions, *unifying* the productive classes in society, instead of following the pattern of "class struggle"; it was a phenomenon that grew out of the fallacy in Marxian predictions related to the above conditions for the growth of Communism.

The Fascist regime in Italy may be divided into two separate periods:

1. A period from 1925 (after three years of consolidation) to 1938.

2. A period from 1938 to the summer of 1943 (due to foreign control and influence, the emergence and the short-lived development of the Fascist Republic in North Italy could be omitted).

The following charts and table illustrate the basic arrangement of the Fascist corporate-state structure with particular emphasis on the functional role of the corporations; note the employers' and the workers' joint participation in the selection of the slate of candidates.

Chart I indicates this arrangement for the period 1925–1938.

Chart II illustrates the 1938–1943 modification with the basic changes in the originally established corporate structure. Note the change which curtailed the legislative role of the corporations and the elimination of the suffrage; also the renaming of the legislative chamber. This action was justified by the Grand Council of Fascism by the approaching war which, coupled with the Fascist awareness of lack of preparedness for war, necessitated a much stricter domestic control to provide needed State flexibility and quick decision-making procedures as well as guaranteeing a minimum involvement in controversial debates.

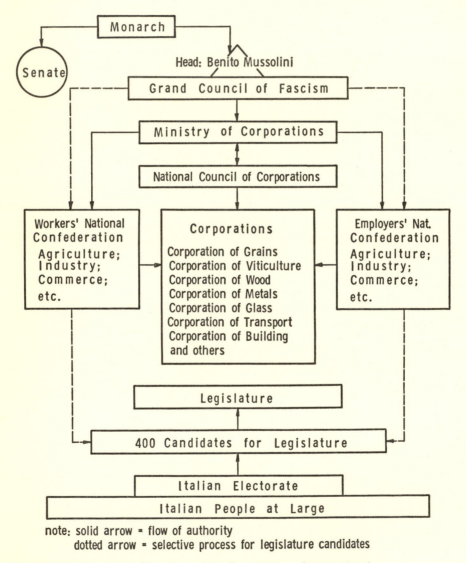

note: solid arrow = flow of authority
      dotted arrow = selective process for legislature candidates

Chart I. The Corporate Structure of the Fascist State (1925–1938)

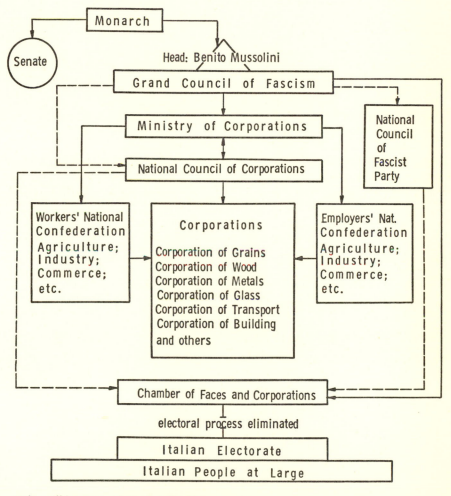

note: solid arrow = flow of authority
      dotted arrow = selective process for chamber of faces and corporations

Chart II. The Corporate Structure of the Fascist State (1938–1943)

THE CORPORATE STRUCTURE

PREPARATION OF THE 1929 ELECTORAL TICKET FOR THE ITALIAN LEGISLATURE (THE CHAMBER OF DEPUTIES)

Corporate organizations, or other organized public agencies	Number of candidates nominated	Number of candidates approved by the Grand Council of Fascism
A. Employers' confederations		
Agriculture	96	46
Industry	80	31
Commerce	48	16
Marine transportation	40	10
Land transportation	32	12
Banks, credit & insurance	24	10
Total	320	125
B. Employees' confederations		
Agriculture	96	27
Industry	80	26
Commerce	48	10
Marine transportation	40	11
Land transportation	32	9
Banks, credit & insurance	24	6
Total	320	89
C. State employees		
Civil servants	28	7
Railroad, post office, telegraph, etc.	9	3
Universities	30	15
Secondary schools	15	5
Elementary schools	10	4
Total	92	34
Total, employees	412	123
D. Other categories		
Liberal arts & professions (corporated)	160	82
War veterans	45	40
Wounded veterans	30	14
Academies of art and science	9	2
National Center (Catholic)	8	4
Fascist Institute of Culture	3	1
Institute of Fine Arts	2	2
Society "Dante Alighieri"	2	1
Navy League	1	0
Colonial Institute	1	1
Workers recreation	1	1
Olympic Games Committee	1	1
Touring Club	1	1

THE CORPORATE STRUCTURE—*Continued*

Corporate organizations, or other organized public agencies	Number of candidates nominated	Number of candidates approved by the Grand Council of Fascism
Cooperative organizations	1	0
Reclamation consortiums	1	0
Public investment	2	1
Total	268	151
Total, syndicates	800	296
Total, public bodies	200	103
Grand total	1000	399

Note: Mussolini's own inclusion in the ticket made the 400th member of the Chamber of Deputies.

Part III
National Socialism

The National Socialist regime is usually presented as a mere Germanic extension of the doctrine that developed in Mussolini's Fascist Italy; but there are indeed some striking contrasts not only between the institutional arrangements but also between the functioning of the two systems. Indeed, one is bound to notice their different attitudes toward racial groups and the use of concentration camps; differences are also detected not only in regard to the international impact created by each regime but also in the motivating factors that brought them into existence. Differences in their motivation would also suggest differences in their functioning and in the goals that each of these regimes expected to achieve.

One of the conclusions that one may draw regarding Fascism is that, in spite of the suggestion by some of a weakness in its theoretical background or ideology, it was an easily *exportable* system of government, one which under certain specific socioeconomic and political conditions would prove attractive to more national states than Italy. Theoretically, and in a broad sense, this attraction may be significant in regard to any country whose internal social and political conditions are similar to those which prevailed in Italy after World War I. In other words, the probability for adoption of a Fascist form of government is greater in a nation that suffers a substantial lack of raw materials and of private capital in an accumulated state for investment and at the same time lacks experience in democratic self-government but, nevertheless, is stimulated to act by an awareness of its own industrial capacity.

Almost perfect illustrations of the compatibility of Fascism to States other than Italy existed in pre-World War II Europe. All the countries of East-Central Europe, with the possible exception of Czechoslovakia, developed Fascist type systems in the period between the two world wars. A detailed study of the sociopolitical systems in East-Central Europe during the interwar period (especially in the mid-1930s) will confirm that most of the elements of Fascism were firmly embodied in at least ten of that area's states. At the same time, it is demonstrable that the fundamental elements of *National Socialism* were not present in those states, or if some of these National Socialist elements did appear, they were either enforced directly by the armed forces of National

97

Socialist Germany or they were implemented only fragmentarily; and this implementation was motivated by vital national political interests related to the requirements for self-preservation of the international political situation. National Socialism, when present at all in East-Central Europe during the interwar period, was never in a developed form.

On the other hand, the exportability of Fascism was quite clearly observable in the ideas expounded by Sir Philip Mosley in England, and by the *L'Organisation de l'Armée Secrète* (O.A.S.), which, one could say, had seceded from Charles de Gaulle's *Rassemblement des Français.*

National Socialism lacks the characteristic of exportability. Its lack of international appeal is easily explained by three factors:

First, anthropologically, it stresses exclusively the mastery of one single race, the Germanic or Nordic race.

Second, ethnographically, it emphasizes the undisputed capability of one single people—the German people and nation.

Third, politically, it singles out Germany as the only national State which combines the above two qualities and, therefore, demonstrates a unique sociopolitical and economic superiority which is destined by fate to lead the way in the progress of mankind.

As a consequence, National Socialism does not appeal to other national States. As a matter of fact, the elements of National Socialism that may be exportable are only those elements which are coincidentally either identical or very similar to aspects of Fascism, namely, a strong and centralized national government, the image of a strong man in power, etc. But these latter concepts are not the property of Fascism and National Socialism alone. They are embodied in any kind of ordinary dictatorship,[18] whether past or present. Hence, they cannot be considered as being unique elements of either Fascism or National Socialism.

One line of argument, however, may be advanced in opposition to the above reasoning. Some would claim that any theory of a sociopolitical nature automatically has within it certain exportable elements.

It would be quite incorrect, however, to single out the guiding principles expressed in *Mein Kampf* as the theory of National Socialism and then proceed to study the regime based on that "theory" alone. By so doing one would, in fact, dangerously limit the likelihood of achieving the desired objectivity. In this particular case it will be necessary to broaden the comparative method beyond the framework of the political analysis of one single country and one single regime.

As indicated above, Fascism also had its own theoretical sociopolitical princi-

---

[18]See Part I, pp. 31–33.

ples. A comparison between *Mein Kampf* and Mussolini's *Fascism: Doctrine and Institutions* will stress the far greater suitability for export of Fascist doctrines.

Because the sociopolitical program of National Socialism, as expressed in *Mein Kampf*, is aimed exclusively at the German nation, its objective was rather restricted. The writings of Mussolini, on the other hand, although the author was directing them to his own people, did not focus exclusively on Italy, and because of that the exportability of the doctrine was not restricted.

Throughout his writings Mussolini refers to what he calls Mazzinian principles. As was emphasized earlier such references are also abundant in Mussolini's political speeches. Those Mazzinian principles, however, were aimed not at Italy alone, but their intent was to awaken the Italian people so that they might enter into competition with France and the somewhat abstract notion of the French mission to Europe and the world, an idea Mazzini had derived from the impulse of the liberal traditions of the French Revolution of 1789, juxtaposed to earlier ideas of the Italian Renaissance. When referring to the mission of France, Mazzini advanced reasons why there should be competition on an international scale; he pointed out that it is not France but Italy that has more to offer, for Italy can draw upon the ideas of the Italian Renaissance. Mazzini contended that the value of an Italian mission is greater and is more widely acceptable. Theoretically, this was a definite element of *exportability*.

Therefore, the first fundamental difference between the doctrines of Fascism and National Socialism is that the former is much more exportable.

Another basic notion of Fascism, frequently emphasized in the works of Mussolini, Gentile, and Rocco, was the Mazzinian concept of Thought and Action. It is a concept which contains no drastic innovation or originality. It is no more than a proposal for a systematically established relationship between decision-making and its application. As was emphasized earlier, it was a proposal for a strictly timed and precise order in the process of conceiving, generating, and promoting human activity.

In its essence, the concept of Thought and Action was analytic rather than creative. It simply claimed that *ideas born* are of no value whatsoever if they remain ideas only. On the other hand, *action* alone, another fundamental aspect of society, is again of no value when it is not based on ideas, because in such cases it only reveals immaturity. Therefore, Mussolini incorporated into the doctrine of Fascism the Mazzinian proposal that in order for human activity to give full value, timing between human thought and human action is exceptionally important. In other words, the birth of an idea should be immediately implemented by practical steps, without any time being spent on its refinement. Such refinement and polishing of ideas could best be achieved through the experience gained in the process of practical application; thus the *momentum* of such ideas would be fully utilized. The application of the Mazzinian idea by the

Fascist regime was claimed by Mussolini to have created the *dynamic* character of Fascism.

Nothing similar can be found in the doctrine of National Socialism as applied in Germany. Instead, we find a psychological concept of an extremely emotional and abstract nature, geared toward an exclusive and narrow Germanism. This typically Germanic idea is the posited existence of a permanent struggle between what is conceived by the National Socialists as *Kultur* and the conventional notion of *Civilization.*

Even before attempting to define and analyze this idea of permanent struggle and the interaction between its component parts, Kultur and Civilization, it should be stressed that Fascism is not only totally disinterested in such a matter, but to the Fascist mind this struggle is meaningless. However, it is fundamental to the outlook and the attitudes of the proponents of National Socialism.

The concept of Kultur denotes the exclusivity of the German environment which resulted in Germanic culture, regarded by National Socialism as far superior to world civilization. The superiority of Kultur was pronounced very dogmatically but the claims made for it have later been tested by sociologists and psychologists; their findings show that such claims hide feelings of inferiority and these are deeply embedded in the notion of Kultur. The very character itself of the idea of a permanent struggle of Kultur vs. Civilization reveals this inferiority complex.

The battle between Kultur and Civilization is not a conventional struggle or competition. It cannot be said to be similar to the Mazzinian idea of the virtue of the Italian mission to the world competing against the universality of French liberalism. In the Mazzinian case, the competition between Italy and France is a conventional one. Indeed, it presupposes that the struggle is based on a common denominator: both parties diffuse ideas of the same type and direct them to the same target; the destiny of both is to carry out a mission. The problem in such competition is only one: which of them, the Italian or the French mission, will be accepted by society as the better and the stronger and be allowed to exert its influence?

In the case of National Socialism, however, the basic conditions for the struggle are essentially different. The outcome of the battle is predetermined because, according to the National Socialist line of reasoning, Kultur by definition enjoys a much higher status than Civilization. The theory begins by totally negating the value of Civilization. Therefore, it is not simply a matter of waging an unrestricted struggle in which both Kultur and Civilization have the opportunity to demonstrate their values and strength on equal terms. It is quite obvious that, theoretically, the concept of Kultur avoids any free and equal competition. The theory assumes that Civilization as it exists is faulty because of its origin and essence, and that it creates an intellectual and spiritual emptiness within society. Consequently, it has to be rejected. When this condition exists, Germanic Kultur will be welcomed to move in and fill the void with its superior intellectual and spiritual virtues.

These preconceived differences in the status of Kultur and Civilization, prior to any struggle between them, are quite clearly expressed by Hitler in the pages of *Mein Kampf,* where he has attempted to establish the meaning of these concepts. There he states:

> By "Kultur" I do not mean what is expressed today by the word "Civilization." The latter seems to be, on the contrary, rather an enemy of the true spiritual and living levels. . .

In a footnote, Hitler makes his explanation clearer:

> Civilization means the application of reason to life. Goethe, Schiller, Kant are reflections of the western mind. The patriots prefer to seek "life forces," the irrational impulses, which seem to them more characteristic of the German mind.

If we carry out an analysis of what Hitler calls "the German mind," it becomes apparent that neither Hitler nor the doctrines of National Socialism applied anything new or original to the German tradition. In fact, the contrast between Kultur and Civilization was probably first advanced at the beginning of the nineteenth century by the German philosopher Fichte. In 1808, in Berlin, he delivered a series of speeches addressing himself to the whole German nation. In these speeches Fichte reached the general conclusion that in its development the mind of Western Europe was not then strong enough in following nationally-oriented principles, but, on the contrary, was displaying an international attitude *par excellence.* Advancing firmly along such avenues, the Western European mind at first conceived, and later fully developed, the meaning of the concept "Civilization," a system of patterns of behavior inspired by, and coupled with, a number of spiritual ideas. The predominant characteristic of Civilization, as defined by Fichte, was that this entire ideological and behavioral system was of a rational nature designed to be universally applicable.

In contrast to Civilization, the German mind had developed the concept of Kultur. German ideology saw in this concept a very direct and intimate union between the German nation, on the one hand, and the *natural forces of the universe,* on the other. Fichte claimed that only the Germans knew by intuition the true means of realizing in a practical way this intimate union and, therefore, enjoying the full value of it. He enhanced the exclusive Germanism of his statement by claiming that the Germans alone were capable of understanding the spiritual interaction which results from this intimate union of the nation with the natural forces of the universe. Since the Germans are the only people that can create such a union, they are the only ones who have the obligation to turn those natural forces into reality for the benefit of mankind.

In explaining the substance of this unusual and exclusively Germanic capability, Fichte maintained that the Germans are the chosen people to realize this union because they alone possess in a highly developed state the *Volk*, a notion whose essence contains much more within itself than the ordinary meaning of "people." The Volk are, indeed, people, but they are also the only people capable of looking with a very high degree of understanding upon the primitive nature of the universe. Therefore, the German Volk has infintely more direct contact with nature than do other peoples. This direct contact makes the *Volk Mind* able to revert more easily to the instincts and concepts of the primitive world.

All other nations have fallen under the decaying influence of two modern concepts, *Classical Thought* and *Christianity*. Under their combined influence, the Western world has created the international concept of Civilization, which has acted as an oppressive factor ever since. These nations have erred enormously in accepting gladly the oppression of Civilization in order to escape from the natural practices and concepts of the primitive world. Fichte claimed that this was, indeed, a great error because they were not any longer able to comprehend the priceless values of that world.

The essence of Kultur seems to imply that the German national consciousness is primarily something different from that of the "Romanized" Mediterranean peoples. The concept of Kultur strongly attempts to present the German Volk as much less "Romanized" than others, this being one of their strongest virtues.

As mentioned earlier, the inherent feelings of primitiveness which according to Fichte constituted the superiority of the Germans when compared to other nations might, indeed, have been only a superficial emphasis designed to prevent the emergence of a true inferiority complex based on the German awareness of being less "Romanized."

This highly abstract line of reasoning was aimed at convincing the German people of their national superiority and was used effectively to help bring about the emergence of the National Socialist regime in Germany. This regime probably enjoyed, at least initially, wide popular support.

The theoretical motivation for Fascism in Italy—the concept of Thought and Action—was used to impress a dynamic character on the regime. No practical aspects were claimed as being applicable to Italy alone, except possibly the Italian origins of Mazzini. Thus, the concept was presented as being a universal one. Here we find the second fundamental theoretical and motivating difference between the doctrines of Fascism and National Socialism.

The third fundamental and the most pronounced characteristic of Fascism, distinguishing it from National Socialism, was the Corporate Structure of the State, based on Saint-Simon's vision of a consolidated producer class, Georges Sorel's practical understanding of Marxism, and Mussolini's Corporate Theory. This theory contained neither an emotional idealization of the Italian Volk nor any abstract nationalistic framework. Instead, it proposed a very realistic (whether right or wrong) method designed to assure better living conditions for the producers in the nation as well as less exploitation of the Italian working class by the rising number of industrial magnates and investors in the new industries.

Nothing of this kind existed in the National Socialist doctrine. Instead, as a counterpart, a highly developed theory focusing on Germanic *racial supremacy* was elaborated and applied by the National Socialist regime. Because of the application of this Racial Theory in Germany, many people who were not of Germanic Volk origin and, therefore, unable to see and implement the "intimate union between themselves and the natural primitive life forces of the universe," were subjected to cruel suffering and torture.

The emergence of the German Racial Theory and its application can be regarded partly as an extension of the idea of permanent struggle between Kultur and Civilization, especially as a consequence of the claimed and uncontested superior status of Kultur in this battle. Thus, while one can rightfully regard the *Corporate Theory* and its practice in Fascist Italy as one of the most important rational elements of Fascism, the *Racial Theory* and its application may be regarded as an equally important counterpart in National Socialism. When a comparison is made on these grounds, with Corporate Theory as an expression of Fascist realism, compared to Racial Theory as an expression of National Socialist realism, Fascism appears to be a much less emotional sociopolitical doctrine, disinterested in racism, with a number of Jewish supporters; among them, Margerita Sarfatti, the official biographer of Mussolini, de Begnac, and others.

Mussolini and his chief theoreticians, mainly Gentile and Rocco, all claimed that Fascism was based on the ideas of Mazzini and that their doctrine was no more than a true expression of Mazzinian concepts. This claim immediately placed Fascism within the realm of emotionalism, romanticism, and idealism, with a nationalistic touch.

On the other hand, when one observes the functioning of Fascism, it is easy to detect realistic features based on pure common sense. This rationality in the functioning of the system was obviously due to the attempts of pragmatic Fascists to remedy the ailing social relationships in post-World War I Italy, and to introduce efficient methods in production.

From its beginning, the Fascist regime attempted to prevent the emergence of the large-scale labor-management disputes that the new leaders of the country expected would take place in conjunction with the push toward more advanced stages of industrial development. As a matter of fact, the precedent for such incidents happening was near at hand, for the occupation of the industrial plants in the northern part of the country by the workers in 1919–1920 was clear evidence of the oncoming conflict. Mussolini managed to take advantage of that crisis and to use it to strengthen his, at that time, small Fascist movement.

The attempt to prevent labor-management disputes, to be effected through the corporate structure of the state, was the most significant and, at the same time, the most important rational element in the doctrine of Fascism. Regardless of its importance, however, it appears to be the only important element of rationality and is far from sufficient to justify the presentation of Fascism as a rational doctrine in its entirety.

Having in mind the predominantly emotional and romantic character of Fascism, we must attempt to explain the origins of the above-mentioned isolated element of rationality. Generally speaking, we may trace this explanation to two important lacks in Italian society:

1. A lack of traditional roots in Italian society. Because of this, the Italians lack ties that bind them together within the framework of commonly accepted emotional concepts derived from the past. The emergence of Mazzinian concepts was only accidental, and their popularization was restricted to a relatively few Italians, while the large masses of people in Central and Southern Italy were never affected by Mazzinian Romanticism.

2. The lack of traditional and common beliefs of an emotional nature provided a perfect opportunity for Fascism to be accepted on realistic grounds. Only after the regime had been consolidated was an attempt made to create a Fascist theory. During the interim period it stayed in the "limbo" between Marxian Socialism and Nationalism.

If we look back into the origins of National Socialism, it is apparent that, contrary to the Italian case, the German tradition is extremely rich in common emotional beliefs that have held the nation together since the beginnings of its history. The entire concept of Kultur is deeply rooted in the minds of the German people, a belief both irrational and emotional, and closely linked to the concept of Volk, also rich in emotional and supernatural elements stemming from German mythology.

The idea of the German Volk was substantially influenced by Myth and Kultur on the road to exclusive Germanism. The *Nibelungen Lied* and German mythology are both significant parts of the concept of German Kultur. However, the transition from mythology to Kultur is not direct. It has passed through an intermediary—the notion of the German Volk. Indeed, Volk is presented as an inseparable, integral part of German mythology and as such, it serves as a strong link between this mythology and the concept of German Kultur.

Individuals from among the Volk who deserved eternal life because of bravery and other virtues on earth, were believed to depart after death for Heaven. Heaven in German mythology is, however, limited only to *warriors*. Therefore, the deserving and good individuals of the Volk live eternally among warriors; this is considered by German mythology to be the highest possible reward and honor for having led a good life on earth. Closely related to this belief, perhaps, is the belief prevalent in many parts of the world that modern Germans are militaristic by nature and cruel toward their enemies in war, while remaining sentimental romanticists among themselves.

One may say that other peoples too have developed beliefs closely linked to their mythology. The ancient Greeks and Romans provide the best examples of societies in which the relations between gods and humans were conceived of as being quite intimate. It would logically follow that the modern Italians and Greeks would have, like the Germans, some kind of Volk legacy as part of their national traditions. A crucial difference, however, does exist in that neither in modern Italy nor in modern Greece has any political regime emphasized such a legacy in order to apply it in practice or to justify its own existence. Italian Fascism never spoke of any liaison between the Italian people and the natural forces of the universe. All studies in Italy and Greece related to their mythological past have been studies of culture and history, without any political intent.

In Germany, however, an entirely different phenomenon took place. Even before the emergence of the National Socialist Party of Hitler, very serious attempts were made to present the German people as distinct and superior to others through the concept of *race*. The essence of the concept of Germanic race appears, in fact, as a modernized form of the much earlier idea of the close relationship between Volk and mythology. Germany's mythology has always been conceived by the German mind as superior to other similar beliefs, and from this awareness it was not a long or difficult step toward the belief that the German Volk, or race, is also superior to non-Germans in modern times.

Thus, not only the ideas of German mythology, unacceptable by the twentieth century, but the much more readily acceptable theory of a superior German race, a modified and more modern extension of the former, has entered as a traditional legacy into the national development of the German people. No longer on the grounds of mythology (whose study nevertheless continued to be extensive) but on the basis of race were the Germans taught, during the National Socialist era, of their alleged uncontested superiority.

During the nineteenth century and the early part of the twentieth, two additional purely Germanic elements were amalgamated with the concept of *Mythology-Volk-Kultur*. This amalgamation led to the psychological build-up of a new and much more refined theoretical concept, which gradually took shape and which one may call the *German State of Mind*. The new elements were:

1. *The Cult of Life Idea* as put forth by the two brothers August Wilhelm and Friedrich Wilhelm Schlegel; the cult idea was derived from the original German Romantic school of the end of the eighteenth century.

2. *The Obsession with German National Unity,* which may be traced to Friedrich Ludwig Jahn, who later in life became known as "Father" Jahn. He also adopted the ideas of the Romantic school, but he directed these ideas toward the goal of German political unification and nationalism.

Both of these elements, added to the original Mythology-Volk-Kultur concept, were products of a distinct kind of German Romanticism. German Romanticism was different than the other Romantic movements of Europe. It was not atomistic, and although romantic in expression, it contained within itself a certain realistic basis. This was particularly evident in both the Cult of Life Idea and the Obsession with German National Unity.

A substantial part of the whole ideological complex that one may call the German State of Mind—consisting of the Mythology-Volk-Kultur concept, on the one hand, and the idea of Cult of Life plus the idea of German National Unity, on the other—finally found its most complete expression, and thus its ability to influence emerging National Socialism, when an additional intellectual refinement had been accomplished by the cultural group known as the *Bayreuth Circle.*

August Wilhelm von Schlegel (1767–1845) and *Friedrich Wilhelm von Schlegel* (1772–1829), writing at the end of the eighteenth century, put forth the Germanic Cult of Life idea which was the core of the special type of German Romanticism. It is precisely this idea that made German Romanticism very different from the other Romantic movements of Western Europe. The Cult of Life idea was the element which contributed a strong tinge of Realism to the prevalent concept of Western Romanticism. In other words, German Romanticism, as propounded by the von Schlegels, was differentiated by the fact that it was an extremely intelligent attempt toward universal knowledge, resting, however, on a strongly Romantic basis. This strange combination of Realism and Romanticism resulted in the typically Germanic concept of *Weltanschauung,* a concept which implies the acquisition of an exact perception of the world through knowledge derived from pleasant and unpleasant practical experiences rather than from academic channels of learning.

This process of experiencing (rather than merely observing) everything in the world before it becomes an object of human rationalization was marked by a great deal of *dynamism,* extracted from *living Nature.* It was conceived of as a process applicable exclusively to the development of the German Volk. Because the Cult of Life idea is rooted deeply in *Weltanschauung,* the latter implies knowing through experience everything in life on Romantic grounds. Goethe's *Faust* is a clear expression of this.

Descending from a noble Saxon family, the von Schlegels were very much influenced by their father, Johann Adolf, who was a poet devoutly dedicated to his duties within the Lutheran Church. Friedrich studied law at the old and famous universities of Göttingen and Leipzig. During this period he produced some experimental literary works: *Lucinde* and *Alarcos.* He later lectured at the universities of Jena and Paris. August began writing poetry at a very early age. After completion of his studies at the University of Göttingen he was elected a professor at the University of Jena. Shortly after his appointment, August and Friedrich undertook the editing of *Athenäum,* which appeared in Berlin from 1796 to 1800. It was a journal concerned with esthetics and art criticism. Marked by an impartial spirit and based on observation of the forces of life, the journal attempted to discover and explain every aspect of the vital development of the human mind. The *Athenäum* provided the two brothers ample opportunity to lead lives immersed in poetry and science. They associated with the greatest German poets and thinkers of the day, men like Ludwig Tieck and Novalis (Friedrich von Hardenberg) and the circles which gathered around them.

A wave of political unrest swept over Germany in 1813, as a result of the military conquests of France. France's conquests in Central Europe were the instrumental factor in the awakening of German patriotism. The von Schlegels were very much a part of this awakening. From 1818 to 1819 Friedrich was actively engaged in political and diplomatic activities, whereas August in 1813 entered the service of Carl Johan, the Crown Prince of Sweden, (the former Comte Bernadotte—a marshal in the French Emperor's army) and became his secretary for a brief period. It was during this service that August Schlegel received the title of nobility, thus, adding "von" to his name.

The remainder of their lives the von Schlegels devoted to studies of the fine arts and the sciences, strengthening their right to be considered founders of the modern Romantic school of German literature. August applied himself especially to the study of the mysticism of Oriental literature. He traveled and studied in France and England, where he worked at Oxford University and at the East India College, and also held the post of professor of art and literary history at Bonn. Friedrich, while in Paris, studied Sanskrit and Indian civilization. Like his brother, he took a very strong interest in orientalism and produced the work *Von der Sprache und Weisheit der Inder,* later translated into English under the title, *On the Speech and Wisdom of Indian Culture.* After 1818, Friedrich went to Vienna where he edited *Concordia,* and lectured on philosophy.

Whereas the von Schlegels contributed the Cult of Life—*Weltanschauung* complex to the Mythology-Volk-Kultur concept and thus helped form an integral part of the German State of Mind, it was "Father" Jahn who brought this idea to completion by providing its nationalistic content based on an obsession with German unity. "Father" Jahn's ideas enjoyed great currency in Germany.

While Mazzinian ideas influenced only a small part of the Italian people, mainly in the North, and remained largely ignored by the peasantry and the lower classes, "Father" Jahn's preachings were accepted by most of the German people and all levels of society. His ideas had an unusual impact on the German students of that day.

"Father" Jahn (Friedrich Ludwig Jahn, 1778–1852) was born in the province of Priegnitz in Prussia. The son of a Protestant preacher, he studied between the years 1796 and 1802 at some of the most famous universities of Germany: Halle, Jena, Greifswald, and Leipzig. At the University of Leipzig he received a doctor's degree in philosophy. Characteristically, his dissertation was colored by strongly nationalistic feelings. Concerned with the German language, Jahn desired to purify it, by deleting all foreign influences, words, and expressions; as a prerequisite he proposed the development within the German people of a consciousness of their superior national status.

As a student he became immediately assimilated into the German Romantic school of artists and writers. He was fascinated by the concept of the German Volk and subjected it to philosophical analysis, and in the process laid the basis for his own rabid nationalism. The term Volk he thought applicable only to an *organic* society; the term described only the existing German society, in contrast to the societies of the "decadent" West which were not of a *Volk* nature but of an *atomistic-individualistic* type.

Throughout his life "Father" Jahn was rather poor, but he was always very close to the masses of the German people, and he was especially intimate with German youth. He earned his living by teaching, public lectures, and private tutoring.

In 1811 "Father" Jahn attempted for the first time to implement his ideas. He founded two different organizations: an open gymnastic society with his students as members; and a secret nationalistic society with a selectively screened membership, called the *Burschenschaft,* which he used to promote his ideas of obedience to *one single* political leader. "Father" Jahn portrayed such a *leader* as one who neither terrorized the masses nor is different from his followers at large. On the contrary, Jahn insisted that this type of leader and the people he leads are, in fact, a single *organic unit.* From there, "Father" Jahn went on to stress the concept of the organic nature of the *leader-followers* combination, that is to say, the full identification of the leader with the masses of people and with the political organization that he heads. "Father" Jahn further insisted that only such a sociopolitical amalgamation of leader-followers is truly Germanic, because it illustrates the organic complexity of the nature of the Volk.

"Father" Jahn was indeed the uncontested leader of this secret society, and he sought to use his leadership to demonstrate the true organic nature of leader and people together, in all of their activities. This practice gained him the title of

"Father," which replaced Friedrich, his first name. His particular brand of German nationalistic activity gradually developed in two different stages:

A stage based on Prussian provincialism, expressed by the profession of his nationalistic ideas in terms of Prussia alone.

A stage based on *all-German* nationalistic unification, expressed through an extension of his original Prussian provincialism.

The repressive system of rule imposed by Metternich was not in sympathy with "Father" Jahn's promotion of ultranationalism, whether in a local or a broader context. As a result he was arrested and dragged from prison to prison between the years 1819–1840. However, in 1848 his work was finally recognized when he was selected to be a delegate to the revolutionary national parliament.

Toward the end of his life, "Father" Jahn's ideas and exemplary actions were enthusiastically acclaimed by his followers, who added two other popular names to his "Father" title. He was occasionally hailed as the "storm trooper of nationalism" and, more often, the "German Jacobin." "Father" Jahn has retained his popularity with the German people, not only because of the lasting impact of his ideas but also because of the example set by his own life.

The addition of "Father" Jahn's ultranationalism and the obsession with German unity, combined with the concept of *Weltanschauung,* to the Mythology-Volk-Kultur concept, brings us closer to a final definition of the German State of Mind. To round out the concept, however, it is necessary to consider another tangible and influential element which was instrumental in shaping that quite unrealistic complexity known as the German State of Mind.

Mythology-Volk-Kultur, linked to the German State of Mind, already expresses the idea of German supremacy over other nations, but the *Racial Concept* came soon after to strengthen and complete this definition. Ironically, credit for this addition to the German State of Mind, important as it may have been in promoting German supremacy, cannot be given to German thinkers. Indeed, a French diplomat and man of letters, Joseph Arthur Comte de Gobineau, and an Englishman, Houston Stewart Chamberlain, son of an English admiral, are the ones who deserve the credit.

Joseph Arthur Comte de Gobineau (1816–1882) is generally regarded as the founder of modern racism. His purely academic interests led him to specialize in Oriental studies in which he earned a reputation as a learned scholar. De Gobineau's theoretical assertions were quite simple. Basing his theories on his knowledge of the Orient, he attempted to compare Oriental races with those of Europe. De Gobineau's study included the evaluation and classification of the eating habits of the peoples of Asia, Africa, and Europe, and then ascertaining the respective degree of comfort required by those peoples for their food consumption and life habits in general. On these grounds he called the African

Negroes (the "Himatics") clearly an inferior race, but de Gobineau hesitated in arriving at any conclusions as to the racial status of the Europeans (the "Caucasians," "Semitics," "Japhetics") compared to the Asians (the "Altaics," "Mongols," "Tartars," "Fins"). In fact, it seemed for a moment that he would proclaim an overall Asian racial supremacy. However, as a consequence of further comparative studies leading him to determine that the Teutonic race in Europe was "superior," he finally decided for West European superiority; thus, it seems quite clear that it was only due to the excellence of the Germanic race that the balance turned in favor of the Western peoples.

Houston Stewart Chamberlain (1857–1927) engaged in both creative writing and musical composition, as well as in racial speculations. His conclusions were voiced in a very frank and aggressive fashion, attesting, too, to the "superiority" of the German race. The point of departure for his racial investigation was the old Roman Empire. Pointing to the vigor, ability, and disciplined behavior of the early Romans, he attributed these qualities to their original racial purity. Thus, unlike de Gobineau, he took a direct look at race and character (instead of constructing vague hypotheses based on eating habits), this being the basic premise for his research.

Chamberlain next turned to the victorious wars of Rome and to the extension of the Empire's political boundaries. The acquisition of new lands and foreign populations, prisoners and slaves of various ethnic and racial groups, resulted, according to him, in the gradual disappearance of the initial racial purity and vigor of the early Romans. Numerous intermarriages between pure Romans and Jews, Orientals, and Westerners poisoned the blood of the people of the Empire. This melange, according to Chamberlain, was the key factor that brought the pure Roman race to a state of extreme weakness, making it an easy prey to the attacks and the invasions led by the racially uncorrupted Teutonic tribes.

One further aspect of Chamberlain's thought is important: he drew upon Darwin's biological theories to reach still another novel conclusion. He voiced his strong regret that the Germanic invaders who poured into the racially decaying Roman Empire, had not completely destroyed the defeated race. Had they done so (not only destroyed the Empire politically but also eradicated the race), Chamberlain asserted, then the German race would have assumed a prime role in world affairs because of its compact racial purity and its vigorous ability to build the future for the benefit of mankind.

The effect of de Gobineau's and Chamberlain's ideas was substantial. One of their effects was the formation of the "Antisemitenliga" in Germany in 1879. It was founded by Wilhelm Marr, himself a Jew converted to the Christian faith. In his work *Der Sieg des Judentums über das Germanentum* (The Victory of

Judaism over Germanism),[19] he attempted to divorce most of the biblical-religious arguments in the racial controversy from sociological-economic factors. The former appeared to him to be quite obscure and irrelevant to the then all-important socioeconomic competition. This idea was further elaborated in another work, in which he said:

"One has no need now to expose religious prejudice when one is being faced by the question of race, when one finds the difference in the 'blood'. . ."[20]

The theory of racial supremacy, as expressed by both Comte de Gobineau and Chamberlain, is the final brick in the psychological edifice and definition of the German State of Mind. All of its component parts, namely, the Mythology-Volk-Kultur concept, the Cult of Life-Weltanschauung, the Romantic idea of the von Schlegels, the extreme nationalism and obsession with German unity professed by "Father" Jahn, and the racial theories of de Gobineau and Chamberlain, were individually highly developed notions in themselves, but only loosely integrated into a broader concept. This whole complex of ideas would have remained unsuitable for the National Socialist regime of Hitler, until, during the last decades of the nineteenth century, it was included in the speculations of the Bayreuth Circle in Germany, centering around the composer Richard Wagner. Only after this unorganized ideological conglomeration had passed through the Wagnerian intellectual machine did it receive a truly compact form which, with all the member concepts strongly interrelated, provided the basis for its practical application.

Of all the basic elements which together make up the German State of Mind, the Mythology-Volk-Kultur concept appears to be the most vague and difficult. The other three fundamental elements, namely, the Cult of Life-Weltanschauung idea, the extreme Germanic nationalism and obsession with unity, and the Theory of German Supremacy, are not difficult to understand, even at first glance.

Regardless of how clearly each of the above basic elements of the German State of Mind might have been perceived by the German people during the nineteenth century, they were mainly looked upon as quite disparate ideas. The only significant link existed within the framework of the Mythology-Volk-Kultur concept.

Being in a raw state (however influential the substance of each element might be), this grouping of concepts did not have the weight of an important ideological doctrine. It could have served only to reflect the cultural value of the

---

[19]Berne (1879).
[20]*Vom jüdischen Krigsschamplatz*, Berne (1879).

German past, mainly on historic grounds, as one might observe, for instance, the Greek and Roman heritage. But it seems most unlikely that a whole sociopolitical movement, like the National Socialist movement, could have emerged with an influential doctrine exclusively founded upon such vague elements. These elements were given national importance and sociopolitical significance only after a means was found to refine them and link them all logically together in compact form.

The fact that all of these elements were accepted as scientific truth and as the doctrine justifying National Socialism, may be explained by their entering the popular mind of Germany in a somewhat simplified but very refined form. These elements had progressed from their raw state and had been transformed into a compact and seemingly logical unit. They were made accessible to the mind of the average German as an ideological unit, and in that way won credence and praise.

This transitional stage, so important to the future political development of Europe, may be traced back to a small group of German intellectuals who, reacting to the international events of their day, were inspired by the mythological and romantic aspects of the German past. This group gathered around the composer Richard Wagner, and during frequent meetings in the town of Bayreuth they discussed these ideas at length. These intellectual gatherings were indeed the first significant attempt to present all the elements of the German State of Mind in systematic form and in a way that would make the individual feel culturally superior and proud to belong to the German nation. The Bayreuth Circle truly built the creed of National Socialism.

However, it is easy to see that if such a philosophy were intended to be applied in practice, the system of values propounded by the Bayreuth Circle had very serious shortcomings. It is difficult to assume that these people, all outstanding intellectuals, could have committed such a grievous error. It is much easier to conclude that their basic aim was *not* to make their ideological foundation serve as the basis for a sociopolitical movement of any kind in Germany. Rather, it seems that they sought merely to preserve these ideas and values in the intellectual realm, for their own satisfaction, and to preserve the historic German cultural heritage. Another fact that supports such a view is that the Circle's official organ, the *Bayreuth Bulletin,* which disseminated their ideas and reported on their discussions, was never widely circulated—at least not widely enough to indicate that an attempt was made to reach a farflung audience. It was a publication distributed primarily to the Wagnerian club members and their intimate friends. From this one can rightfully deduce that the Wagnerian circle, as originally conceived, did not desire to indoctrinate anyone outside its own membership.

If the circle had intended otherwise, that is, if its system were to be implemented socially and politically, then major shortcomings are readily apparent:

While its system of thought was fashioned in an almost perfect manner, the
Wagnerian Circle allowed the entire framework to rest on *emotion* and *irrationality*. It created a system, but it did not make any serious attempt to strengthen it
by introducing, or even considering, at least one realistic and easily applicable
concept. Much later, on rather superficial grounds, an attempt was made to cure
a similar shortcoming in the actual functioning of the National Socialist regime
in Germany. However, compared with the doctrine of Fascism, the cure attempted by German National Socialism appears quite insufficient. As shown
above, Fascism, although emotional in its major parts, has at least one very
strong realistic and efficacious element, namely, the Corporate Structure of the
State. Indeed, in states with directed economies such a structure is highly
applicable.[21]

Paradoxically, the attempt to bring a remedy to the shortcomings of the
ideological system of the Wagnerian Circle is seen in the only element in
Germanism which is *not* of typical German but rather of old and well known
universal origin. And this element refers to the National Socialist Party structure
and functioning, which provide for a modernized form of a strong, centralized,
stable, and dictatorial supreme authority over the nation and the State. Such
authority is, in fact, universal, that is, it is inherent in any totalitarian sociopolitical system, whether of German, Italian, Spanish, South American, or any
other origin. Thus, it *turned* the Wagnerian Circle's intangible theories into a
practical political doctrine allowing a *dictatorial* rule.

Another aspect of the shortcomings of the system propounded by the Wagnerian
Circle (again, provided one is inclined to assume that its goal was to promote its
theories in practice), is the fact that *no real attempt* was made by the
Circle members *to put their ideas into effect*. Indeed, the whole system of
Germanic thought was simply looked upon, and probably intentionally so, as an
intellectual exercise or speculation. It was only under the impulse of Adolf
Hitler that the members of the National Socialist Party attempted to put into
practice the intellectual speculations of the Wagnerian Circle, and to use them as
a weapon of massive indoctrination.

The Wagnerian Circle, although it never changed either its ideological foundation or the structure of its membership, can nevertheless be examined in two
different stages of development separated by the year 1883. This is the year that
marked the death of its most influential member, Richard Wagner, and it also

---

[21]It might, for instance, be very helpful to an England governed by the Labour Party.

brought a formal change in the name by which the circle had been unofficially known since 1876. In 1883, the group became known as the Bayreuth Circle, after the name of the town where the group's meetings were most often held.

During his lifetime, Wagner was the uncontested leader of the Circle. He was also the master mind for the elaboration of the Circle's ideas, and their refinement. After his death, his widow, Cosima, attempted to play the role of her late husband. However, while she was nominally accepted, she was never able to exert the same influence.

The death of Wagner presented a real opportunity to modify the ideas basic to the Wagnerian system of thought. A rather unrestricted reinterpretation by the rest of the members became possible but no important change took place. The intellectual speculations of the members seem to have faltered and the system itself became more doctrinaire, as each one of Wagner's followers tried to assume authority by showing *greater loyalty* to the system rather than modifying it, thus trying to demonstrate his own qualities of leadership within the circle. During this undeclared competition no one was able to achieve the uncontested preeminence of Wagner, and the changing of the name of the club became the most convenient way to open the door to leadership to anyone but Cosima Wagner, the former leader's wife. What was actually happening could in part be compared to the process of de-Stalinization (destroying the "cult of personality") in the Soviet Union, without however, a concurrent tendency to disgrace the fallen leader, or criticizing him, or even attempting to change his thought. The only immediate change was the elimination of Wagner's name from the Circle's name in order to make room for another, should someone succeed in becoming the new leader. No one succeeded in such an endeavor, with the exception perhaps of Rosenberg or Hitler himself.

Membership in the Circle was from the first, and for most of its existence, naturally restricted to an exclusive group on account of its high-level intellectual domain; it never had a direct or significant influence upon the masses of Germany. Its impact was tangible only among a certain class of Germans, and during the time of Wagner this influence was exerted chiefly through the somewhat also naturally restricted circulation of the *Bayreuth Bulletin.* For all practical purposes, there were no personal contacts between the Circle and the masses. The members, being at that time loyal followers of Wagner, did not regard themselves as either able or worthy to individually propagate the club's ideological foundations over the head of their leader. Thus, Wagner's personal leadership, masterminding the whole organization and enjoying enormous prestige, at the same time served to restrict the direct propagation of the Circle's ideas. After 1883, this restriction disappeared, as one would expect; through their competition for leadership, the individual members of the Circle began to use their journal more effectively in order to promote their ideas through direct contact with the German masses. Among the most prominent members of the Bayreuth Circle who individually promoted the Wagnerian ideas after 1883 were Cosima Wagner, the leader's widow; Winifred Wagner, the leader's daughter-in-law; Siegfried Wagner, the leader's son; Houston Stewart Chamberlain, the leader's son-in-law; Dietrich Eckart, responsible for acquainting Hitler with the Wagnerian system of thought; Alfred Rosenberg; Joseph Goebbels; and somewhat later, after 1923, Adolf Hitler.

For a time after 1883, Wagner's widow, Cosima, became the nominal leader of the circle. His son, Siegfried, died after the First World War, but Siegfried's widow, Winifred Wagner, was formally recognized as a leader during the National Socialist regime. Throughout the duration of the regime she was assigned the important function of being the permanent master of ceremonies at the plushy Wagnerian festivals. In performing this function, Winifred gradually became one of the closest friends of Hitler, this friendship giving rise to rumors that Hitler wanted to marry her.

Of the original Wagnerian group members, the most instrumental in the emergence and functioning of the National Socialist regime were Eckart, Rosenberg, and Goebbels.

Dietrich Eckart helped to popularize the Wagnerian ideas among the German masses. He was a gifted poet, soaked in German Romanticism and accustomed to heavy drinking in beer halls. These personal characteristics made him very popular among the people of Munich. There he freely propagated the Wagnerian system of thought. Eckart was one of the founders of the new German Workers' National Socialist Party, which Hitler came to lead. Eckart's association with Hitler resulted in the latter being indoctrinated with the theories of Wagner, especially the de Gobineau-Chamberlain emphasis on Germanic-Aryan racial purity. Since Hitler proved such an enthusiastic student, Eckart in 1923 brought him into the Bayreuth Circle.

Alfred Rosenberg was of a rather uncertain Baltic-Prussian origin that prompted a series of rumors that his family was of Jewish descendent. Not connected with the rich Baltic barons, he had a mixed proletarian and petty-bourgeois origin. In spite of his upbringing and education in the capital of Estonia, Rosenberg became a fervent German patriot.

With the outbreak of the competition for leadership within the Bayreuth Circle, Rosenberg became the main rival of Goebbels. The two possessed forceful personalities so that their rivalry resulted in the formation of two separate wings within the Circle. The Rosenberg-Goebbels rivalry never died down; indeed, it later reemerged in Hitler's National Socialist Party, the effect being a split among the party members. Within the loyal rank and file of National Socialism, one wing was led by Rosenberg, the other by Goebbels.

Being devout National Socialists, both Rosenberg and Goebbels were in agreement in relation to National Socialist fundamentals: both were against bourgeois capitalism; both were anti-liberals; both were against Democracy. Indeed, they had no differences, especially in respect to the interpretation of the meaning of Democracy in the contemporary Western world. To them Democracy meant, in reality, *Pluto-democracy,* a mere tool of *Plutocracy,* a capitalistic system of society secretly run by world Jewry, working through hidden forces exclusively for the benefit of the Jews the world over.

However, Rosenberg and Goebbels differed substantially in other respects, primarily of a tactical nature. Throughout the period of National Socialism in Germany, Rosenberg was regarded as the leader of the *moderate* National Socialist wing. He was opposed to violent actions of the Bolshevik type. If one uses as a model the traditional Socialist split and compares it with the division within National Socialism, Rosenberg's wing may be looked upon as a National Socialist moderate wing in a *Social-Democratic* sense. He represented the old Teutonic knights' tradition of National Socialism, based economically on agrarianism rather than on industrialization. According to Rosenberg, the spark of life in society stemmed from the countryside. Politically, he was most vigorously anti-Slav and anti-Russian, and although being anti-capitalist, he was *not* a firm opponent of the West.

His followers maintain that he won two major political victories over Goebbels:

Hitler officially recognized Rosenberg's importance to the regime by proclaiming him the *philosopher of National Socialism.*

And Hitler's war against the Soviet Union was regarded as an outgrowth of the Fuehrer's approval and support of Rosenberg's anti-Slavism and anti-Russianism. Rosenberg was praised by his supporters as having influenced German foreign policy to the extent that the German-Soviet war became the major German war between 1939 and 1945. The start of this war was considered internally to be a very heavy blow against Goebbels and his followers.

In fact, Rosenberg did not win any real victory in his rivalry with Goebbels. The status he received from Hitler represented the Fuehrer's attempt to appease both Rosenberg and Goebbels, and to *neutralize* the excitement their strife stimulated among the rank and file of the National Socialist Party. While Rosenberg was proclaimed to be the official philosopher of National Socialism, Goebbels was appointed by Hitler as Minister of Propaganda of the Third Reich, thus giving him a major means of presenting his views directly to the German people. But still, in order not to allow *too* much direct communication between Goebbels and the German people, Rosenberg was entrusted from 1921 on with the editorship of the official political party organ of National Socialism, the daily newspaper *Der Völkische Beobachter.* In addition, Hitler regarded Rosenberg as the chief of the entire educational system of the National Socialist movement. Rosenberg's "influence" in launching the attack on the Soviet Union could be easily explained, not on the grounds that his ideas should merit any special recognition in the formulation of the foreign policy of National Socialist Germany, but rather because of the coincidence that Hitler simply momentarily happened to have the same views in that regard.

In contrast to the political moderation of Rosenberg, Goebbels was regarded as the leader of the radical, "National-Bolshevik" (revolutionary) wing of National Socialism. He advocated violent political action basing it on proletarian premises. He was anti-agrarian and supported the proletarian big-city point of view. He looked upon industry as the most important element in human society. Contrary to Rosenberg's anti-Slavism and anti-Russianism, Goebbels stressed a vigorous anti-Western stand in foreign policy. While the transfer of the major weight of the war from West to East could be regarded as a blow against Goebbels, on the same grounds one could discover a blow against Rosenberg in the signing of the August, 1939, Treaty of Non-Aggression and Mutual Assistance between Germany and the Soviet Union.

If Rosenberg's views had no real impact or influence on Hitler's political decisions (the attack on the U.S.S.R. being regarded merely as a coincidental phenomenon), there is, on the other hand, no concrete evidence to the effect that Goebbels had any particular influence either.[22]

Rosenberg and Goebbels were the only important members of the National Socialist ruling circle about whom rumors were spread that they were of Jewish origin. However, these rumors have never been verified. Since both Rosenberg and Goebbels were the most vigorous racist and anti-Semitic leaders of National Socialism, it has been thought that they both assumed this role in order to counteract such rumors.

In spite of the importance of Eckart, Rosenberg, and Goebbels, in terms of popularizing the Bayreuth Circle's ideas (thus providing the doctrinal base for National Socialism), the most outstanding member of this intellectual club was its creator and leader, Richard Wagner.

Richard Wagner (1813–1883) was not only a musician but also a political commentator of note. In the columns of the *Bayreuth Bulletin* he presented point-by-point the Wagnerian system of strict Germanism. It was all based on the elements making up the German State of Mind. However, the limited circulation of this journal, fragmentarily disseminating the club's ideas over a large number of issues, gives us a quite inappropriate, but not impossible basis for research.

On the other hand, it may seem at first glance rather difficult to relate an analysis of librettos of operas with political research. However, Thomas Mann recorded in an article his view that not only an investigation of the language used

---

[22]E. K. Bramsted, *Goebbels and the National Socialist Propaganda*, East Lansing (1965).

in Wagner's operas but also a study of the maestro's music would be very revealing as to Wagner's political ideas.[23]

One really does not have to go so far as to analyze his music alone. A selection of the easily available issues of the *Bayreuth Bulletin,* combined with a thorough analysis of the plots and language of Wagner's operas, will establish sufficient evidence to bear out Mann's contention. Merely the lyrics of three of his operas are enough not only to justify his conclusions but also to trace the three most important stages in Wagner's political evolution. The opera *Rienzi* could be taken as a very illustrative example of the first stage in the evolution of Wagner's political views. *Die Meistersinger von Nürnberg* typifies best the second stage of his political development. Finally, one should look at the opera *Tristan und Isolde* in order to discover the third and final step in the evolution of Wagner's political ideas.

Very much like Benito Mussolini prior to reaching the stage of Fascism, but on a much more pronounced irrational and romantic basis, Richard Wagner passed through a process of sharp contradictions and ideological transformations before arriving at the system presented in the *Bayreuth Bulletin* and in his music.

Some scholars on National Socialism have maintained that Richard Wagner's starting point in the field of political theory was very obscure and vague, and consequently, of no importance for the future bent of his mind. The initial political confusions in Wagner's mind could be attributed to two factors:

1. A lack of practical knowledge of politics in general, especially inexperience in the art of scientifically systematizing political ideas.

2. The highly emotional and sensitive nature of Wagner's own character and personality, and his easily getting excited over matters of secondary importance.

The formative years of Wagner's political development were dominated by the influence of the following doctrines:

Philosophically speaking, Wagner belonged to the Young Hegelian wing and as such firmly adhered to the *Feuerbachian* School of Thought that modified the original philosophy of Hegel (see Part IV, p. 179).

Sociopolitically speaking, he was a sort of *democrat-internationalist* with a slight Socialist tinge. He became so excited by the 1830 Revolution in France that he virtually proclaimed that he *in spirit belonged to it.*

Wagner was also strongly influenced by another event, namely, the flow of Polish refugees escaping the rule of Imperial Russia. While he was a student at the University of Leipzig he met and associated with many of them. The influence of these associations led him to proclaim that he was nothing less than

---

[23]T. Mann, in *Common Sense,* New York, January 1940: "I find an element of Nazism not only in Wagner's questionable literature; I find it also in his music."

a *world revolutionary.* At the same time, however, Richard Wagner was a full-fledged member of, and firm believer in, the *Burschenschaft,* "Father" Jahn's secret *nationalistic* students' league.

This combination of ideological influences made it indeed difficult for Wagner to develop an unambiguous sociopolitical viewpoint. He was hesitant and confused during the formative period of his development. This is the type of confusion which has been sometimes called *obscurity* and *vagueness.* Therefore, while Wagner's state of mind was confused indeed, it is not difficult for us to gain an understanding of it.

Confused as he may have been, Wagner's political development during its initial stage was characterized by a predominant tendency toward some sort of *democratic Socialism* and *revolutionary internationalism.* This leaves entirely out of the picture, for the moment, the indoctrination received through the *Burschenschaft.*

Wagner published his first essay during this uncertain stage of his sociopolitical development. It appeared in 1834 and revealed a strong bent toward *internationalism.* Carried away by romantic dreams, Wagner made bold to predict the future development of the world! He envisioned the rule of a *new master* who would speak and write neither in Italian, French, nor German. The master would be *art* itself, who would be above any kind of national unity or national vanity. He would rise up and excite humanity on nothing less than a *universal* scale.

Also influenced by the Revolutionary French ideas of freedom, Wagner adored France and especially the free French press. In 1839 he left Germany for Paris.

His stay there brought about the first modification, the first radical switch, in his spiritual growth. Unexpressed until then, the subtle influence of the teachings of the *Burschenschaft* now came into their own. To a great extent this change was impelled by Wagner's association in France with German intellectual exiles: Heine, the composer Meyerbeer, and Borne—all of Jewish blood.

Falling entirely under their influence, especially of Heine and Meyerbeer, Wagner's mind quickly began to clear itself of its original state of confusion. It began gradually to effect a transition from *internationalism* to Germanic *nationalism.* Heine and Borne were the political leaders of the exiled organization *Young Germany,* already mentioned in the section on Fascism in connection with Mazzini's secret society *Young Switzerland.* Under the strong influence of Heine and Borne as well as the *Young Germany* group, a pronounced trend toward nationalism took place in Wagner's mind. This change was apparent by 1842, only three years after he had arrived in Paris.

Wagner's personality was to have a strong impact on this new spirit of German nationalism. It took on an emotional character which found its justification in an anti-French feeling. Thus, Wagner's display of emotional nationalism rested on a negative basis rather than on the positive need for German nationhood.

A positive approach to nationalism would have required the assertion of the values of the German nation, possibly with exaggerations, but without the necessity of degrading the contributions and status of other nations. Wagner's approach was, however, quite different. It was negative in the sense that he acquired a violent anti-French animus prior to the realization of national values in Germany.

Wagner expressed his anti-French feelings for the first time in 1843, when he wrote his autobiography. His leitmotif was his emphasis on the reasons which the French had for writing music. Wagner asserted that the French write music only for gold. Since music is above all based on spiritual values, this monetary motivation could only indicate French decadence. Wagner was already convinced of his own musical ability, but he failed to gain recognition for his music in France. He concluded that the French were unable to appreciate the spiritual value of music.

To Wagner, it was predominantly the Jewish element in France who had established gold as criterion of the quality of music. The composers of France could produce nothing better than what Wagner called "Jewish Music," music which was, in reality, called forth by materialistic standards, but which claimed to contain spiritual values. From then on, Wagner began to make a sharp distinction between what he termed "Jewish Music" and "German Music." The former was, of course, materialistic and the latter was based on spiritual idealism. As a result of this distinction, gold became the symbol of materialism and of evil in all the major operas he wrote after his return to Germany.

In his autobiography Wagner concludes his tirade on Jewish and German music with a personal confession. This confession suggests the emotional basis for the emergence of at least part of his anti-French sentiments; he relates:

1. That he lived in poverty and misery in Paris because the music he composed was not appreciated and for that reason he was not paid enough money for it.

2. As a result of lack of money, he felt homeless and developed feelings of nostalgia toward his German fatherland, to which he then swore eternal fidelity.

Thus, the period from 1830 to 1843 introduced the first modification in Wagner's view of the world. The period 1843–1851 brought a second modification in his ideological development. This second modification in his mind and ideas consisted of a transition from pure emotional nationalism toward a not less sentimental but this time "organic" nationalism. The homelessness and loneliness which Wagner had experienced during his stay in Paris had led him to hate all kinds of individualism. His feelings of nostalgia for the German fatherland were, indeed, no more than *a drive to belong,* an impulse to be part of an organic whole, that is, a national and ethnic unit which would recognize him as a constituent part of itself. At this point we find the key to Wagner's "organic" nationalism.

Organic integration of individuals suddenly appeared to Wagner as something that could be accomplished only within the German cultural domain through the semi-mythological Volk, of which *all* German-blooded people are a part. The intermediate role of the Volk in this integration was of such magnitude, in his view, that once he arrived at this conclusion he made all his writings and all his music, especially the librettos of his operas, express the German-Volk-Soul. The finest expression of this view is *Die Meistersinger von Nürnberg* which he started to write in 1845.

Die Meistersinger is based on an all-Germanic Volk motif, in sharp contrast to Wagner's earlier opera *Rienzi,* where the concept of idealistic *internationalism* was strongly pronounced. The impact of *Die Meistersinger* upon Wagner's contemporaries and upon later generations of Germans was unparalleled. The opera became the favoite musical work of the National Socialist Party and also became the particular favorite of Adolf Hitler. The fundamental message of the opera is a warning to all the German Volk against the penetration of their society of the dangerous, insidious influences coming from the decadent "Welsch," a term Wagner used to identify a hybrid between Latin and French individual values.

During the Saxon Revolution of 1848–1849, the city of Dresden was seized in May, 1849, by a group of revolutionaries belonging to the Saxon parliament. Wagner joined in this uprising, whose leaders included the German writer Rockel and the Russian anarchist Bakunin. Wagner shared some of the ideas of this group. All of them were anti-capitalist, and Wagner's former sentiment in favor of internationalism provided no obstacle to his joining a revolution which might bring about Socialism. In the end, however, the revolution was suppressed, with much bloodshed, by the Prussian army.

This incident in Wagner's life should not be construed as evidence that he accepted the ideological framework of Marxism. He was definitely not a Marxist. He had by then renounced his previous attachment to the Feuerbachian-Young Hegelian School of Thought, and by 1849 he had already advanced far along the line toward the all-Germanic Volk concept. Thus, the actual reasons for Wagner's active participation in the revolution were known only to himself.

He then believed that all class distinctions should be abolished (although not for Marxian reasons) and that poverty should be eliminated among the German Volk. To Wagner, this was the prerequisite for the well-being of the German Volk organism. Abolition of all class distinctions and of poverty, Wagner often repeated, will lead to the strengthening of the Volk which eventually would become united within a single all-German *super state.* In this respect, he did not favor a world revolution nor the "classless society," such as Marx advocated, but he sought in a limited fashion to benefit *only* the German Volk.

Within the national realm, Wagner wanted to abolish money as a means of exchange, as the most precise symbol of Jewish-gold standards of regression. Abolishing money, he argued, was one important prerequisite for the emancipation of the German Volk. Wagner refrained from indicating what would replace money if it were abolished in Germany. He decided to rely on God's enlightenment. This idea of Wagner is a clear reflection of some of his early influences: of the impracticality of the French revolutionary Socialist Blanqui, and the utopianism of Rousseau, (both to be discussed in Part IV, pp. 144–151 and 161–166), and it is an indication of Wagner's own emotional irrationality.

Wagner's thinking may seem similar to Marxism, or rather Socialism, in another respect, but again Wagner was concerned only with Germany. He stressed the need for equality in respect to the work performed by all the individuals of the Volk. He proposed to arrive at such equality by abolishing the unproductive leisure classes. Although this was the chief Saint-Simonian goal (see Part II), Wagner's long-range intent was quite different. When all members of this class were forced to work, the producers' load represented by labor would be reduced considerably. Then, the economic satisfaction of German needs would be possible with fewer hours of work by each individual. Wagner prophesied that the time thus gained by the Volk would be devoted to the pleasures of art and music.

This was Wagner's vision of an all-Germanic life harmony, somewhat analogous to the Marxian world utopia of the second stage of Communism. While in Marx some sort of impulsive free labor relations are to ensure the ideal harmony of mankind, in Wagner *art* alone is to be the governing principle in the German super state. In both cases, however, the freely given labor (in Marx) and art (in Wagner) are visualized as pleasurable, harmonious activities, fulfilling the nature of the individual to the highest possible degree.

Although Wagner was exclusively interested in the well-being of the German Volk, in one case his emotionalism carried him to the point where he timidly stated that many more "small" Germanys of that harmonious kind could be set up all over the world!

The year 1851 brought another modification in Wagner's ideological framework. He came under the influence of Schopenhauer, and gradually he began to repudiate many of his former notions. Now he opposed his own faith in the reason of the revolution. He also pointed out that this rejection of Feuerbach and the Young Hegelians was due to the futility of their materialism. Wagner did not, however, associate himself with the original Hegelianism, which would have been a logical step as an expression of his anti-materialistic attitude, and would have been even more fitting because the concept of providential determinism was held in common by both Hegel and Schopenhauer.

In this new stage Wagner began to believe that reason cannot guide men toward progress. To reason is no more than a futile exercise, because everything is governed by what Schopenhauer had identified as his concept of the *Will.* On such philosophical grounds Wagner developed a narrow, all-Germanic political theory. He held that all parliaments and elections were futile instruments for the Volk. It is the Will which ultimately determines everything, including politics and law-making. The revolution in which Wagner had participated he now dismissed as futile, terming it *un-German* in nature, a product of French-Judaic influence.

This new trend in Wagner's thinking led him to discover the primary element that distinguishes the Volk. He thought of the Volk as being only those people who were able always to act correctly, on an *instinctive,* not a rational, basis. By acting according to their instincts alone, they in fact *obeyed* the Will. Thus, they were not unnecessarily burdened with a futile rationality, which is very often fallible.

Although every member of the Bayreuth Circle who was still alive during the interwar period contributed substantially to the formation of the doctrine of National Socialism by popularizing the Circle's ideas, it was nevertheless Richard Wagner who did the most. This is true in spite of the fact that he was not alive to witness the formal creation of National Socialism, the political creed that based itself on the loose idealization of the Germanic heritage as systematized and strengthened by him. It seems paradoxical that Wagner, who was the oldest man of the group, contributed the theoretical foundations and it was Adolf Hitler, the youngest member of the Circle, who joined only in 1923, who proved the most instrumental in applying the Wagnerian system of thought. Wagner was the architect who designed the matrix of the ideas; Hitler was the chief constructor who put it into practice. The other Circle members proved to be little more than valuable helpers.

Adolf Hitler (1889–1945) was born in Braunau, an Austrian town across the border from Germany. As he grew up he became firmly convinced that he was a gifted artist, and he persisted for some time as a painter, despite the fact that his achievements went unrecognized. When he sought admission to an art academy, he was rejected.

During World War I his patriotic feelings were strongly aroused, even to the point of exaltation. When he was drafted into the army, he made great efforts to distinguish himself as a fierce patriot. As a result he was awarded the Iron Cross (the highest wartime decoration, not available as a rule to enlisted men), but he did not go beyong the rank of corporal.

At the close of the war, his mood was one of bitter disappointment. Once again he turned to art, but he was not more successful than before. This final disenchantment led him to wander aimlessly through Austrian and German towns, where he joined the large masses of unemployed. While in this depressed state of mind, even before his meeting with the poet Eckart from the Bayreuth

Circle, Hitler accepted an idea which had gained currency among many hot-headed, demobilized, and unemployed war veterans: that Austria-Hungary and Germany had not been truly defeated in the war. What in their view actually had happened was that both countries had been betrayed and stabbed in the back, even while fighting bravely, through the attraction the German armed forces and their government had felt for President Wilson's Fourteen Points. Hitler became convinced, along with many other veterans, that the Fourteen Points had played somewhat the same role as the Trojan Horse in the ancient Trojan War. Had it not been for Wilson's program, both Austria-Hungary and Germany would have continued the war instead of capitulating, and would have eventually won it.

A large number of works about Hitler attest to his poor mental state and disreputable character. Pointing to his life of poverty and failure, combined with grandiose and unrealistic ambitions, most of these works have attributed to him limited intellectual ability and serious defects of character. Hitler has been labeled a "psychopathic person," "political charlatan," "demagogue," "sadistic maniac," "homosexual," not to mention derogatory terms of a more scholarly nature.

A few authors, however, have stressed other elements in Hitler's character. In this regard, it is important for students of National Socialism to become acquainted with H. R. Trevor-Roper's introduction to his *Hitler's Secret Conversations,* as well as the stand taken by Professor André Le Jules of Paris. According to their interpretation, although Hitler lacked formal education because of his talent for absorbing learning easily and his extensive reading interests, he was a self-educated man. Thus he had a mastery of the main ideas of the social sciences. In part Hitler was at the same time historian, political scientist, economist, sociologist, anthropologist, and even philosopher. In each of these fields he had developed firmly established views supported by his own arguments.

Indeed, it would seem to be a more popular and journalistic than scholarly attitude to uncritically support those who attribute to Hitler all of the most negative character traits. Regardless of what the majority opinion is, one must consider carefully two important factors which have necessarily contributed to the above negative view of the man:

1. The low degree of objectivity and rationality possible among the masses after a damaging and exhausting war, such as World War II.

2. The low probability of a man with (supposedly) so little mental ability as Hitler was reported to have had, becoming a member of a select, highly intellectual group such as the Bayreuth Circle. This Wagnerian group was, indeed, an intellectual group *par excellence,* of which even the philosopher Nietzsche was for some time a member.

It is very difficult to determine what Hitler's ideas on life and politics were before he joined the Bayreuth Circle, and, thus, to what extent they were modified by this group. One thing seems certain, and that is that Hitler's ultranationalism must have been irresistibly attracted to the sophisticated Germanic Volk concept of the Wagnerian system. In any case, Hitler's mind, as shaped or merely refined by Wagnerianism, made these ideas an inseparable part of the National Socialist doctrine. The basic elements that can be detected in National Socialism are: (a) *the Leadership principle;* (b) *the Party movement;* (c) *the Volk principle.*

Hitler saw two basic entities in political life: the political philosopher and the practical politician, who were entirely different phenomena. But Hitler did not exclude the possibility that in the long process of history they may join and, at some point, merge into one; thus would arise the incontestable and popular political leader.

Hitler maintained that the closer this union becomes, the closer one nation is to having an incontestable political leader, the greater will be the political difficulties encountered in the life of the country. This increasing number of difficulties would arise from the inevitable conflict within the leader: a conflict between a *theoretical element* (stemming from the political-philosopher entity) and a *practical element* (evolving from the practical-politician segment) within the leader.

In order to neutralize his inner conflict so that he may fulfill his responsibility to the nation, such a leader would, in a crisis, naturally be inclined to listen to the counsel of his people. This would be natural because there would be no ruling groups, learned in the theory and practice of politics, to advise him. But in spite of this natural inclination, the leader must bear his burden alone without trying to satisfy the demands of the masses. Were he to do the opposite, he would usually receive very poor advice from the unintelligent masses.

Therefore, the political leader must shun inappropriate advice and influence and work toward goals which often are comprehensible only to him and possibly (but not necessarily) to a few select people, gifted by nature with extraordinary intelligence and forming an elite within the nation. In especially difficult situations, the leader may reach his goals by methods comprehensible to no one else; but these goals must always be for the good of the majority of the people, who do not always know what is good for them.

Hitler recognized two leaders of this type in history, leaders whose mission it was to work with an elite for the good of the majority:

Genghis Khan, who because of his mental superiority and organizational talents succeeded in uniting all of the Mongol tribes, the effect being *good for all of them.*

Charlemagne, one of the greatest leaders in history. By the use of force combined with organizational talent, he succeeded in uniting *for their own good* even the Germans. They resisted him in this effort because they were unable to see the good that he was bringing to the majority.

In this part of Hitler's philosophy there are two elements quite clearly observable, namely, the concept of a *rule of by an elite,* and the concept of a *leader* apparently separate from the masses as well as from the elite.

Hitler probably acquired the concept of the rule by an elite through reading uninfluenced by the Bayreuth Circle. There is nothing exclusively Wagnerian in this concept, except that the Circle considered itself to be an intellectual elite within the German nation. Hitler probably acquired this concept from reading Jean-Jacques Rousseau, especially his idea of the *General Will* (see Part IV, pp. 144–151).

The concept of *individual leadership* is, however, purely Wagnerian. It seems to flow directly from Wagner (and possibly from "Father" Jahn) to Hitler, and from Hitler to National Socialist doctrine. As early as June, 1848, Wagner made a sharp distinction between the terms *Monarchy* and *Kingship,* and also between *Democracy* and *Republic.* According to Wagner, both Monarchy and Democracy were bad forms of government because neither of them serves the interests of the people. Monarchy serves the interest of the aristocracy while Democracy serves the interests of the elected democratic elite.

On the other hand, Wagner accepted Kingship and Republicanism as good forms of government when they are *combined* into one. In this respect he insisted on abolishing Monarchy and emancipating Kingship. His reasoning was that a given monarch is nothing more than the first among his aristocracy, while a given king is the first among the Volk and not merely among the aristocracy, which is a limited class created by the monarchs, not by nature. According to these differences, the good king will care for the whole Volk. Therefore, all class distinctions must be abolished along with the Monarchy in order to create Kingship.

Wagner also sharply distinguished between a Republic and a Democracy. For him, republicanism did not involve any kind of constitutional-parliamentary rule; Democracy, on the other hand, involves direct or indirect representation. Republicanism does not need any representation because it represents itself through the Volk. In Democracy, however, the Volk must be represented in a parliament and in the executive branch of government. But such representation automatically involves strong favoritism for a certain class of people because the nature of the electorate is a determining factor.

In republicanism the Volk does not have to be represented because republicanism *is* the Volk. In Wagner's mind *res-publica* and the *Volk* are one single *organic* unit. Following this line of reason, the king, who is the first of the Volk, is by himself the *Volk* and the *res-publica.* Therefore, directly and collectively *the king becomes the Volk.*

This Wagnerian reasoning is the exact basis for the leadership principle in National Socialist doctrine and for the whole National Socialist regime in Germany. The only refinement of this concept was the replacement of the term "King" by the more timely one of *Fuehrer,* a leader who is in exactly the same way identified with the Volk.

Probably after reading, and possibly receiving inspiration from, Hegelian philosophy (although Hegel was never mentioned in positive terms either in Hitler's writings or in those of the leading National Socialists), Hitler expounded upon his own ideas of the meaning of history. In Hitler's eyes, history is nothing more than a regular succession of different eras, each one of them marked for eternity by a specific culture. By culture, Hitler does not mean *Kultur,* but rather like Saint-Simon:

1. The totality of each era's predominant ideas which characterize the historical period; and

2. The era's social organization.

Therefore, consistent with his earlier line of thought, he conceives culture as a structure composed of a theoretical element (the political philosopher—the ideas) and a practical element (the practical politician—the social organization).

In a broad sense there were in Hitler's mind two basic eras in history, identified by the following cultures:

The ancient culture of Greece and Rome.

The modern capitalist society of Western Europe.

Although he recognizes the culture of Greece and Rome as being more glorious, Hitler believed, like Chamberlain, that it collapsed because of infiltration of *Jewish Christianity.* While this view was Hitler's official stand, he kept to himself certain doubts which bothered him until his death. His personal emotions were probably the source for this doubt, because he admired the Greco-Roman era far above any other period.

The capitalistic society of Western Europe had displaced the *good* German culture at the time of the Renaissance because the Germans let themselves be too much influenced by the characteristics of the age. Therefore, the Renaissance brutally and unjustly interrupted the development of German culture and, as a consequence, prevented it from accomplishing its great sociopolitical mission in the world.

At the end of World War I, Germany was swept, along with the rest of Europe, by the fashionable political trend toward decentralization of authority, and by Democracy. The creation of the Weimar Republic, with a liberal constitution, was a serious attempt to organize German society along democratic lines. The Weimar Republic, however, failed to combine the German people's desire for political Democracy with their basic economic needs. What resulted from the new system was a series of crises of political, social, and economic nature.

Article 48 of the Weimar Constitution is often pointed to as the chief reason for the collapse of the republic and the emergence of National Socialism. This article gave emergency powers to the executive branch of the government, allowing it to rule by decree—laws during times of national crisis. It is instructive to note that a similar provision in the constitution of the Fifth Republic of France, in its *Article 16,* allows the executive to assume power in case of a national emergency.[24] In the case of France, the power provided by Article 16 was used effectively, the emergency passed, and the National Assembly resumed its constitutional powers. French Democracy was not in the least damaged by the use of the emergency powers of the executive.

A similar situation (not provided for in the U.S. Constitution) occurred in the United States during the depression years. To combat the economic crisis, President Roosevelt did assume, temporarily and without official decree, extraordinary powers until there was a greater degree of stability.

It should be clear, then, that it is not the institutional aspect of the Weimar system of government that should be blamed for the collapse of the German Republic and the rise of National Socialism, but the functional aspect, because the German state, when faced with a crisis similar to those faced by France and the United States, acted quite differently.

Much of the responsibility for the collapse of the Weimar Republic must be attributed to the various German social groups and their leaders. Furthermore, the German people were totally inexperienced in democratic self-government, and there were numerous vestiges of authoritarianism still remaining as conditioning factors and stimuli. During this unstable period, a series of political parties directed the life of the country. The Socialist Party, the Communist Party, the Center-Catholic Party, the Conservative party, and the German Nationalist People's Party (DNVP) were the most important among them.

Influenced by the ideas of the Bayreuth Circle, transmitted through Rosenberg, Goebbels, and Hitler himself, the National Socialist movement appeared and began to grow in strength. Unlike the Fascist movement, which actually grew within the Socialist Party, the National Socialist movement gradually prospered in the midst of *all* the conventional parties as a result of their inability to provide a stable political regime and a sound economic basis for the German nation. Hitler quickly assumed leadership among a disenchanted people who were looking for a strong and responsible leader.

---

[24]Indeed, this provision was used by President de Gaulle during the crisis over Algeria in 1960–1961, when there was danger of an airborne invasion of Paris by the army stationed in Algeria.

The Socialist Party was the backbone of the Weimar Republic, but all of its efforts failed to halt bitter inter-party quarrels. Faced with deteriorating economic conditions, the republic was failing. This provided the grounds for various intellectual groups to seek to replace the Weimar system by some other, not clearly defined system, but one that had proved itself in Germany in the past—an *authoritarian* state based on national solidarity. With this in view, this movement began to call for a "conservative revolution."

Taking advantage of the growing popularity of authoritarian ideas in Germany, and taking note of the activity of those seeking a conservative revolution, the Communist Party became more insistent in its demands for a "proletarian dictatorship." The National Socialist movement found the time ripe to organize itself formally into the German National Socialist Workers' Party. It copied much from the Communists, but instead of a proletarian state it called for a "national dictatorship" of *all* Germans.

In 1923 the party, incited to act by the enthusiasm of its members and by the prevalence of political radicalism, attempted a *coup* against the provincial government of Bavaria. The National Socialists were unsuccessful in the face of army resistance, but large rallies occurred in support of the *coup,* demonstrating the party's growing popularity.

The National Socialist Party participated in the general election of 1928, but its vote was only 2.6 percent of the total vote. All anti-Weimar, non-constitutional parties, as well as those who called for a complete authoritarian system, received a combined popular vote of less than 15 percent.

But the country's instability continued to increase. Under similar conditions the industrial workers in Italy had occupied the plants in 1919, not long before the march on Rome and the advent of Fascism. In Germany, though, a different course of action was followed. The workers began to submit mass resignations, sheltering themselves financially behind the Weimar government's liberal provisions for unemployment benefits. Simultaneously, with plenty of free time, they assumed an active radical role in the work of the Communist Party.

The consequent substantial decrease in output from the factories provoked massive layoffs of white-collar administrative personnel. Added to these workers who now joined the ranks of the unemployed, there came the large new crop of intellectuals from the universities who were unable to find work. These two groups, the administrators who had lost their jobs and the new intellectuals, faced with the specter of unemployment and misery as the answer to their great ambitions for academic and social status, also embraced an extreme radicalism, but one different from that of the Communist factory workers. Instead of Marxian protest, they adopted rightist or conservative revolutionary ideas. This trend proved socially contagious; soon the white-collar workers found their ideas strongly supported by the insecure middle class of the nation. Since a large percentage of the members of these classes moved openly to support National Socialism, one could detect a very basic difference between the social composition of Fascism and that of National Socialism: the former was at its beginning a mélange of capitalists and factory workers (the Saint-Simonian producers' class), while the latter was predominantly a middle-class phenomenon—intellectuals and former civil servants, etc. The totalitarian movements grew very swiftly into great strength.

The radical pressure began to cause ruptures within the coalitions of the political parties, reaching a dimension which finally broke the Weimar regime. The beginning of the end of the Republic could be detected in the gradual drifting away of the traditional constitutional parties from constitutionalism and Democracy. Most significant in this respect was the very large decrease in the membership of the Socialist Party, upon which the regime was founded. The bulk of their lost members joined the Communist Party. However, the biggest gains in popular support during that period were registered by the National Socialists.

The year 1930 represented the crucial moment of the sociopolitical crisis. It was an election year during which all the totalitarian parties registered substantial gains at the expense of Democracy. While the National Socialists had won only 12 seats in parliament in 1928, in 1930 they won 107 seats.

Faced with what seemed a hopeless situation for the continuation of Democracy, the chancellor, Heinrich Bruening, began to rule by emergency decree. Choosing to exercise the power provided by Article 48 of the constitution, President Hindenburg had delegated all power to the chancellor. The strong Socialist parliamentary group did not object to the implementation of Article 48 because such an objection would have constituted a vote of nonconfidence, and would require new elections. Such elections were very much feared by the Socialists, whose popularity was clearly and rapidly waning in favor of the Communists. The Socialists were quite certain that they would lose a new election to the totalitarian parties. The National Socialist Party was growing stronger in membership and popularity, and was also winning local elections.

Despite the Socialist Party's reluctant attitude toward new general elections, they were held in July, 1932. The returns made the National Socialist Party by far the strongest single political party in the country. They won 230 seats in the parliament.

These results incensed the Communist Party, which was competing with the National Socialists in courting the people's favor. Protest riots conducted by young Communists followed. Such disturbances were counteracted by militant National Socialists, even before the government had the chance to intervene.

Increasing instability threatened to create complete disorder. As a measure of internal political appeasement, President Hindenburg decided that a new government had to be formed, a government reflecting past German concepts of political stability, one based on a military-conservative orientation. Hitler immediately offered to create such a government. His offer was substantially strengthened by a formal message of support he received from the German Nationalist People's Party. He also enjoyed the support of many of the President's military and civil advisers. Thus, on January 30, 1933, Hitler was formally appointed by the president to the post of chancellor. He was to be the last chancellor of the Weimar Republic.

Very quickly the National Socialist Party began to consolidate its newly won power, promoting a series of totalitarian concepts based on the following principles:

1. *Concentration of power within the hands of the leader.* In practice this was the Wagner-"Father" Jahn leadership principle. It was applied by permitting no limitations on the power of the leader, no definition of administrative jurisdiction, no autonomy in local government, and no checks and balances between the three branches of government.

2. *Atomization of society.* In National Socialist terms this involved the dissolution of all existing public organizations. Thus, the social and professional security of the individual was undermined, rendering him fully dependent on the power of the new regime.

3. *Coordination of the individual.* This measure was designed for the moment when the individual was considered to be beyond the stage of atomization of the entire society. Now he was reorganized in semi-political and semi-military social groups sponsored and exclusively controlled by the National Socialist regime. Thus, the state was to substitute for the public organizations.

4. *System of psychological thrust.* This principle referred to the elaboration of large-scale state propaganda to publicize the then only alleged existence of a powerful secret police. The object of this propaganda was to stifle any thought of rebellion among the people.

5. *Extensive propaganda.* This involved the establishment of complete state control over all access to information in order to create and guide the country's public opinion. It was used as a very effective tool for the indoctrination of each individual.

Unlike Fascism, the National Socialist regime did not seek to present itself even nominally as a regime based on constitutional principles. Consequently, the old Weimar Constitution was proclaimed void and was not replaced. In a true Wagner-"Father" Jahn fashion, the leadership principle became the supreme idea in National Socialist Germany.

Instead of the elaborate system of the corporate state (the Fascist structure between 1925 and 1943), no provisions of any kind were made for selecting candidates for the legislature prior to actual elections, nor were the economic relationships of the nation systematically regulated. The Fuehrer appointed and dismissed officials of all ranks. Even the executive branch of the government ceased to function collectively as an institution. Almost no cabinet meetings were held, and no votes were taken at such meetings. The cabinet ministers were transformed into technical experts who were constantly at the full disposal and mercy of the Fuehrer. In the name of the leader, according to the inherited active power of the Weimar Constitution's Article 48, most of the country's legislation was issued by decree. Occasionally, for the sake of appearances abroad, some laws were left for adoption by the parliament. Elections were seldom held, and when they were, a single list of candidates was presented to the electorate for approval (much as in contemporary Communist nations). The candidates were not selected, as under Fascism, by a special procedure designed to consider every economic class or profession. It was the Fuehrer alone who made such selections, with the help of the inner party circle.

The following three charts provide a visual representation of the structural form of the operative hierarchy of the National Socialist Party (III); the state-party relationships in National Socialist Germany (IV); and the state-party control over the youth organizations, a group of highly indoctrinated and state-controlled youth organizations which were created to build support for the policies of the regime (V).

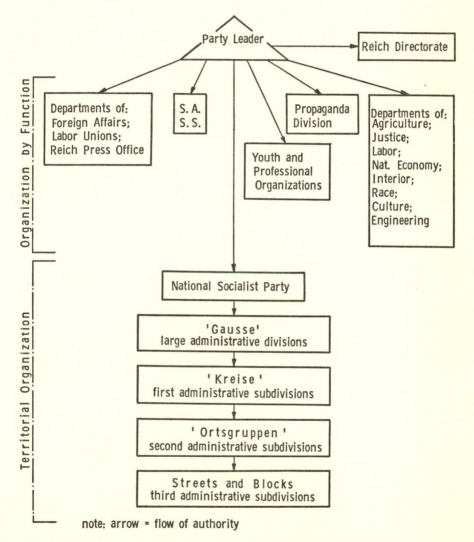

Chart III. The Operative Hierarchy of the National Socialist Party

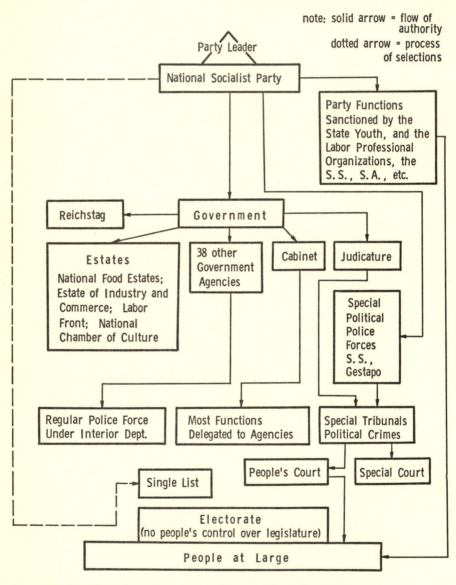

note: solid arrow = flow of authority

dotted arrow = process of selections

Chart IV. The State-Party Relations in National Socialist Germany

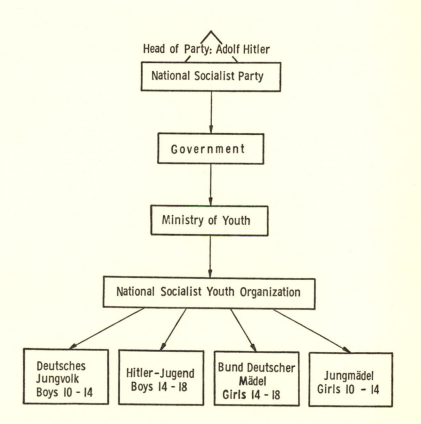

Head of Party: Adolf Hitler

National Socialist Party

Government

Ministry of Youth

National Socialist Youth Organization

| Deutsches Jungvolk Boys 10 - 14 | Hitler–Jugend Boys 14 - 18 | Bund Deutscher Mädel Girls 14 - 18 | Jungmädel Girls 10 - 14 |

note: arrow = flow of authority

Chart V. The State-Party Control over the Youth Organizations in National Socialist Germany

Part IV
Marxian Communism

Any study aimed at an objective comparison between the three modern sociopolitical regimes of a totalitarian character—Fascism, National Socialism, and
Communism—must perforce be firmly grounded in reality. This reality constantly reminds us of the fact that Fascism and National Socialism are already a
part of the respective Italian and German political past; Communism, on the
other hand, is still the chief motivating force which directs the sociopolitical and
economic development of the Soviet Union, China, and other states and,
incidentally, affects significantly the sociopolitical life of many non-Communist
countries. In other words, Fascism and National Socialism were both confined to
an international development which ended with World War II. Communism was
also a part of the above-mentioned era (and even preceded it) but has gone
beyond it and is very much a part of the present.

This imbalance in regard to the time and setting of the three regimes, naturally
leads to difficulties when one attempts to make a parallel and systematic
comparison of their ideological roots, the first two (Fascism and National
Socialism) having been restricted to a political environment, circumstances and
ideological conditioning quite different from the current stage of national and
international evolution. Thus, when attempting comparisons, one should make
an allowance for these diverse ideological and political circumstances.

It would then be clear that in judging Fascism and National Socialism one
would be likely to commit an error if one compares them with Communism on
the basis of present ideological criteria. The data related to the first two would
carry within themselves a *negative*, restrictive factor while the data on Communism would be free from it and would in fact have a *positive* element, an element
going beyond the point of time at which Fascism and National Socialism
interrupted their evolution.

One could rightfully expect, then, that the positive side of the comparison
would give an advantage to the investigation in terms of providing it with the
opportunity to draw information from up-to-date data on Communism, that is,
to make full use of currently relevant variables and findings, along with all the
modifications having had to be made regarding the original Communist doctrine.
Such an opportunity could be highly rewarding; it would provide simultaneously

a valuable basis for discovery, isolation, adjustments, and subsequent explanation of the changes and of their motivating factors. Therefore, this positive aspect offers almost all of the elements needed to gather, integrate, and interpret the past and present development of Communist political theory, leading to a clear view on pertinent ideological patterns.

The negative aspect, on the other hand, places limitations on this type of comparison because of the current absence of Fascist and National Socialist political regimes. The interruption (as a result of World War II) of their normal sociopolitical development now prevents the extraction of current data to be used for a point-by-point comparison (either of the theoretical and/or institutional-functional realm) with the parallel, relevant developments in Communism. Because of these limitations a substantial portion of the material on Communism (the post-World War II period) must be, on account of methodological considerations, either treated alone on a non-comparative basis, or simply omitted. However, since the focus of this work deals with theoretical foundations, predating the functioning of all three regimes one could use data on *Marxism,* comparing it on an equal footing with the *ideological roots* of Fascism and National Socialism. To do otherwise would mean to compare *current* ideological developments of Communism with what *would have been* the pertinent evolution in Fascism and National Socialism, provided that these regimes were in existence today to function on the currently quite different international scene. Methodologically it would mean a distortion in the analogous structures.

Due to this limitation, which from the start deprives us of a suitable common denominator directly and equally related to the three major modern sociopolitical totalitarian systems, one would be forced to accept one of the above-mentioned alternatives, thus escaping, as far as possible, from the limiting factor. The theoretical domain appears as the most likely area within which one might discover what they have in common because it predates the functioning of each one of the regimes and, also, because it provides substantial indications of respective psychological motivations.

A number of writers have concluded that neither Fascism nor National Socialism really possessed any substantial ideology in the true sense of the word. Indeed, in spite of the availability of theoretical material (such as that included in the two preceding parts), some authors have attempted to point out that what may appear on the surface as Fascist and National Socialist ideologies (as in Mussolini's *Fascism–Doctrine and Institutions* and Hitler's *Mein Kampf* respectively) were in fact nothing more than a reflection of particular national "states of mind" which were coupled with rigid sociopolitical programs, all aimed at the achievement and preservation of a strong and permanent state institution.

There is no such disagreement relating to the Soviet Union's sociopolitical and economic system. Indeed, if one looks at it from a theoretical or functional point of view—that is, if one concentrates on Marxism, or on its application in the U.S.S.R. since 1917—one could always find an abundance of statements relative to the building of the final, ideal stage of Communism which is to be characterized by the total absence of a state institution as a regulating force in the man-to-man, man-to-state, and state-to-state power relations.[25] Such statements and goals automatically suggest the existence of two possible hypotheses:

1. There is a drastic difference between Fascism and National Socialism, on the one hand, and Communism, on the other, setting the latter distinctively apart in terms of the regime's theoretical goals; and

2. There has been added a substantial amount of theoretical *utopian* thinking to Marxism, since currently no one is able to observe in operation such a stateless society as that proposed by Marx.

The latter proposition normally brings to mind shades of *Anarchism,* and rightfully evokes the question of whether Anarchistic overtones could be, indeed, rooted in the doctrines of Communism and of Socialism as well. However, the student of Communism is bound to discover many examples of past and present Communist officials firmly denying any possibility of such Anarchistic influences or overtones. Only Socialism is advanced as the true prerequisite for the achievement of the ideal Communist stateless society. In any case, the verification of these denials should include a close look at Anarchism; at least theoretically, it is a part of this topic, the tracing of the paths that supposedly lead to a Communist society. The professed vision of a stateless society, held in common by Anarchism, Communism, and also in some instances, by evolutionary Socialism, is quite utopian and would eventually suggest that one must construct the basis for the analysis on the concept, role, and functioning of pertinent *utopias.*

While constructing the initial framework of such a study one does not have to go as far back as the utopias of Antiquity; neither does one have to take Plato and Xenophon into consideration. It is enough to select a somewhat well developed stage of utopia, a stage which has incorporated and taken into account the pertinent essential elements of thought of Antiquity and yet presenting them, along with new concepts, in a modern and sophisticated form. So formulated, this developed status of utopia seems to have evolved somewhere in the period between the end of the sixteenth and the beginning of the

---

[25]According to Lenin, rural electrification was the primary factor to be accomplished prior to the withering away of the state institution. According to Stalin, the capitalist encirclement of the U.S.S.R. was a real danger which had to be eliminated prior to proceeding with the withering away of the state institution. According to Khrushchev, the danger from mainland China was the roadblock to fulfillment of the Marxian prediction of the withering away of the state institution in the U.S.S.R.

nineteenth century. This is the same period to which is attributed the crystallization of the theoretical motivations underlying Fascism and National Socialism.

If we relate the meaning of the term "utopia"—*no place*, (that is, an ideal,
chimerical, a visionary product of human imagination)—to the fact that no one
can find in existence today the type of stateless society envisioned by the
doctrine of Communism, we have arrived at the basic justification for the study
of utopia in relation to Communism. Indeed, the relation of utopia to the study
of Communism is as pertinent as the German Mythology-Volk-Kultur concept is
relevant to National Socialism. Similarly, just as the latter crystallized into a
sociopolitical doctrine through the intellectual help provided by Fichte, the von
Schlegels, "Father" Jahn, and the Bayreuth Circle of Richard Wagner, plus the
racial theories of de Gobineau and Chamberlain, utopia developed into its most
sophisticated form—the notion of a stateless society—through the philosophical
elaborations found in Early French Socialism and later in Kant, Hegel, Feuerbach,
and Marx.

In spite of its dubious meaning, the term utopia denotes one of the most noble
and sincere drives of man's nature: its final target is always the betterment of
societal life. It is an expression of man's speculations about a better world (not
just a nation or a country) and the hope of achieving it. Therefore, the author of
a utopia is not merely a "lost dreamer," not a "sleep walker," but an international social ideologist, a political reformist, a literary satirist, and, above all, a
determined driving force for the betterment of societal relationships on a
universal scale. Consequently, one would not err in stating that the actual
development of utopian thought is in fact a reflection of the social, intellectual,
political, and economic development of mankind.

If one places the aims of the doctrine of Communism into such a context, one
could not lightly dismiss its central prophecy of the stateless society. Its
"utopian" goal is quite clear. One would seem to have to start from the premise
of expecting that this entire theoretical structure will carry a great deal of
international appeal aimed not at a single nation but at mankind as a whole. In
fact, the international appeal, that is, the character of universality, the exportability of the Communist doctrine, may be regarded as its major asset.

However, the term "utopia" (as used in this context) does *not* signify a
limitless endeavor of human vision in relation to society. Not all kinds of
visionary and chimerical writings and expressions fit within the framework of
this noble drive aimed at the betterment of human relationships. The numerous
writings which portray imagined adventures in space, romance on Mars, or in a
rocket ship traveling to the planets, cannot be regarded as utopian in the sense of
the word as used here. Indeed, the finite line that may have a criterial significance in establishing the fundamental difference between that kind of literature,
totally the product of man's imagination, on the one hand, and the term

"utopia," used in the political context, on the other, may simply be the extent of dynamism in the character of the literature in question. If the author's main concern is the action, the *dynamic* action, if he has a clearly discernible *plot*, involving a small group of *heroes*, then the writing may be classified as pure fantasy with no significance whatsoever for our topic. A true utopia in the sense used here has no story to tell, has neither heroes nor performers; it is related in vision to the historic era in which it is written, aiming at the improvement of the then existent societal relationships whether of political, social, or economic nature. It is an overall dream, involving a large society of humans, projected through time from a base definitely determined by the pertinent characteristics of the given era in which the utopia has been written.

Although entirely fictional, a utopia would always describe a particular state of *human* society or community. It would not be a particular philosophy or theory in the proper sense because such philosophies and theories, if they are a part of utopia, are envisioned by the author as already implemented ir. the imagined institutions and the like procedures of the societal structure. On the other hand, pure political theories or philosophies are only propositions; they are not presented in an implemented form.

Utopian themes are descriptive, always pertinent to the political and social structure and the functioning of fictional politically organized communities, and do not stress in their context either dynamic action or adventure.

On the other hand, a utopia, as fictional as it may be, does not mean a complete freedom of imagination for the author. He always must "keep his feet on the ground" because he deals with human beings, not with a society of ghosts or other *humanoid* creatures. Moreover, a given utopia always has a certain resemblance to the existing circumstances of the time in which it is written and to the particular type of politically organized society in which the author has lived. However, in any case, such an era (or society) is always the subject of the author's criticism. In fact, his work reflects its shortcomings and his wishes for their correction.

One can broadly place the major utopian writings in two categories:

(1) *progressive* utopias; and

(2) *retrogressive* utopias.

A *progressive* utopia usually looks toward a politically organized society which is projected by the author as existing in the future, far ahead of his time. Since an improvement of societal relationships over the current reality is always the dream or goal of the author, one could also classify this kind of utopia as *optimistic*, reflecting his positive attitude and faith in human development.

A *retrogressive* utopia usually describes a society imagined to have existed in the past. The tone is usually nostalgic and implies what might have been accomplished if errors had been avoided.

This division into "progressive" and "retrogressive" utopias is indeed important in as much as one can detect the advocacy of political tendencies of quite different natures emphasized in each of these two categories. For instance, a progressive utopia usually stresses *centralizing* political ideas as the major cure for sociopolitical upheavals. On the other hand, the retrogressive utopia seems to recommend *decentralizing* political methods as most suitable for correcting sociopolitical injustices.

If one attempts to relate these characteristics to the current sociopolitical problems of society, one can see that, at least in the Soviet Union and in the U.S.A., they still determine the domestic political issues in both countries. In broad terms, one may say that "centralization of power" in the hands of the central authority (whether party, government, or both) vs. "decentralization and delegation of such power" is the underlying factor separating the periods of Leninism from Stalinism, and of Stalinism from the post-Stalinist period in the U.S.S.R., while in the U.S.A. the very same problem has been in existence since the American Revolution but in the form of federal rights vs. states rights.

In addition to progressive and retrogressive utopias, one may also run across (although quite seldom) a kind of utopian literature based on hypotheses in which the author focuses on future experimental application of proposed societal arrangements. Such writings can be classified as *experimental utopias,* formulating a certain creative force which encourages the setting-up of communal relationships that might prove more advantageous than the currently accepted sociopolitical arrangements. Owen, Hertzka, Cabet, in part Fourier, and other authors with similar goals in mind could be rightfully regarded as promoters of this idea.

Thus, once accepting that the utopian writer is not merely a "lost dreamer" and a "sleep walker" but an international social ideologist, a political reformer, literary satirist, and a determined driving force for the betterment of societal relations on earth, one may go further in completion of this assertion by adding that the actual evolution of utopia could be regarded as the reflection of the social, intellectual, and political development of mankind.

When one places within such a framework the final goals of Socialism and Marxism—and of their most advanced product, Communism—(those goals being the professed withering away of the state institution), one can then concentrate on examining those utopian propositions closely related to the basic motivation of Socialism, an ideology claimed as the common prerequisite to the last two ideologies. This prerequisite would in turn lead to a clearer understanding of the Communist politically organized societies.

Du contrat social of Jean-Jacques Rousseau, first published in 1762, contained in its title the word "social" with the connotation of *socialized man,* a term close to what then might have been the meaning of Socialism. Indeed, it would be quite difficult to trace the precise moment in which this term first appeared. The year 1803 has, however, sometimes been accepted as the year in which the term appeared in print for the first time (in Italian). Rousseau's *Social Contract* contained the word "social" although not "Socialism." The argument exists that even as late as 1803, the sense given to this term was entirely different, and one should say, unrelated to the meaning which Socialism came later (and currently) to have.

Moreover, it has been quite convincingly argued that the 1803 appearance of the term *Socialism* in Italian print was nothing more than an accident. Supporters of this line of argument have said that this was evident because no further trace of this term was found until 1827. During that year, the word "socialist" made its way into the *Cooperative Magazine,* a magazine supported by the followers of Robert Owen. The word was then used with the meaning of a special cooperative group. Thus, the term did approach the connotations which it is given today.

The next appearance of the word "Socialism," in a sense much closer to its present meaning, occurred in 1832. It was used by the editor of the French periodical *Le Globe,* Pierre Leroux, who made that magazine the principal organ for the followers of the Saint-Simonian doctrine. From that moment on (especially till the end of the 1830s), the term has been used widely in France with the connotation of something opposite to "individual," that is, *social* versus *individual.*

Gradually, after having been used rather freely in France, the word passed into the English dictionary. The term seems to have appeared next in Germany and some of the other European countries, and reached the U. S. at a somewhat later date.

Pierre Leroux and his periodical, *Le Globe,* are both part of what is usually referred to as Early French Socialism. One might say that this type of Socialism which followed the 1789 Revolution in France, appeared as a reaction to that event, as a protest against the failure to achieve the prescribed revolutionary goals. Indeed, the French Revolution had succeeded only in part. With the exception of the elimination of the Monarchy, the greatest revolutionary success occurred in the countryside rather than in the urban areas. In the country, the liquidation of French feudalism appeared as one of the major revolutionary accomplishments—indeed, almost as the essence of the Revolution. The socio-economic order in the urban areas, however, was not substantially modified, at least not to the extent of the sweeping revolutionary changes in French agrarian society. Therefore, one might generalize by saying that, with the exception of the elimination of the Monarchy, the Revolution was only half successful; that is, almost 100 percent successful in the countryside but close to 0 percent in urban areas with large cities. This would appear to explain the emergence of Early French

Socialism as a distinct *urban* phenomenon. Its main goal was to correct urban inadequacies. For the purpose of clearer understanding, the period of Early French Socialism may be studied in several respects. For instance, one may observe the existence in postrevolutionary France of a Socialist wing characterized by *revolutionary radicalism.* Simultaneously, one may observe the development of an *evolutionary* branch of French Socialism, and still, in between these two groups, one may see the ideas of *Anarchism* flourish.

As indicated earlier, the rather rich and complex socioeconomic scene in France emerged as a result of the 1789 Revolution. However, one should not omit, at this point, the influence of Jean-Jacques Rousseau on both the Revolution itself, and the various branches of the early French Socialist movement. For instance, the evolutionary branch of Early French Socialism could be easily and correctly categorized as a Rousseauan type of Socialism. Indeed, it bears all the characteristics of Rousseau's School of Thought. On the other hand, the radical-revolutionary branch of Early French Socialism could also be looked upon as influenced to a substantial degree by Rousseau but only in an adverse fashion. Indeed, it appeared as a discontented reaction to Rousseau's ideas. The third branch of Early French Socialism, Anarchism, may be considered a subordinate form of evolutionary Socialism. It may also be looked upon as a side-effect of Rousseau's impact on French society.

Jean-Jacques Rousseau (1712–1778) may hardly be regarded as a true philosopher in the modern sense of the term. However, he did fit the eighteenth-century French type of philosophy quite well. In any case, whether one looks upon him as a true philosopher or not, one must admit that he had an extremely powerful *influence* on the philosophy, literature, human tastes, manners, and politics of his time. Therefore, whether he was a philosopher or not would be of less importance than to recognize his immense influence and impact on society. Indeed, Rousseau is regarded as the founder of the well-known *Romantic movement* in political philosophy. It is a system of thought arranged and expressed in such a fashion that modern scholars have come to a variety of conclusions regarding his ideas, these conclusions quite often conflicting with one another. Indeed, some have described his political philosophy as a *pseudo-democratic dictatorship;* others have called his ideas *true totalitarianism;* still another group looked upon Rousseau as the *friend of despotism.* One should also mention that his philosophy has sometimes been referred to by the rather confusing term *totalitarian democracy.* And to make the diversity in the interpretation of Rousseau more complete, it should also be mentioned that some refer to him as a *true* and *very good* democrat.[26]

---

[26]G. Kateb, "Aspects of Rousseau's Political Thought," *Political Science Quarterly,* No. 4, December 1961.

If we even today can observe such great diversity as to the interpretation of Rousseau's thinking, it can easily be comprehended that his power and originality quickly created a split in the thinking of prerevolutionary France. Thus, one can observe the emergence of the evolutionary group of Early French Socialism which was to form the pro-Rousseauan group; and also the stirrings of the radical revolutionary group, regarded as a non-Rousseauan group. It seems that theoretical Anarchism, appearing in its basically nonviolent, *Proudhonian* aspects, rather belongs in the pro-Rousseauan group. Saint-Simon and Fourier may both be regarded as the most important promoters of the non-Anarchistic pro-Rousseauan ideas; thus, they too belong with the evolutionary branch of Early French Socialism, while the radical revolutionaries, Babeuf and Blanqui, represent the non-Rousseauan branch. In addition to this split within the social philosophy of the time, another split also occurred, this time along the lines of Socialism versus capitalistic Individualism (as opposed to Anarchistic individualism). Even today one can witness the existence of this division, still very much along the lines of the rupture that occurred in postrevolutionary France.

No lengthy research is required to learn the details of Rousseau's life or of the psychological forces that shaped his mind and character. He, himself, readily volunteered this in great detail in his *Confessions.* In reading Rousseau's work, one is left with the impression that, indeed, there is no lack of objectivity. Rousseau definitely does not attempt to conceal his evil endeavors throughout his life. On the contrary, if one looks for a bias, one will get the impression that Rousseau enjoyed very much presenting himself to the public as a great sinner and as an unorthodox nonconformist. If there is some lack of objectivity in Rousseau's autobiography, it is related to exaggeration of the negative aspect of his character. Whatever the extent of evil or goodness in him, one can be certain that Rousseau did not possess ordinary human virtues. His life was one of constant manipulation of circumstances and taking full advantage of environmental reality in a not-very-honest manner.

Rousseau was raised in Geneva as an orthodox Calvinist. His father simultaneously held two professions: watchmaker and dancing master. His mother died when he was a child, and he was brought up by an aunt. At the age of twelve, Rousseau left school to become apprenticed in a trade. In fact, he was continuously apprenticed in various trades, not holding any one of them for long, later commenting that he had hated them all. At the age of sixteen, he fled from Geneva and settled in Savoy. There, he was for a while without means of subsistence. The solution he found was to secure an audience with a Catholic priest to whom he sincerely expressed his wish to be converted to Catholicism. Later on, Rousseau admitted that his motives for that act had been completely mercenary. Then he somewhat joyfully reminisced that he was at that point committing an act of banditry. One should take note of the fact that when he was writing the *Confessions*, Rousseau had been "reconverted" to Calvinism. During another period of his life, Rousseau served as a lackey to the grand lady Madame de Vercelli. She died while he was in her service. On this occasion, he was found in possession of one of her expensive ribbons and was, therefore, accused of having stolen it. Madame de Vercelli also had a maid with whom Rousseau claimed to have been in love. Responding to the accusation, Rousseau quickly stated that the ribbon had been given him by this maid. He was believed, and the maid was punished. Later on, Rousseau admitted that, in fact, he was the one who had stolen the ribbon; but his act of blaming the theft on the maid was, in his view, the best proof of the love he had for her! He stated that when taken by surprise, her name was the first that came into his mind. Consequently, he loved her more than anyone else.

Except for the maid in this case and also another servant girl in a hotel in Paris, all of Rousseau's relations with women seem to have been quite carefully selected. Indeed, they were all helpful and instrumental in helping him stay on the upper levels of society. Once, through the help of such a noble lady, he was appointed secretary to the French ambassador to Venice. There he worked conscientiously and efficiently. However, he was not properly paid for this work by the French government, in the sense that the embassy owed him for some time a certain amount of money. Unable to settle the problem locally, he used the occasion of one of his trips to Paris to try to get help from the authorities and the courts of justice. There was no question that Rousseau was right in his claim—everyone recognized the legitimacy of his case. However, a great amount of red tape and bureaucratic formalities were involved, and Rousseau had to wait a long time before he got his due. This delay and inefficiency have sometimes been advanced as having had something to do with Rousseau's rejection of the government of France.

Rousseau's first literary success came in 1750. The Academy of the French city of Dijon announced a contest, a prize to be awarded the author of the best literary essay on the question, "Have the arts and sciences conferred benefit on mankind?" Rousseau eagerly entered the competition. He developed an essay with a very negative emphasis concerning the above question, and he won the prize. Among the other ideas he advanced in that prize-winning work was the argument that science, letters, and arts appear to be the worst enemies of morals. In addition, he contended that science, letters, and arts automatically create wants and desires and, therefore, they are sources of slavery. He also opposed human Civilization as it was then institutionalized. Rousseau admired what he called "man in his *noble savage* state." Such primitive men, he contended, could, indeed, easily be defeated in war by sophisticated and civilized Europeans, but this defeat did not increase the value or worth of the victors. He also maintained that science and human virtues are incompatible, and in fact, contrary to each other. In this respect, he stated that all sciences have an evil origin. He went on to say that astronomy derives from the superstition of astrology; eloquence comes from ambition; geometry, from avarice and stinginess; physics, from vain curiosity; and ethics, from sinful human pride. Therefore, education, in the form as it existed then, and the art of printing are things to be deplored. Everything that distinguishes civilized man from the native barbarian is the worst evil. Only the state of nature still retained in the development of mankind has an unsurpassed value.

The prize awarded Rousseau by the Academy of Dijon made him famous. He decided to exploit his new asset by demonstrating publicly his ideas. In one instance, he publicly sold his watch while stating that, being a naturalist and realizing the virtues of pure nature and, simultaneously, the evils of Civilization, he no longer needed to know the time.

In 1754 Rousseau published another work, *Discours sur l'origine de l'inégalité* (*Discourse on Inequality*). In it he elaborated further on his previously published ideas; but this time Rousseau failed to win a prize. In the *Discourse on Inequality* he maintained that man is good by nature. He does evil, however, not because of his inner forces and inclinations, not because of his nature, but because of the institutions created by Civilization. All these institutions among which man is forced to live have, in fact, conditioned him to become bad.

It would be useful to leave Rousseau for a moment and emphasize that this kind of thinking was strongly reflected at a later date in the Marxian School of Thought, that is, in the theory underlying Communism. In Marx's thought men are good by nature, but they act in an evil way because of the long conditioning they have undergone in a world of capitalistic institutions. According to Marx, to fulfill the ideals of Communism would mean to eliminate, once and for all, such institutions. Once they are destroyed, the natural goodness of man will prevail. There will be created a natural world of total fulfillment and harmony, with happiness and satisfaction for every one. Like Rousseau, Marx believed that institutions are bad, because, as he saw them, all institutions were capitalistic by nature. Therefore, they must be destroyed. But the State, with all of its agencies, is also an institution. Therefore, the Communist State should serve only as the means for an orderly destruction of all institutions, at the end including itself. Thus, the final stage of Communism appears as quite utopian. It is characterized by the withering away of the State institution, this same State institution, this same dictatorship, which is to be used in the immediate postrevolutionary period for the destruction of capitalism.

There is also parallel between Rousseau and Karl Marx related to the question of private property. While Rousseau only seemed to *pose* the problem and deduce that private property is a retarding force in the development of mankind, Marx went further in his elaboration by pointing out how man can *eliminate* private property. Marx prescribed that in the immediate postrevolutionary period private property should be confiscated by the State. However, the State, being in itself an institution, is also destined to wither away—it is doomed to vanish. As a result of this process of withering away, therefore, private property will disappear along with the disappearance of the State.

Rousseau, on the other hand, was much less sophisticated in this respect. He did not admit that there were any proper means for doing away with private property, but only pointed out that it was, in fact, a societal evil. Rousseau held, for instance, that metallurgy and agriculture are both things to be deplored: both connote the idea of private property. He stated that Europe is the unhappiest continent on earth, only because it has most of the iron and most of the agriculture of the globe. In order to undo that evil, Rousseau, lagging very much behind Marx's sophisticated systematizations, unrealistically recommended that one had only to abandon Civilization. One should do so because man is a good being by nature, and man can reach his natural goodness only by living in accord with Rousseau's notion of the *noble savage*.

One can discover in Rousseau a suggestion of the Marxian theoretical definition of the *second stage* of Communism—a stage characterized by a total lack of institutions, a stage where men live alone as individuals with no frictions among them, with no conflict of interests, in a state of total happiness, fulfillment, and harmony.

The idea of going back to nature was so strongly developed in Rousseau's mind that it affected his relationships with what could be called his friends. One example is his relations with Voltaire. There is evidence enough to point out that at first they admired each other very much. In 1755 a violent earthquake took place in Lisbon, an earthquake which inspired Voltaire to write a poem about the disaster; in it he deplored the deeds of nature. Rousseau read it and burst into fury. He answered Voltaire by stating that it was not at all the fault of nature but of the people of Lisbon. They did not have to live in seven-story houses; and if they hadn't done so, they wouldn't have suffered from the earthquake. If they had lived dispersed in the forests in the state of nature as humans should do, they would have survived the earthquake and would probably not have suffered at all. What had happened was not worthy of Voltaire's poetic effort; the people of Lisbon, living in a civilized manner, deserved this cataclysm. In addition, Rousseau claimed that it is a good thing that a certain number of people get killed now and then to alleviate the population pressure.

This was the end of the friendship between Voltaire and Rousseau. In his reply, Voltaire treated Rousseau as a mischievous madman; Rousseau retorted that if there was nothing in Voltaire that he could honor but his talents that was not a fault of his.

In 1762 Rousseau published two works, *Emile* and *Du contrat social (The*

Social Contract). Emile treated the problem of education according to the principles conceived and promoted by Rousseau. In that work he also included a part entitled "The Confession of Faith of a Savoyard Vicar." In it he set forth a series of principles for a natural religion. This irritated both the Catholic and the Protestant churches. *The Social Contract*, on the other hand, contained ideas that might prove dangerous to Rousseau; in it he advocated a type of neo-Democracy which totally rejected the divine right of kings.

Adverse reaction to both *Emile* and *The Social Contract* reached such a magnitude that Rousseau was expelled from France. He attempted to go to Geneva, his native city, but Geneva didn't want him either. He then attempted to go to Berne, but again he was refused asylum. Therefore, he lived for a while at Motiers, but not for long. He was driven away by a mob which accused him of murder. The only country which accepted Rousseau was England. Indeed, there he achieved great social success amidst English high society. His fame increased, and George III granted him a pension. Unfortunately, his having been accused of murder seems to have affected his mental stability. Apparently unprovoked by anything in England, he conceived the idea that there was a plot against him; therefore, he "escaped" from London and went back to Paris. There he lived for a few years in great misery, and died in circumstances which have made some people suspect suicide.

Almost all of Rousseau's political theories are reflected in *The Social Contract.* There he paid lip service to Democracy, but actually tended to justify totalitarian types of states. One general characteristic of *The Social Contract* is the lack of sentimentality and romantic emotion that otherwise characterized the rest of his writings.

In that work he expressed his preference for small city states over large politically organized areas. In terms of political organization, Rousseau advanced Democracy as a superior form of government for small city states. His idea of Democracy, however, was a *direct* Democracy, not one based on representation. For medium-sized states, Rousseau advocated Aristocracy as the most suitable political regime. Oddly enough, what he means by Aristocracy is something very close in essence to what is known today as *representative* Democracy. For large states, though, Rousseau recommended Monarchy as the most appropriate form of government.

One of the opening sentences of *The Social Contract* is "Man is born free, but everywhere he is in chains." In spite of this implied call for freedom, liberty seems to have been only a nominal goal for Rousseau. It is quite clear that he would gladly sacrifice it for equality. *The Social Contract* focuses on the abstract idea of the total alienation of each man, together with all of his rights and possessions, from the entire community. The individual's interests being quite similar to the interests of the other individuals in the community should not interfere negatively with human associations. Here we take note of a very interesting idea, which later became one of the foundations of Modern Totalitarian Dictatorship, namely, the *identification* of the individual with the community. Thus, the societal arrangements and accepted ways of life became, in fact, an obstruction to the individual's progress since they reject the value of a separate individual existence if it is not in step with the community's view. The individual's values are, in Rousseau's view, only achieved *through* and *within* the societal unit. Very close, indeed, is "Father" Jahn's advocacy (see Part III, pp. 107–109) of the *organically* combined leader-masses principle; this Rousseauan notion also seems to relate quite closely to one of the basic features of National Socialism.

Such a social association in which each individual is totally alienated from his own self and is instead entirely given over to the mercy, wishes, and interests of the whole community, Rousseau defined as a *State*. But, according to Rousseau, this definition of a State applies only to those cases in which the association is passive. When it is active, he defines it as a *sovereign;* and when it is placed in a state of interaction with other similar associations, then Rousseau referred to it as a *power.*

As an extension of this concept, Rousseau advanced in *The Social Contract* his idea of the *General Will* in the community. In his view, the General Will is something quite different from what would be the *will of all,* and it is not necessarily identical to the idea of the *will of the majority.* The concept of the General Will is one of the most important in the totality of Rousseau's ideological system. The mechanics through which one can arrive at this concept involves an almost mathematical cancelling out of opposing *individual* wills. As a matter of fact, they can be identified by giving them mathematical signs of pluses and minuses with various but corresponding "identities," thus indicating the degree of their opposition in relation to each other. This cancellation process of individual wills is to continue until cancellation is no longer possible; that is, until there are no more contradictory wills, at least contradictory enough to warrant labeling them by the respective plus or minus signs. This sum total of man's opinions and desires, likes and dislikes, is, according to Rousseau, the *General Will* of a given community. It does not appear necessarily to be the will of the majority. Rousseau tends quite clearly to make the concept of the General Will seem to be a totalitarian notion because in addition to the above, he openly stated that the General Will is always infallible—a totalitarian interpretation *par excellence.* Another totalitarian aspect of his thinking was his advocacy that all men should be forced to join the General Will in their thought and action because of its infallibility and also because such an adherence will show them the only way which can make them free. In other words, they should be *forced* to become free. To force somebody is always a totalitarian action even though this action could be for somebody's own good. (See Part I, p. 19.) To decide what is good for somebody else is also a totalitarian concept, central not only to the Fascist and National Socialist regimes but also very much in evidence in the practice of Communism, that is, the adjusted application of Marxism.

There are some indications that Rousseau's theory had more than a passing impact on the French Revolution of 1789. Although it is not possible to measure the exact degree of such an influence, one cannot doubt that such an influence did exist. One can even suggest that, although currently unmeasurable, his influence must have been quite significant, because there were in France, after the first revolutionary wave, several schools of thought based on a Socialist ideology quite closely associated with Rousseau's ideas. In fact, one can detect in postrevolutionary France the emergence of the three Socialist schools frequently referred to as Early French Socialism. These three schools appear even more as a Rousseauan product through their division into two groups—the pro-Rousseauan group following in general most of the Rousseauan recommendations for society, while the non-Rousseauan group emerged as a reaction to the alleged inefficiency of these recommendations. As stated earlier, the main thing is that, whether pro-Rousseauan or non-Rousseauan, both were influenced by Rousseau. While the first group was mostly in agreement with him, the latter was a reaction to the Rousseauan ideas. In any case, it was Rousseauism that provoked the reaction. In this sense, both are related to the Rousseauan impact on French society in the revolutionary era.

François-Marie-Charles Fourier (1772–1837) of the pro-Rousseauan group emerged as one of its main exponents. Like Rousseau, this group had no taste for violence or revolution, and also displayed a streak of utopianism. One can argue the point whether this early French evolutionary Socialism was independent of the classical type of Anarchism, or whether the Anarchistic School of Pierre-Joseph Proudhon was a part of it. On the other hand, the non-Rousseauan school of Early French Socialism counted among its adherents men like Cracchus Babeuf and Louis-Auguste Blanqui. The principles of that second school were, in some cases, not less utopian, but the major non-Rousseauan characteristic was that they all advocated a *revolution* and other violence as a means of achieving their final goals.

Within the evolutionary wing of Socialism, Fourier emerged as the most important representative. His writings importantly influenced Karl Marx, whose few brief recommendations related to the final stage of Communism substantially reflect the Fourier-like type of a free and harmoniously happy society. While the notion of the actual process of the withering away of the State institution in Marx is based on a certain logic, the description of the society which is to follow that event is indeed extremely vague, and carries within itself all of Fourier's overtones.

Fourier propounded his ideas in four major writings: *Théorie des quatre mouvements et des destinées générales* ("The Theory of the Four Movements"), which was published in 1802; *Traité de l'association domestique agricole* ("The Domestic Agricultural Association"), published in 1822, and republished during 1823–30 under the title: *Théorie de l'unité universelle; Le nouveau monde industriel et sociétaire* ("The New Industrial and Societarian World"), published in 1829; and *La fausse industrie mercellée, répugnante, mensongère, et l'antidote: l'industrie naturelle, combinée, attrayante, véridique, donnant quadruple produit* ("The Phony Industry"), which appeared in two volumes during 1835–36.

These titles make it quite evident that Fourier's recommended remedy for the oppressive socioeconomic and political conditions in France at that time was based on work performed in small dimensions. Indeed, Fourier placed great emphasis on this smallness during the beginning stages; the remedy might eventually but *naturally* diffuse itself and take on a somewhat larger dimension, although its size was left completely undetermined by Fourier. Fourier was predominantly preoccupied with the problems of man as an individual rather than as a part of society. He contended that if the problems of each individual were solved, they, in turn, would automatically create a happy society. Therefore, he searched for the grievances of the individuals as separate units and systematically attempted to discover and propose remedies for the individuals, again one by one. In this respect one may classify Fourier's method as fully inductive.

Fourier hated the large-scale industrial organizations, which he frequently referred to as "monstrosities"; and he was not a bit interested in technology. On those grounds alone, Fourier's position emerged as being very close to the Rousseauan ideas of nature and of Romanticism. Additional characteristics of Fourier, which again place him close to Rousseau, were his pacificism and his dislike of wars, revolutions, upheavals, and sociopolitical disturbances of any sort. In this respect he is quite close to Saint-Simon.

Fourier was of middle-class origin, being born into a merchant family. His family possessed a small fortune; they lost all of it during the Revolution. However, Fourier managed to formulate his basic ideas and to write them down in leisure because he did not have to work for a living during his youth and later he had an easy position as a clerk for a businessman. There is no evidence of Fourier being influenced by earlier Socialist writings except for those of Rousseau. On the contrary, the available evidence seems to point out that Fourier formed his social ideas all by himself, on the basis of personal observation. Unlike many of his predecessors and contemporaries, he avoided looking upon the entire society as a unit but, as mentioned above, focused his attention on the individual and his problems. His first conclusion from this kind of observation was that along with the many recognized human rights, the indisputable, the most important, and the most natural right for man was not his right to freedom, liberty, or life, but his *right to pleasure*. This idea of man's right to pleasure became the very basic tenet in Fourier's writings. In fact, his entire system is based on this fundamental principle.

Fourier realized, though, that the individuals' right to pleasure, when placed on a societal level, may clash with another's right and bring the community into disharmony. Disharmony was most likely to occur when man's right to pleasure was curtailed, and the chief factor for such curtailment would predominantly stem from *displeasure*. Asking himself what is the true origin of displeasure, he thought he had discovered that labor is one of the chief origins. Therefore, if labor is to be reorganized and promoted through other than the usually accepted displeasurable channels, it will decrease the amount of displeasure usually felt by the working man. But since the goal of labor is to guarantee men the means for subsistence, Fourier thought that if the process of achieving this goal could be changed, then the whole essence of labor would automatically be modified.

Showing a substantial similarity to Rousseau's naturalism, Fourier stated that man is a *creative* being by nature. This meant to Fourier that when fully satisfied, from a material point of view, man will still be inclined to perform labor for the sake of labor, that is, for the *pleasure* of doing it. Here, an analogy may be drawn with Marxian theory, which begins with the premise that while man is good by nature, man is also essentially a creative being. Further developing his naturalistic theory of labor, Fourier stated that since pleasure is nothing else but an *attraction*, reorganized labor should also be based on attraction, rather than on necessity. In sustaining this basic idea, he incorporated a short discussion of God, Who has vested all men with the natural drives for attraction. Thus, man's task on earth should be no more than to discover God's wish and God's plan for society, and then simply to put it into practice. Fourier's hypothesis was that God meant for men to work with pleasure.

He also saw an analogy in the work of Newton who had discovered the "Law of Attraction" in reference to the physical universe. Now the time had come, Fourier implied, for men to discover and to apply that very same law in the world of social living and in the world of ideas. This could bring nothing but total harmony, happiness, and satisfaction to man.

As far as the notion of labor was concerned, through this solution human society would avoid all the waste of energy which is spent daily through man forcing himself to work without benefit of love or pleasure. One may rightfully regard Fourier's ideas as the inspiration for Marx's second stage of Communism.

The Fourieristic solution, being entirely based on the principle of attraction, proposed that the natural division of all labor fall into two categories, a division by *age* and a division by *sex*. As an illustration, Fourier contended that the mother's attraction toward her child is naturally founded to the extent that she feels more pleasure caring for it than the child's father would. On the other hand, a child will have a passionate attraction toward unclean places and games. These two particular types of attraction are quite illustrative, Fourier seemed to imply, of his proposed division of labor by age and by sex. The attractions can be used so that, in the above examples, both mothers and children can perform useful work for society, and at the same time, perform it with pleasure. Children could be given unclean and messy work which they would love to be engaged in and which adults, on the other hand, dislike. The fruits of this labor would, in turn, benefit the entire society.

In furthering these basic ideas, Fourier became aware of the time element which could be a very important factor in the preservation of pleasures. The question of how long an individual would enjoy doing the work to which he is naturally attracted became the next crucial point to be considered. He stated that while human nature strives always toward pleasure, it is also *natural* for human nature to become bored even when it feels attraction for something. Therefore, he resolved that the reorganization of labor in society should be limited to the extent to which man *could* perform attractive work, and only for as long as he performed it with pleasure. The fact that each man has more than one area toward which he is attracted would provide a natural guarantee against boredom. It would provide him with a pleasurable variety as far as labor is concerned. He should be able to change, on his own, the kind of work he is performing for another, as soon as he wishes to do so. This natural interchange in the societal labor process would assure, according to Fourier, full-scale production for society, and the production would also be performed with pleasure.

An overall assumption which Fourier added to this entire proposition, in order to make it practical and feasible, was that consumers would have no need of luxuries in order to reach and maintain their state of happiness. The state of nature is never luxurious. Desire for luxuries is a part of Civilization, not of nature, and therefore they are unnatural and superficial. Man desires luxuries only because he sees other men possessing them and thus accruing prestige and fame. In his imaginary society, Fourier contemplated the production of no luxuries of any kind. The societal economy, according to him, would consist only of good food, warm clothing, and suitable living quarters for everyone. This strong Naturalism on the part of Fourier is, indeed, very Rousseauan. It follows automatically that he would not care at all for big industrial enterprises with a large output of goods. All that Fourier emphasized was the comfort one derives from the goods and their quality. In this respect, he was very much against the competitive system of production because he detected that under such a system products are made to wear out rapidly with an eye toward the market created by the need for constant replacement. In other words, in his view, the competitive system of production does not result in long-lasting products of high quality.

Fourier concluded that, above all, luxury goods are not very pleasurable to make. This would seem evident because the process involved in their production is more difficult and requires an extensive training to make the needed refinements. Therefore, in the economy of luxuries there can be nothing but waste of effort and energy. One can easily see that this particular argument is also very Rousseauan.

Fourier's entire Naturalistic stand merely suggests that he was above all against overemphasizing industrial development in any nation's economy. Indeed, he stressed agriculture, which could naturally provide the basic, most important, comfortable but not necessarily luxurious, needs of life; these were good food, warm clothing, and suitable group surroundings. All this calls for a productive process on a small scale.

In the realm of youth education, Fourier seems to have again followed the same basic line. Accordingly, education should be based on a standardized, inflexible curriculum, but structured according to each one's ability and according to each one's "attraction," most essential to his vocational trade. Therefore, Fourier proposed a very pleasurable educational process, which also would be easier for the students because of its focus on simple matters related to each one's future occupation. In this respect, he had stated that the best way to make children learn is to give them a free choice in learning what they want. He seems to have been convinced of the soundness of young children's decisions concerning their curriculum because he believed that by nature they would possess two deeply developed tendencies: first, to create things; and, second, to imitate adults. If a freedom of choice is given to children in deciding exactly what they should learn, they most likely will combine these two natural drives and, thus, will receive the best possible training, with an overall achievement characterized by pleasure.

In order to provide the physical surroundings for this ideal society, Fourier went into considerable detail in planning the physical plant where such happy communities were to live. He gave them the name of *Phalanstères,* a French adaption of the Greek work "phalanx." One of the major characteristics of life in the Phalanstères was that there would *not* be equality for all. Fourier argued against equality because individuals have, by nature, different attractions toward different needs. Here one can see a clear departure from the Rousseauan foundation, which would be emphasizing "equality." The Phalanstères would consist of one or more buildings with all the facilities open to common use. There would be apartments of various sizes suited to the needs and desires of the various families. There would be no regulation as to the families' (or their individual members') use of those facilities. One could use at will either one's own apartment, or the facilities available in the common section. Most probably the stand against a regulated use of the available facilities reflected Fourier's own basic attempt to assure the individuals of pleasure. Regulations are only possible through limitations, and limitations bring about displeasure.

The loose organization, or rather the lack of organization, as described above also indirectly suggests that Fourier was not a partisan of economic equality. On the contrary, the apartments might be occupied not only according to each family's wish, but also according to their respective level of financial capability. In terms of finances, Fourier developed a peculiar scale according to which special rewards were to be paid to the higher skill, the greater responsibility, and the more efficient managerial capacity demonstrated.

The Phalanstères would not be granted or built by the State or by any other governmental or welfare agency. Fourier proposed that each one interested in his plan should make an investment for the achievement of this community of happiness. Each investor would then receive a share in the common capital when such accumulated capital was put into operation. The Phalanstères would be predominantly engaged in agriculture, a Naturalistic idea again very close to Rousseauan thinking. Fourier developed detailed computations in order to calculate exactly how many people were needed to live in a community in order to assure full-scale natural and pleasurable production, mutually satisfying to the needs of all. Allegedly through the use of the laws of probability, he suggested that 1,800 persons should live in one Phalanstère, cultivating about 5,000 acres of land. The remuneration for their success would be on the same scale for men and women; he stressed quite strongly women's emancipation. The reward payments for work varied in Fourier's mind. Originally he stated that for labor one would receive 5/12 of the total value produced, but later he changed his recommendation to be 1/2. For returns from the capital invested in the community no variation developed in Fourier's mind: one would always receive 4/12 of the profits. For remuneration of special talents and special services performed, Fourier recommended at first 2/12 but later changed it to 3/12 of the total value produced.

Fourier was very careful not to allow for capital accumulation in anyone's hands. He found that accumulated capital would reverse the cycle and bring back the deplorable conditions which he wanted to rectify. Thus, Fourier insisted that the rate of capital return would vary according to the size of each individual's holdings; the more investments one made above the needed norm, the less proportion of shares he would receive on each additional investment share. Profits from investment would thus be placed on a regressive scale.

Fourier did not provide for any government, for any State organization, or any strict authority to run or head these communities. He called, however, for the existence of a very loose federal structure with a governor, whom he called *Omniarch,* to supervise the Phalanstères' development.

Being totally voluntaristic in his approach, Fourier appealed to the capitalist class of France to help get his project started. He ran an advertisement in the press and used other kinds of publicity, giving to each one interested in his project an appointment at a given hour in a specified café in Paris. A firm believer in the goodness of human nature, he expected a crowd of investors to flock to see him with the intent of investing in the future happiness of mankind. All accounts show that he was very regular and prompt in keeping the advertised hours for the rest of his life. However, no one came.

As an extension of the pro-Rousseauan group of Early French Socialism, that is, as an extension of evolutionary Socialism, one may include the birth and growth of Anarchism. In terms of the influence on Marx exerted by the evolutionary and the revolutionary branches of Early French Socialism, Anarchism, too, had its impact.

Pierre-Joseph Proudhon (1809–1865) is regarded as the founder of Anarchism. His father was a brewer in the French countryside near the town of Besançon; his mother was of typical peasant stock. Whatever knowledge their son acquired was arrived at through self-education. Young Proudhon was fully aware of his low-class origin, but instead of concealing it, as did many of his contemporaries, he felt quite proud of it. During the process of his self-education, Proudhon placed, at first, a very strong emphasis on theology, but he did not neglect other fields of study. As a matter of fact, he studied well and persistently. However, with neither guidance nor a predetermined and planned curriculum, his study was rather disorganized. At the same time, during his youth, he earned his subsistence as a proofreader in a printing office.

The result of such a disorganized self-study was that when Proudhon began to write (an endeavor probably influenced by his job as proofreader), his writings were also disorganized. His mind, too, while well reflected in his works, was far from orderly. Indeed, he was never able to elaborate an acceptable, orderly system of ideas.

But young Proudhon was excellent when criticizing the endeavors of others, whether those were ideas, literary publications, or systems. One may say that this critical faculty came to him naturally and logically because of his ability to observe with precision any matter he touched upon. Indeed, only a talented observer can accomplish a good deal of self-education with no guidance or help. As in Fourier's case, Proudhon's method of observation was mostly of an inductive nature, that is, he would begin with a simple fact and analyze it thoroughly before reaching a generalization. Those analyses of Proudhon were usually very well done. Proudhon was extremely critical of the evolutionary Socialists of the Saint-Simonian and the Fourierist types, as well as the revolutionary Socialists of the Babeufist and Blanquist groups. In other words, he strongly but equally disliked the utopian and revolutionary branches of French Socialism. Primarily, this intense dislike centered around the fact that whatever systems the Socialists elaborated, they always assumed the establishment of some authority. According to Proudhon, authority, or the enforcement of decisions of authority, was the basic evil of society. The fundamental Proudhonian idea, however, much in the line of Saint-Simon and Fourier, was that society must be organized in terms of labor, not on the grounds of political regimes or structures of State power. Therefore, while one can easily see that he did not differ much in fundamental ideas from either Saint-Simon or Fourier, he, at the same time, criticized the fact that they called for some kind of organization or regimentation of labor instead of leaving it free to be expressed by the individual. Even Fourier called for an institutional framework of human labor; though claimed to be pleasurable, such a framework clearly still existed in connection with the Phalanstères. Proudhon greatly feared that in practice all such plans would lead to the establishment of some kind of authority.

The proposed Proudhonian society of labor was to be based on two predominant elements: *liberty* for the individual with no harmful limitations of any kind; and *justice,* being the essential idea of the French Revolution of 1789. Very much attracted to analysis, Proudhon broke down the notion of justice into two parts, and stated that justice consists of *mutuality* and *reciprocity* taken together. Therefore, the combination of liberty and justice will necessarily lead to only one limitation related to the individual: a necessity for "sharing" and "give-and-take." In fact, this would mean full and unrestricted liberty to each individual, but one based on a mutual and reciprocal foundation; or otherwise stated, enjoying full individual liberty while allowing the same liberty to others.

Proudhon wanted to see his system operate as a servant of man, by no means as his master. Therefore, he strongly emphasized the idea that whatever he himself proposed, it could, under no circumstances, be enforced upon the individual. In fact, this is in essence the *true meaning* of Anarchism. Proudhon was the first to introduce this word into political terminology.

In order to illustrate the disorganized quality of Proudhon's thought, we can point out an apparent contradiction in it. He liked and upheld the idea of a freely and directly elected National Assembly, which he envisaged would rise above what could be conceived as a State institution. He vigorously argued against critics suggesting that such an assembly would contradict his basic idea which presupposes no authority of any kind. In defending his argument he emphasized that such an assembly would be nothing but the product of individuals' work in free and direct elections. It seems, however, that in reality this would still be an authority *par excellence,* even though Proudhon gave it the status of something much higher and looser than the usual authority of the State.

When Proudhon spoke of the "individual" as being the basic cell of society, he usually meant the individual *plus* his family. Therefore the *individual* is a unit consisting of something more than one person. He seems to have used this terminology in order to stress his idea of a *natural* division of labor. Proudhon pointed out that such a division could by no means be based on law, on customs, or tradition, or need for efficiency of production, but only on nature. In every family (which is his complete understanding of "individual") there is a natural division of labor. Each member naturally engages in the type of work which is most suitable for him. Here again one can see a reflection of the ideas of Fourier as well as those of Rousseau. This notion reappears in the second stage of Marxism, at a somewhat later date.

When Proudhon attempted to analyze his ideas of labor by moving from the basic family unit to the best interests of society as a whole, he found that there seemed to be some built-in contradictions. He thought there might be a conflict of interest between individual-family and society. Proudhon attempted to solve this new dilemma by relating it to a proposal for a *fair exchange* of individuals' labor, but an exchange exclusively geared toward goals of self-realization of the individual. Once engaged on this track, Proudhon could not avoid arriving at two other basic conclusions: (a) like Fourier, he became a staunch opponent of economic equality in terms of individual equality; (b) like Rousseau, he endorsed the elaboration of a social contract among individuals with the sole purpose of decreasing to a minimum the conflict of interests conceivably emerging between the individual and society.

In relation to his stand against economic equality, Proudhon maintained that since individuals perform unequal labor, they are bound to receive unequal rewards. At this point he endeavored to convince himself that such an arrangement in reality would mean nothing more than a natural establishment of full harmony based on his fundamental idea of *mutually* and *reciprocally* expressed justice. He even stated, in this respect, that the lower laboring class, from which he himself had emerged, was fully aware of the necessity of economic inequality. He argued that only the intellectuals and other members of the intelligentsia were unable to understand this basic law of nature since they were the ones who most often objected to economic inequality. Proudhon implied that the intellectuals amounted to nothing more than "theorists" and, as such, they will never know the real problems of the masses of people on whose behalf they claim to speak.

As to the necessity for a social contract among individuals, Proudhon upheld a formula based not only on his theory of natural division of labor, but also on the added notion of a *gratuitous credit*. The gratuitous credit formula was to be arranged through free contracts, which would bring about the creation of a new credit system. He maintained that such a system would assure an *equal opportunity* to each individual according to his capacity and ability to produce labor.

Thus, he again rejected the notion of equality. In 1848 Proudhon published his work *Solution du problème social* in which one can find his theory on credit in its entirety.

Midway in the 1840s, when Karl Marx was visiting Paris, Proudhon met with him. Marx seems to have been very much impressed by Proudhon's thinking, and he decided to ask Proudhon to work with him in the field of Socialism. This friendship, however, did not last long. Marx began to introduce Proudhon to the Hegelian system of thought, which he maintained would provide the essential basis for their future success. Within this context, Marx endeavored to explain the mysteries of Helgel's thought along with the basic idea of Dialectical Determinism. It appears that Proudhon did not accept Marx's interpretation of Hegel, and soonafter their friendship and cooperation ended in a series of bitter quarrels which related in part to Hegelian matters. Finally, Marx charged Proudhon with misunderstanding Socialism, and also with an inability to grasp the true meaning of Hegelianism. This altercation took place because Proudhon, contrary to Hegel, maintained that contradictions in society cannot be solved. Indeed, for Proudhon, compromise is not possible because contradictions are the foundation of his whole idea of the necessity for economic inequality. There-fore, in Proudhon's mind there was no room for Hegel's notion of *synthesis.*

Proudhon, on the other hand, must have felt that he had understood and interpreted Hegel better than Marx, this in spite of the fact that both Hegel and Marx were Germans—Marx even having had a close and personal association with some of Hegel's philosophical disciples. In 1846 Proudhon published another work on his economic ideas with the title *Système des contradictions écono-miques.* Soon after its publication Proudhon changed its title to *Philosophie de la misère* ("Philosophy of Misery," "misery" to connote "impoverishment"). When Marx had a chance to read Proudhon's book, he became furious. He replied by writing, a year later, a rebuff in which he rejected, one-by-one, most of Proudhon's major points. Ironically, Marx entitled this essay *Misère de la philosophie* ("The Misery of Philosophy") again with the meaning of "impover-ishment" for misery.

The revolutionary branch of Early French Socialism was quite different than either the Anarchistic or the Fourierist brands of evolutionary Socialism. Among the evolutionary Socialists the ultimate desire for peaceful change was much emphasized (as in Saint-Simon and Fourier), while this was of no concern to revolutionary Socialism. On the surface it seems difficult to find substantial utopian elements in the means recommended by the revolutionary branch of Early French Socialism. Indeed, it was this type of Socialism which gave, for the first time, the term "Communism" a realistic foundation. It called for political action—a situation in which people follow and obey a leader in whatever decision he makes. This aspect of early French revolutionary Socialism took the place of the voluntaristic approach which was the foundation of evolutionary Socialism. This type of movement was imbued with a certain realism: when a leader begins to be followed by loyal supporters—all united around a radical idea, or cause, demanding a change in present conditions—the outcome is quite often a *revolution,* and revolution is something very tangible and real.

Louis-Auguste Blanqui (1805–1881) is an excellent example of the revolutionary branch of Socialism in France. His philosophy seems to have had little influence on Marx (where utopian theoretical elements are clearly in evidence), but must have influenced Lenin a great deal, particularly in regard to the structure and role of the Communist Party which Lenin created for the U.S.S.R. Young Blanqui was born into a revolutionary family. His father was a long-time revolutionary who had sided with the Girondins. Later on he was on good terms with Napoleon I, who made him a provincial sub-perfect. However, the French Emperor's defeat and the subsequent restoration of 1815 ended his official career. Fortunately, his wife had, at that time, a rather small but profitable estate—with no means of his own, he depended entirely on her. Blanqui's mother was known as a woman with a violent temper and a domineering character. In order to keep young Blanqui away from his father's revolutionary influence, she had to send him away to Paris as a student. There, at the age of 16, young Blanqui joined the revolutionary secret society of the Carbonari. As a member of this group he later had a chance to join an uprising and he was wounded. He also served as a reporter and a feature writer for the Socialist paper *Le Globe,* edited by Pierre Leroux.

In addition to his revolutionary background and family tradition, which upheld and implemented revolutionary ideas, Blanqui also happened to live and work in an extremely agitated political era. The entire environment left its mark upon him; his family, friends, or events of the time, all were conducive in setting Blanqui's mind on the road to revolution. Indeed, his developing years were marked by a series of revolts by the textile weavers in the city of Lyon, lasting from 1831 to 1834; several republican uprisings in Paris in 1830 and 1834; further, a series of other sociopolitical disturbances all over France which pointed out the extent of the discontent prevailing among the republican and working classes under the French bourgeois monarchy.

All this agitation was organized by numerous republican societies and secret clubs all over Paris. They demanded that the spirit of the Great Revolution not only to be maintained but also substantially advanced. They wanted to turn French society back to the early revolutionary years and reawaken the Revolutionary tradition. The most important of these republican societies was the *Society of the Friends of the People.* Blanqui joined it, and even before the Paris uprising of 1830 he was already involved in a number of plots. As a result of his first conspiracies, and also because of his subversive writings, he was arrested in

1832. He was brought to two successive trials and sentenced to one year of imprisonment.

A significant incident occurred during his first trial which clearly illustrated his frame of mind, his enthusiasm, and the pride which motivated his actions. He was asked by the judge to state, as was the custom, his name and profession. Blanqui stated only his name. The judge reminded him again to state his profession. Then, after a moment's hesitation, Blanqui proudly announced: "Profession, proletarian." Blanqui was again prosecuted in 1834, but was on that occasion acquitted. Soon after, he again participated in a conspiracy. The "Society of the Friends of the People" had by then lost much of its influence, and was on the verge of breaking up. Consequently, Blanqui shifted his attention away from it, and in 1835, he allied himself with another social revolutionary, Armand Barbès. Both organized another republican secret society, which they gave the name: the *Society of the Families*. This name alluded to the society's secret structure, small groups acting independently of each other. Upon its formation, the "Society of the Families" set itself at once to prepare for new insurrections. As a first step, it established in the heart of Paris small factories to make powder and cartridges. In 1836, the Parisian police discovered most of them, and Blanqui, along with most of his men, was again arrested. Coincidentally, a bill calling for a general political amnesty had by then been adopted. Blanqui and his friends were released, only to begin plotting again. They found that the "Society of the Families" was in hopeless disarray because of the activity of the police. Blanqui founded a new group and called it the *Society of the Seasons*. It was organized on the basis of a strict hierarchy and chains of command; it consisted of groups with separate leaders who were named after the days of the week, the days of the month, and the seasons of the year. Membership in this society was mixed, composed chiefly of students and workers; the workers, however, prevailed.

Due to his previous experience and a growing awareness of the state of affairs in France, Blanqui began to shift gradually away from the old cherished republican enthusiasm and tradition. He began to orient himself particularly toward the working-class movement. In 1839 Blanqui had under his leadership about six hundred men ready to follow him in revolt, and he started an insurrection. At first, Blanqui ordered an attack on a gunsmith shop in Paris. That portion of the coup was entirely successful, and the rebels supplied themselves with modern weapons. The second order by Blanqui was to attack the central police headquarters in the Latin Quarter of Paris. Blanqui had underestimated the actual size of the police force, and was surprised when his men were stopped and beaten off. In the midst of their retreat Blanqui suddenly ordered them to storm and occupy the Paris City Hall which was located along their route. After capturing and holding it, Blanqui expected that large bodies of workers would enthusiastically join their rebellion. This move, Blanqui thought, would give him decisive victory. However, nothing of this kind happened. The government collected forces strong enough to counterattack and recapture the City Hall. Blanqui's associate, Barbès, was wounded and was made a prisoner. Although Blanqui escaped and lived in freedom for a few months, he was finally discovered, apprehended, and, along with Barbès, sentenced to death. In the meantime, however, while they were awaiting execution, the sentences of both Blanqui and Barbès were commuted to life imprisonment. Accordingly, Blanqui was confined to the fortress-prison on the island of Mont Saint-Michel, where he remained until 1844. During that year, his health declined to the extent that the prison physicians predicted his imminent death. The government offered him his freedom on the basis of a pardon, but Blanqui refused to accept any clemency. Consequently, while still a prisoner, he stayed in a hospital until 1847, at which time the government simply set him free. One year later, the revolution of 1848 broke out. Blanqui immediately went to Paris where he found numerous followers ready for action. Prior to this, he had quarreled with Barbès in regard to mistakes in strategy committed during the 1839 uprising. Now they were rivals, though not enemies: Blanqui led a group called the *Central Republican Society,* while Barbès was at the head of the *Club of the Revolution.* Of the two, Blanqui's group was regarded as the most radical and dangerous, while that of Barbès appeared moderate. Both Blanqui and Barbès advised their respective groups to remain calm for the time being and not to initiate open revolts; both were convinced that in view of the prevailing circumstances such revolts were bound to fail.

At this point, Blanqui's lively biography reflects aspects of his ideological orientation which were running through his mind amidst the changing political circumstances in France. The provisional government of the country had proposed immediate, free national elections. Blanqui firmly opposed this plan. Indeed, he never believed in the suffrage as a means of determining the democratic will. On many occasions he clarified his view by stating that people who, for a long time, had been subjected to the rule of reactionary forces cannot be expected to vote for real Democracy and personal freedom since they had no way of knowing in practice what real Democracy and freedom were. Political Democracy would mean nothing to such people until they had been conditioned through a special process of education in the ideas of Democracy. A significant analogy could be drawn at this point between Blanqui of France and Lenin of Russia, an analogy related to the gradual preparation of people in accepting Communism. The educational process proposed by Blanqui appears, indeed, as quite analogous to the first stage of Communism as proposed in the teachings of Marxism-Leninism. In reality it refers to indoctrination preparing the masses for the acceptance of the second stage of Communism. Blanqui called himself a

Communist, and even before Marx he stated that Communism could be brought about only in stages. In each ensuing stage, people would become more ready for it than they had been during the previous stage, this evolution being due to gradual education in "republican" ideas. In this respect, Blanqui viewed a period of *political dictatorship* as indispensable to the carrying out of the above educational process. The similarity on this point between Marxism and Leninism and the earlier Blanquism is striking. One further similarity: Blanqui envisaged, during the period of the peoples' education, the launching of a ruthless attack on the Church as the foundation of a false social doctrine.

During 1848, although delaying the attack on the provisional government of France, Blanqui did not give up the idea of revolution—he only modified it. He was now thinking in terms of a *coup d'état*, a coup perpetrated by a small group of efficiently organized, disciplined revolutionaries taking advantage of the element of surprise. He envisaged a group of revolutionary specialists, members of a small, secret, and centralized organization; they were to be obedient and excellently trained in promoting conspiracies and in using weapons. It seems, indeed, that during the 1906 Congress of the Russian Socialist parties in London, Lenin was actually advocating Blanquism as the fundament of the Communist Party. During the famous intra-party controversy, Lenin, by siding with what became known as the Bolshevik wing of the Russian Socialists, did, in fact, promote Blanquism.

In an attempt to further illustrate the Blanqui-Lenin analogy, one could also emphasize that in his drive to create a reliable party, Blanqui had refused to accept newcomers without examining them. Their desire to belong to the conspiratory group and help the revolt was not enough. Like Lenin, who seems later to have followed Blanqui's technique, Blanqui was not enthusiastic about having a mass party organization. All he wanted was a small, very reliable group of selected men representing true expertise among the revolutionary elite. Indeed, under Lenin's leadership, such a group became the nucleus of the first Russian Communist Party.

According to Blanqui, only such a party would be capable, in a ripe moment, of effectively executing the coup d'état, and would at the same time be able to provide the leaders for the workers' trade unions and other public organizations. The party was not only to guide them with tact and appropriate strategy along the right revolutionary course, but by way of the temporary political dictatorship to reeducate and re-create society. Lenin, indeed, seems to have entirely copied Blanqui's ideas in promoting the 1917 Russian revolution; he even gave a special name to this type of revolutionary elite: Lenin called them *professional* revolutionaries. The essence of the idea, though, seems to have been Blanqui's.

While Blanqui was awaiting the opportune moment to appear again on the French political scene, continuing to build his party according to the above principles, the leaders of several other French revolutionary societies were not willing to wait. Consequently, in May of 1848 a significant uprising broke out, an uprising that was unprepared and planless. Blanqui's immediate reaction was a firm command to his society to stay away from the rebellion because he was convinced that the revolt would collapse. But, ironically enough, while Blanqui was trying to create a party that was disciplined and, above all, obedient to its leader, he was unable to make himself obeyed by his own men, who were all affected by the wave of high revolutionary enthusiasm. Momentarily, in spite of Blanqui's advice, his secret society found itself actively engaged in the uprising. Blanqui had no choice but to join, which he is reported to have done very unwillingly.

The uprising began with popular demands upon the government for French intervention on behalf of Poland against Prussia and Russia. Blanqui's colleague, Barbès, was leading another society which took an active part in the uprising. Barbès, with his men, succeeded in capturing and occupying the City Hall of Paris. At that moment victory seemed assured. Consequently, Barbès proceeded from the building to publicly proclaim to the assembled revolutionary, or simply curious, populace the dissolution of the government of France. In the meantime, however, a large police force had secretly entered the building, and they arrested Barbès at the very moment in which he was proclaiming the dissolution of the French government. Elsewhere in Paris Blanqui was also apprehended, and all the clubs and secret societies were prohibited by special government decree.

Blanqui was tried first and sentenced to ten years of prison. While there, he was allowed books to read and paper to write on. Upon his release, he immediately began to organize secret societies. This caused him to be thrown back into prison in 1861. In 1864 Blanqui managed to escape to Belgium where he immediately resumed his plottings. Two more uprisings were organized by Blanqui during the French war against Prussia, but both were unsuccessful.

Shortly after Napoleon III's surrender, and in face of the national defeat of France, Blanqui appeared in an entirely new role—this time as a French patriot. He even began to publish a patriotic journal called *La patrie en danger*, i.e. "The Fatherland in Danger." In its columns he demanded a national rally in defiance of Germany.

It would appear that Blanqui could not have played this role well, and he was not effective. Thus, he found himself again immersed in his normal revolutionary agitations. In 1870 he joined forces with another dangerous revolutionary, Flourens, and with a section of the Paris National Guard attempted to overthrow the government. The coup was momentarily successful. A new government was formed which, according to Blanqui's principles, was dominated by workers. Unfortunately, there is not enough available data to predict how this new regime would have developed. It collapsed because of internal betrayal. Flourens unilaterally came to terms with the old government and undermined the new regime.

During these developments, Blanqui's health again rapidly began to deterio-
rate. In addition, the conditions created by Flourens's dealings with the old
government forced him to escape to the countryside. However, he was discovered, apprehended, and sent to jail during the time of the Paris Commune.
The Communards approached the government of Thièrs with the futile offer to
exchange him for the Archbishop of Paris whom they held as a hostage. Instead,
in 1872, Blanqui was sentenced to life imprisonment, but stayed in prison only
until 1879. In that year, the authorities were forced to set him free, because
during the national elections, while still in prison, Blanqui was elected to the
French Parliament by the republicans in the district of Bordeaux. His election
was disallowed, but he was set free. Again Blanqui did not waste time. He
immediately began his usual work, and founded a new journal entitlted: *Ni dieu,
ni maître,* i.e. "Neither God Nor Master." Blanqui's life ended on New Year's
Day of 1881. Shortly before he had become ill again at 76 years of age, 33 years
of which he had spent in jail.

His party continued its illegal life for a while, but later came into the open
because of a general political amnesty in France. The party lasted formally until
1905, when it approved a decision to join the new political amalgamation known
today as French Socialism. Thus, it became a part of the current French Socialist
Party which calls itself "united."

Although quite instrumental in framing the ideas of Marx (mostly through its
evolutionary branch) and the application of Marxism (chiefly through its revolutionary wing), Early French Socialism alone cannot explain the Communist
phenomenon. Communism in practice, that is, the initial application of Marxism,
appears as being partly based on the revolutionary branch of Early French
Socialism. However, the ideological, the motivating aspects of Communism, as
contained in Marxian teachings, are also quite strongly attached to both the
early French evolutionary wing of Socialism and German philosophy of the
1800s. It was chiefly Hegelian philosophy which provided this ideological link.
However, the Kantian system of thought may be taken as an appropriate
introduction to Hegel. While much simpler in its substance, it will clearly
introduce one of the basic concepts of Hegelianism. Therefore, it seems that an
understanding of Kant must substantially facilitate the essential meaning given
by Hegel to that particularly important concept—the idea of human *alienation.*

Immanuel Kant (1724–1804) built the nucleus of his theory around his belief
that man's nature reflects a very high state of morality. Thus, one may say that
the spiritual substance in the nature of man provided the foundation for the
Kantian system of thought. Therefore, man may be looked upon as an essentially spiritual and, even, a holy being. This highly idealized man was also
presented as an intelligent man; he had superior powers of reason and, above all,
a number of senses. The latter are, indeed, presented by Kant as the only factor

which makes man *fallible*. Man becomes a fallible being as soon as he places reliance on his physiological senses, which are *not* ideal in proportion to his spiritual nature; they are in a sense material. Thus, Kant admitted a certain *duality* in man:

man, the *ideal* being, with a high state of spiritual morals, who equals the *real man;* and

man, *distorted,* because of the use of his material senses, who equals the *apparent* man. The latter is only one *form* of man, as he usually appears to be; it is *not* his real form.

Thus, we can immediately draw an analogy between Kant and Rousseau. The latter, too, based his theory on faith in the goodness of man. According to Rousseau, man is a very good being by nature. However, his goodness appears distorted in reality, he becomes an evildoer, because of bad influences stemming from the inadequate institutional arrangements of society. Therefore, if one succeeds in eliminating the institutions of Civilization, then the goodness of man will prevail.

Kant posits essentially a similar proposition. The only important difference detectable at first glance is found in the substitution of the Rousseauan notion of "Civilization" with Kant's perception of "human senses." These senses play the same fatal, evil-promoting role as institutions do in Rousseau.

While Rousseau did not engage in pure philosophy to discover the essence of man, Kant concluded on philosophic grounds that man has a *dual* nature. Further analysis seems to have revealed to Kant that man is constantly attempting to reach perfection; this urge in man is viewed by him as a drive toward man's *real* status involving a high state of morals. This status is reflected in the concept of Kant's "ideal" man, the man based on nothing but goodness. However, once engaged in the process of reaching for perfection man always encounters a permanent insurmountable obstacle in achieving that goal. It is derived from the use of his senses. According to Kant, the human senses are the all-important factor which represent the focal point of all man's weaknesses. Man develops those weaknesses which force him to do evil because, through his senses, the world's temptations are revealed to him; thus, man, in spite of his continuous determined attempts for perfection, is constantly prevented from reaching his natural potential, a state of high morals.

The real man, based on naturally high morals, was named by Kant *Homo Nuomenon.* Man as he appears to be in his daily material activites, the imperfect human being of weakness, is referred to as *Homo Phenomenon.*

Concentrating on this basic fragment alone, one should be able to see as clearly implied man's constant battle with his conscious self, aimed at his own perfection. In other words, one may say that Kant has described on philosophic grounds the image man creates of himself, the desire for perfection which man

has within himself, a perfection reflected in the image of his own Homo
Nuomenon. It seems that the picture of himself painted by man's imagination is
viewed by Kant as being the real man; on the other hand, the actual activities of
man as they appear on earth are accepted by him as those of the distorted man,
a distortion resulting from their being perceived through man's physiological
senses.

Thus, Kant viewed the entire substance of man's nature as a *half* perfect and
half imperfect, half good and half bad. The good image of man is the real man
because he constantly strives to reach that high status. If the bad appearance of
man was the real one, Kant seemed to imply, then he would be satisfied with
himself and would *not* have the desire to struggle against it.

Therefore, according to Kant, man has a dichotomous existence: man
Nuomenon, man intelligent—the real man, could be entitled "*I,*" while man
Phenomenon, man empirical—man in his appearance, could be called "*Me.*"

The constant battle of man against his own conscious self, aimed at reaching
his natural potential, was viewed by Kant as an internal struggle between the
nuomenal and the phenomenal portions of man in his determined striving to
fully achieve the status of Nuomenon. In this battle the rationality of man is the
brutal force which orders man's "Self" to become perfect.

This portion of the Kantian philosophy is invested with a non-philosophic,
realistic element of reasoning. It is reflected in Kant's clear admission that man
Phenomenon can never win his own battle completely; he can never achieve a
total victory and place his own "Self" in total harmony and identification with
man Nuomenon. Only a *relative* victory of this kind is possible and this only for
a certain group of individuals. Therefore, the above would mean that man can
reach and enjoy only a certain degree of perfection.

This portion of the philosophy of Kant, namely, his theory on the duality of
human nature, served as the foundation of the Hegelian mystical notion of man's
spiritual *alienation;* it is an important notion because from there it passed to
Marx and became the stepping-stone for his thoughts on man's alienation from
his "Self" through the process of labor.

Georg Wilhelm Hegel (1770–1831), is the giant among German philosophers.
His influence is, indeed, far-reaching. In fact, the study of Hegel could bring one
very close to the essence of Marxism. It is practically impossible to understand
the entirety, or at least the fundamental portion, of the teachings of Marx
without first getting acquainted with that part of Hegelianism which directly
influenced the basic concepts of Marxism. As we shall see later, in its essence
Marxism is not an original system of thought; it is mostly borrowed from Hegel
and from the evolutionary branch of Early French Socialism—more precisely,
from Fourier. Understanding Hegel, however, is quite a difficult task. Indeed, he

had a brilliant but at the same time very diversified, complicated mind, a mind which is usually discovered either in a genius or in a psychopathic personality. Of course, no suggestion is offered here that Hegel was a psychopath, but one can surmise that one day psychiatrists and clinical psychologists might begin to pose questions along that line. In any case, Hegel represents the culmination of German philosophy, making a very heavy impact in any field he cared to touch upon. A number of students of philosophy, and of political theory, have devoted their entire lives to studying and interpreting Hegelianism, and at the age of retirement have openly admitted that the span of human life is not long enough to permit the completion of such a study. For this reason alone, a resumé in this book of Hegel's thought in its entirety would be neither possible nor commendable. Instead, we will confine this discussion to that fragment of his thought which is important to understand Marxism, thus avoiding venturing into the depths of pure philosophy. Many Protestant theologians have accepted Hegelian doctrine and, similarly, Hegel's philosophy of history has affected the development of political theory. Marx was, at first, a follower of Hegel, and although criticizing him later, he retained many Hegelian features in his thinking.

Hegel's biography is rather placid and lacks the dramatic events so characteristic of the French Socialist revolutionaries. During his youth, Hegel's main personal drive was his strong attachment to mysticism. This influenced his further development and may later be seen reflected in his theories. Indeed, in all of them he tried to intellectualize and rationalize all that had at first appeared to him as mystical. The Hegelian School of Thought is, indeed, a true attempt in that direction.

Hegel taught philosophy as a *Privatdozent* at the University of Jena, Germany. There, just one day before the Battle of Jena, he finished the writing of one of his most important works, *Die Phänomenologie des Geistes* i.e., "The Phenomenology of the Mind." Later on he taught at the University of Nürnberg. Shortly thereafter, he was promoted to the rank of full professor of philosophy at the University of Heidelberg. There he stayed for two years, from 1816 to 1818, when he moved to the University of Berlin and remained in that teaching position until his death.

During his younger years, the Germanic Hegel despised Prussia and admired Napoleon I. His admiration for the French emperor was of such a magnitude that he openly rejoiced over France's victory at Jena. During his later life, however, Hegel, like Wagner, seems to have reversed his attachments because he emerged as a patriotic Prussian and a very loyal servant of the Prussian state. In return, the Prussian government recognized Hegel's scholarly brilliance and philosophical preeminence. This reversal has been sometimes explained as being opportunistic instead of reflecting a true Hegelian preference. However, there is much to be said for and against such an interpretation and one can hardly reach a clear conclusion on the matter.

Hegelianism is mostly based on two concepts. First is Hegel's firm belief in the *unreality of separateness*. In this respect, Hegel sees the ultimate reality as being based on the *union* of things. The second important concept was his strong belief that everything in the world is history *developing in stages*. In this respect, Hegel stated that there is nothing outside of history, and he further implied that history would end with the end of his own time because he believed that his era would bring the ultimate self-realization of history; that is during his time history would complete its *last* stage of development; and once fully developed, there would be no more need of history.

A few more words should be said about Hegel's first concept, that is, that of the "unreality of separateness." Hegel maintains that the world and the universe are definitely not a collection of hard units (whether material atoms or souls), each of them living and developing in a self-subsistent manner. Indeed, according to him, and Kant also, they only appear to be real because of the limitations of the human senses. In reality they are definitely *unreal*, while they are in their state of separateness from each other. The apparent self-subsistence of all those separate units living and developing in one's environment is, according to Hegel, nothing but sensual illusion. In fact, they have a greater or smaller degree of reality; that is, one is subject to a greater or smaller degree of illusion, but nothing is ultimately and completely real except what Hegel begins to call the *Whole*. The Hegelian conception of the Whole is not a simple substance reminiscent of the views of Spinoza, but is a complex system of the sort which one may call an abstract organism.

Hegel's strong belief in the reality exclusively confined within the Whole, brought him logically to his firm disbelief in any reality which is expressed in terms of *time* and *space*. Hegel rationalized freely at this point by implying that if the notions of time and space are taken as reality, this immediately would involve a reality of separateness and multiplicity. One would have, then, two different things, time and space, and they cannot be real by themselves when taken individually. One may suggest that Hegel probably envisaged his concept of the Whole as being no more than one spherical thing which would include within itself all of the unreal units, thus, transforming them into one single reality. Such a suggestion, however, would seem to contradict Hegel because he appears to have rejected it flatly. He did so on the grounds that the acceptance as real of the existence of one spherical thing would definitely be a self-contradictory conception. It would be self-contradictory because when one thinks of a sphere, one sees it as separate from the rest which is not in the sphere. Therefore, one sees the sphere as possessing boundaries; and if it possesses boundaries, one therefore admits subconsciously, and by association, the existence of something else besides the sphere. If nothing else, one admits the existence of empty space.

The idea of the Whole, which is so deeply rooted in Hegel's mind, is later on referred to by him as the *Absolute*. This Absolute is, according to Hegel, an abstract or a spiritual thing and, therefore, cannot have boundaries. This is very much an expression of his non-Spinozan views.

In addition to this complicated way of defining the meaning of reality, Hegel also has two other characteristic features which separate him from his contemporaries. One of these features is his emphasis on logic. He says that the nature of reality can be deduced from the consideration that reality must not be self-contradictory. A student of Hegelianism could easily see that logic in Hegel is something much closer to metaphysics than to logic as it is currently understood. Hegel used his understanding of logic to point out that any ordinary unit, if taken as expressing (or as he states—"qualifying") the essence of the whole reality, would automatically turn out to be self-contradictory.

The other feature strongly characterizing the Hegelian system of thought— quite closely connected to the first—is his famous *triadic movement* called his *Dialectics*. In this respect, Hegel developed the following thought: if one thinks of some existing and apparently real *object,* one is automatically conscious of himself as being the *subject*. Indeed, one automatically thinks of oneself as the subject because one is aware of perceiving or doing the thinking about that particular object; therefore, one is the subject. One has, at this point, the Hegelian apparent existence of: (a) the subject, which he also calls the *thesis;* and (b) the object, which he also calls the *antithesis* because it is contradictory to the thesis from the fact of its being aware of something other than the subject.

The apparent existence of both the subject and the object, that is, the thesis and the antithesis, is emphasized by Hegel as contradictory and, consequently, no full consciousness of reality is possible in that divided state. However, through the simultaneous development of both the subject and the object, they join together to bring about the existence of another notion, which Hegel called the *synthesis.* In the final synthesis related to the universe, there will be no more limitations to the consciousness, according to Hegel. The final synthesis, however, reflecting the Absolute, is on a universal scale. Its fragments consist of an infinite number of syntheses, which are a part of the Whole. In each small synthesis, the enlargement of the field might be possible and only the total would make up the Whole. Each one viewed separately only brings about an appearance of reality. For instance, to use Hegel's example, one might say that the idea of an *uncle* is the Whole. This is impossible, Hegel maintained, because it is a thesis and, as such, is a point of contradiction. If there is a concept of an uncle, there must also be the concept of a *nephew*. One cannot be an uncle if there is not a nephew. Therefore, the nephew will appear as an antithesis.

Together the uncle plus the nephew would form a synthesis. At this point, although the unity, or a sort of *apparent* reality, had been achieved according to the dialectical process, the self-contradiction will still continue to exist—one cannot accept the mere existence of the uncle plus the nephew as Absolute. The self-contradiction would exist because there would always be the implication that when there is an uncle and a nephew, there must also be a *larger circle* of the family, or kin, such as sisters, brothers, etc. Therefore, one can begin to apply the dialectical method, the Hegelian triadic movement, in an ever wider and wider circle until all of the family, and then in turn all the universe, is included. The product of the final synthesis, therefore, must be so complete, so fulfilled, as to leave no implication whatsoever of the existence of something else, not even space. Only then, Hegel admitted, could one arrive at his concept of the Absolute, and at the same time, at his concept of reality. Such a complete product reflecting the only reality could be, indeed, nothing else but a *Thought.* Again, however, Hegel showed himself quite capricious. The Absolute cannot be any kind of thought. In order not to be self-contradictory, the thought must be by definition an active thought: the characteristic activity of a thought is to think and if it thinks, that should imply that it thinks of something other than itself. Therefore, it creates an object, and it cannot be the final synthesis because it admits the existence of something else. The Hegelian idea of the Absolute could be looked upon as a thought, but a thought so complete that there will be nothing else available outside of itself to think of. Since the only activity of the thought is characterized by thinking, then the notion of the Absolute in Hegel's mind would be a complete self-realized thought, self-realized to the point that it cannot think of anything else but itself, because there is nothing else left available to think of. Therefore, the Hegelian Absolute appears to be something selfish, constantly preoccupied with itself.

Close to the above described Hegelian belief based on his idea of the unreality of separateness, is his second belief affirming that everything in the universe is history developing in stages. The consecutive working-out, through the dialectics, and the discovery of an ever-increasing number of syntheses, brings one closer and closer to the Absolute. This process, however, is a systematic process. It is systematized by its division into stages, each one ending with the discovery of a new historic synthesis and containing in itself the total of all previous syntheses. All this, according to Hegel, is nothing but the *self-realization* of history passing through various stages. The driving force of this process of self-realization of history is not caused by humans because they, too, cannot by themselves be real. It is caused by the *Weltgeist* (the World Spirit). In fact, Hegel maintained that the continuous process of self-realization of the *Weltgeist* could be nothing else but its search for freedom. To make a broad division of these stages in history, as envisaged by Hegel, without going into some of the details which will be briefly discussed later, the historical process of self-realization is divided into three main stages: First, the stage of *Orientals;* second, the stage of *Greece* and *Rome;* and third, the stage of the *Germans* (meaning the Prussian Monarchy).

During the stage of Orientals, according to Hegel, only *one* was free; while during the stage of Greece and Rome, only *some* were free. During the last stage, however, that is the stage of the Germans, *all* would be free under the Prussian Monarchy. It may appear quite inconceivable today to equate Aristocracy with Democracy. Hegel, however, maintained that both Aristocracy and Democracy belong to the stage of Greece and Rome, a stage where only *some* were free. On the other hand, Hegel lavishly praised Rousseau for having discovered the notion of the General Will, that mystical force in society which is the best, and always infallible. It seems that Hegel saw the General Will of Rousseau's ideological elaborations as embodied in the Prussian Monarchy, while Aristocracy and Democracy would belong either to what Rousseau would conceive as the Will of All, or Will of the Majority. When one bears in mind the fundamental triple division related to the stages of development of history, one could now proceed to examine in some detail the actual division of the historic stages as stressed by Hegel. Indeed, Hegel divided these stages into five segments.

The first was the *Oriental* stage, in which, Hegel emphasized, history began in Asia or more concretely, in China. The major characteristic was the *suppression* of the *individual.* Within the same stage, in its evolution the important historical development moved to the Persian Empire, where the established chief characteristic was the *caste system.* Still within the first stage, the final move of historical development within this stage appeared in Egypt, where the caste system was retained but was somewhat *less emphasized.*

In this detailed subdivision of the development of history, Hegel still retained the stage of *Greece* and *Rome* as the second stage of historical development. Within it, he stressed that the Greek system represented *youth,* while the later Roman system introduced *maturity.* There, the monarch was retained but with *no emphasis* on caste system whatsoever. During the second stage, there appeared for the first time democratic institutions with an accent placed on *individual* ability and individuality, not in terms of man versus nature, but of man versus his own government. While this rise of individuality, indeed, marred the second stage with continuous conflict, in general, however, harmony still prevailed.

The third stage of this historic development was, according to Hegel, represented by the rise of *Christianity.* The chief characteristic of this stage was that the individual did not find himself *any longer in opposition* to the universal, because Christianity is universal. On this premise of universality, the stage was generally characterized by an individual uniformity.

The fourth stage of historical development, as seen by Hegel, was a short-lived stage, indeed. It is chiefly characterized by the fact that during that stage man began to break away from the feudal system. Therefore, it could be looked upon as a *transitory* stage.

The fifth stage was characterized, according to Hegel, by *Germanic Kultur* (see Part III). This is implied to be the most important stage in all history. As a matter of fact, this stage, when it was fully developed and refined, would bring about the end of history. The stage is divided, according to Hegel, into three substages. The first substage is in relation to the *formation* of the German State. The second, reflects the development of the *Reformation* period. The third, the most important, relates to the state of affairs of *Prussianism*. The ultimate development and refinement of Prussianism would bring about the end of history. The connotation is that Prussianism would bring human relationships so ideal for mankind that there would be no more need for development, or betterment, of these relationships. Since there would be no more need for development, in a sense this would be the end of history.

In Hegel's mind, it seems that God is the World; but the World itself is history, and history is developing in stages. Therefore, God is developing in stages also; and with each step of His development He *becomes* a better, more clearly defined God; that is, He becomes closer to achieving His full potential, His state of Absolute. Hegel placed philosophy much higher than religion. It seems that for this reason he avoided the extensive use of the term God. He preferred to replace this term with *Geist* (Spirit or Mind) or *Weltgeist* (World Spirit). The spirit by itself was, in Hegel's mind, essentially a result of activity. In Christian theology, God is regarded as something separate from humanity when this whole idea is taken in an earthly sense. Hegel, however, tried to break down this understanding. He stated that God is always inside the nature of man. Since man is not perfect and God is inside the nature of man, God could not be perfect either. Man's chief characteristic, then, could be ascertained as a continuous drive toward perfection (see Kant, pp. 166–168). In this attempt man is doing nothing more than working toward his own self-realization. But unlike Kant, Hegel saw this activity as acknowledging man's desire to acquire *knowledge of himself* and of his environment. Therefore, acquisition of *knowledge* by man would equal a process of self-realization of man which, in turn, would also be analogous to the Kantian view of achieving perfection of man. On account of Hegel's conclusion that God is a part of man's nature and that He is in man, while man is working toward his self-realization, God, too, is working toward His self-realization by attempting to acquire knowledge of Himself in order to *become* a true and perfect God.

According to Hegel, there is a conflict between the *idea* (which in its essence is an absolute, constant notion), and the *consciousness* which is something vari-

able, other than the subject, something other than one's self. It is something
alien. Here one can find Hegel's thinking reflecting again a great deal of Kantian
philosophy. Indeed, from this Kantian-Hegelian view emerged the concept of
one's alienation from one's self. Therefore, man is in a state of alienation. Only
by acquiring knowledge through self-realization (*Weltanschauung,* see Part III)
and striving for perfection can man conquer this dilemma, since *to know* would
be to recognize the *object* as part of the *subject.* In other words, here one has
the proposition for the achievement of *one synthesis.* The synthesis, if it is not
the last possible synthesis, would generate again a new thesis, which would
receive its counterpart, a new antithesis, and through the same process—acquiring knowledge of one's self and striving toward perfection—still another synthesis would be achieved. Thus, the process would continue from stage to stage
until all cultures in the human development have joined in a final synthesis.
Then, man will become fully self-realized, conscious of himself, and perfect,
along with the *Geist* who, in a parallel fashion, will become the Absolute
together with man.

It is now clear that Hegel had formulated his idea around the proposition that
everything is history and that history is developing in stages. By this, he actually
meant that everything is God, or the *Weltgeist,* and God is developing in stages.
These stages, however, also have periods of *transition* in between them, which
are also a part of the process of historical development. Those periods of
transition are not less important for the final goal than the stages themselves.
Therefore, the *Weltgeist* is as much involved in them as in the fundamental
building of history through stages. As an illustration of the involvement of the
Weltgeist in these periods, Hegel stated that each transition period is characterized by the deeds of a particular outstanding man characterizing that particular
transition period. Thus, Hegel maintained that three important men characterize
the three most important transition periods; that is, Alexander the Great
(transition between the Asiatic and Greek Culture), Julius Caesar (transition
between the Greco-Roman world and the rise of Christianity), and Napoleon I
(transition between Feudalism and the Germanic *Kultur* culminating in Prussianism). However, since, according to Hegel, nothing but the Absolute could be
real, he clearly implied that those men were not real men, but only a reflection
of the *Weltgeist,* a reflection of the same God who appeared in three different
forms, in three different human bodies in order to create each time a new
culture in the world. The extreme depth of Hegel's belief could not be better
illustrated than by Hegel's own statement in reference to Napoleon, implying the
unreality of the entire substance of the so admired by him at that time, French
emperor. In referring to him, Hegel stated that while taking the shape of
Napoleon, he was, in fact, the *Weltgeist* riding a white horse.

The role and the importance of the transitional periods in the development of history were not only related, according to Hegel, to bringing new historical stages but also, by bringing about these new stages, to destroy the old, formerly existing order. Indeed, this development fits perfectly with the Hegelian proposition concerning the usefulness and *inevitability* of contradictions in the process of achieving progress. Thus, logically one could clearly arrive at the idea that the periods of transition between the stages of history are *revolutions.* In fact, the *Weltgeist* had destroyed the existing empires in order to create new sociopolitical and economic orders, which progressively appeared to be more developed and more perfect. A secondary deduction that one may make at this point is that Hegel also strongly promoted the idea of the glorification of the State. This could be seen in the sense that the individual was identified only as a part of the State. Indeed, Hegel did not deal much with individuals as such, but he dealt with them only as incarnated into the State which, along with the *Weltgeist's* development, was in the processs of achieving the Absolute.

According to Hegel, in each human society there are three basic elements: family; civil society; and State. The Hegelian civil society seems to correspond strikingly to what Marx later called the *bourgeois* society.

Corresponding to these three elements, ever present in any sociopolitically organized human community, Hegel also distinguished three principles of morality. In this respect, corresponding to family would be Hegel's reference to *individual* morality. It related to the moral relations between persons. Corresponding to the civil society would be *social* morality which, in Hegel's mind, referred to group moral relations in society. In the third place, corresponding to the State would be what Hegel called the *Sittenrichter,* which referred to a sort of "judging" the *collectivity* of moral customs. Therefore, once again one sees the triadic movement of the Dialectics in full operation. That is, the thesis which is the family as opposed to the antithesis, which is the civil society, are brought together by the synthesis that is the State. The idea of glorification of the State in Hegel could not be more clearly expressed since he showed that the State institution is the only means of achieving the synthesis.

In reference to the civil society, viewed later by Marx as bourgeois society, one may say that it was for Hegel the antithesis which was atomistic. It was, in his view, an economic machine in which each individual was a total egoist, since in that society he was doing nothing but promoting his own selfish interests. Therefore, the civil society is a society of selfishness. As mentioned above, Karl Marx viewed it as the current bourgeois society. Hegel stated that when this civil society, on account of the character of its selfishness, is left to develop freely without interference, it could not help but break into two factions. This will be imminent, Hegel implied, because of the multiple rivalry of individual interests. Thus, there will be, in the future, first a group of wealthy men, and second, a group of poor men. Although Hegel did not call the second group proletariat, he nevertheless clearly developed this idea which was borrowed and skillfully developed by Karl Marx. For Hegel, this second group did not consist just of an amorphous mass of poor people, but a group of men which powerfully negated the present society of wealthy men, and had all the potential power of reaching the *Weltgeist* during the next stage of history. All this later came to help form the foundations of Marxism. Marx repeatedly stated that the proletariat was not composed of just poor people viewed in an amorphous state, but that they were proud and very well defined, potentially strong, poor people. Indeed, this argument revealed itself as early as in the years immediately following the French Revolution of 1789. The reader will recall that Blanqui, when asked by the court his name and profession, proudly stated that his profession was that of proletarian. In further developing this Hegelian idea, Karl Marx stated that the proletariat is a new phenomenon in the development of history, a new phenomenon threatening not just another revolt, but a potentially strong phenomenon in the process of deciding to overthrow the entire concept of life and relations in the existing society. In other words, he promoted the concept of massive revolution, *not* just another revolt.

In his criticism of Hegel, Karl Marx pointed out that one of the points on which Hegel was wrong was that he did not see *civil society* as his own contemporary economic society. In describing the civil society, Hegel viewed it, according to Marx, as something different. In this criticism, Marx stated that the Hegelian civil society was in reality nothing but the current system of man-to-man bourgeois relationships which were based mostly on an economic foundation.

One very important implication of the Hegelian School of Thought was that in all stages of history God was in a process of creating Himself, thus, producing Himself. He was in a constant state of *becoming* until the Absolute would be formed during the last synthesis, which in turn would reflect the end of history, and would then symbolize the ultimate progress. Thus, progress becomes the result of the historically inevitable, *deterministic* dialectical contradiction.[27] Therefore it was Hegel (not Marx as it is often mistakenly understood) who developed the notion of *Dialectical Determinism*. Influenced by this portion of the Hegelian School of Thought, Marx later developed the idea further by admitting that all relationships in human society are based on creation, that is, on *production*, and also, like Hegel, he stated that they are based on acquiring knowledge. Karl Marx clearly recognized what he called the creative energy of man as closely related to the concept of *appropriation*. By this concept he meant for man to *gain knowledge* of something which has already been created, that is,

---

[27]See for comparison the disagreement between Marx's view on Hegel and the Proudhonian foundation of the Anarchistic theory; pp. 159–160.

produced by him. Man was claimed to be the one who had produced himself throughout history; so had God. During this process, both were respectively acquiring knowledge of themselves—a knowledge, progressive from stage to stage, of what they have created in themselves. Therefore, whatever was first produced by man was later appropriated by him. Men were beginning to understand this. In this whole process of production and consequent appropriation, God was externalizing Himself; He was alienating Himself from His own being in order to gain knowledge of Himself, that is to appropriate Himself. Therefore, one can rightfully simplify this Hegelian matter to the point of stating that the whole purpose of the *Weltgeist* in building a civilization in history was to appropriate itself, to get to know itself. However, in order to get to know itself, the Spirit first started with productivity. Things must first be produced in order to become known. Such production, however, could start by the process of externalization of one's self. Therefore, in the Hegelian system of thought, God was, indeed, a God; He was produced, but He Himself must come to know it. God's endeavor to acquire this knowledge of Himself was reflected in the development of the history of mankind in stages.

Finally, one may rightfully conclude that Karl Marx acquired two fundamental processes from Hegel, which served him in the building of the theoretical foundation of Communism. The first was the *process of creation*, of *production*, or *alienation*, and then the *process of appropriation*, that is, the process of acquiring knowledge of one's self, thus, becoming conscious, or aware of one's self. The second process is exactly contrary to the first; it is contrary to alienation. Alienation is a splitting movement, while appropriation implies a trend toward unification. Therefore, both taken together would represent a synthesis. One can look on the former as a thesis and the latter as the antithesis.

In regard to the notion of infinity, Hegel distinguished two kinds. One, he called *false* infinity, the other, *true* infinity. Here again, the triadic pattern in Hegelian philosophy was never broken. One might say that the definition of two infinities could well correspond to the distinction made within his notion of reality when he insisted that nothing could be real but the Absolute; living units outside the Absolute are only real in appearance. Hegel's argument about the false and true infinities began with his statement that some people have concluded that finitude would mean *here*, while infinity would mean *far-there*. He maintained that to accept this would be, indeed, a very ordinary, elementary and in fact, a false conception. Hegel's answer to this common method of defining infinity was that only the continuous alternation of finitude and infinity could rightfully reflect the true infinity. Thus, one can see again the basic dialectical pattern of the Hegelian concept of thought. The triadic movement is again consistently applied: finitude (the thesis); infinity (antithesis); and the continuous alternation of finitude-infinity (the synthesis).

When the development of history finally arrives at a situation in which no object can be formed, that is when no antithesis can possibly be generated by the status quo, then this will be the ideal situation; this will be the Absolute consisting jointly of the *Weltgeist* and mankind. Only in arriving at a new culture is the subject producing itself through alienation into the object in order to form a synthesis, which once formed, begins to generate all over again another subject, which again alienates itself and so on. The whole process of development will continue from historic culture to historic culture until the Absolute is formed through the final synthesis.

The Hegelian System of Thought created a whole philosophic movement at the University of Berlin, later to spread all over Germany and the world. This movement, originating with Hegelian disciples and students at the university, later split into two directions. One wing continued to preach original Hegelianism with no alterations, and referred to itself as the *Conservative Hegelian School of Thought.* The other made a considerable amount of modifications by interpreting in a radical fashion the Hegelian propositions. It became known as the *Young,* or the *Left Hegelian School of Thought.* The major modification of Hegelianism introduced by the Left Hegelians was the especially pronounced emphasis on Hegel's breaking-down of the God-man distance. Feuerbach emerged as one of the leaders of this Young Hegelian movement.

Ludwig Andreas Feuerbach (1804–1872) and his group, while preserving intact the basic Hegelian structure and the idea of alienation, modified the Hegelian dialectics simply by reversing them. The Left Hegelians maintained that it would be wrong to accept the idea of primary cause as being essentially spiritual in substance. The notion of the Hegelian *Weltgeist,* however, was such a spiritual proposition. Closely approaching the Kantian view of man projecting himself into his own conscious, Feuerbach stated that *man* was in reality the thesis, while the *Weltgeist* was his antithesis, that is, the *Geist,* instead of being the *subject,* was the *object* of man's alienation. The synthesis was accepted on the same grounds as was the Hegelian understanding of it: a union between the thesis and the antithesis, between man and *Geist.*

The chief impact of the contribution by the Left Hegelian group was to relieve the whole Hegelian system of its heavy spiritual emphasis. It removed the spiritual substance by substituting a material notion as a primary cause in the development of history, thus, it developed the notion of *Dialectical Materialism.* Now the material notion—man—became the primary cause; man was proposed to be the one who alienated and projected himself into the *Geist.* Instead of the *Weltgeist* creating and then using man, now the whole order was reversed: Man was creating and using the *Weltgeist.*

Karl Marx (1818–1883) was the most important thinker in the development of the philosophy of modern Communism. He was at first the *collector* of many of the preceding utopian or abstract theories and ideas, to which he later attached his own interpretation, the latter marked almost entirely by the impact of the Hegelian-Feuerbachian and Fourieristic heritage. This entire entity was to become known as the system of thought called Marxism.

It would be useful to indicate from the very beginning that an all-important division, or split, exists within the Marxian School of Thought. One, can, indeed, divide Marxism into two: the *Early* and the *Later* stages of Marxism, or, as it is sometimes casually referred to, *Original* and *Developed* (or *Mature*) Marxism. The major criterion which sets apart these two types of Marxian teachings may be described as a division related to the chronology of the writings. Original Marxism, appropriately, is expressed in Marx's early manuscripts. The general impression that one gets from them is their predominantly philosophical nature. Marx's preoccupation during the early stage of his writings was not with man in general, not with social class or professional status, not even with workers. Indeed, he dealt with the essence, the movements, the role, and the activity of the *Weltgeist.* Mature Marxism, on the other hand, is contained in all Marxian writings related to a somewhat later period of his ideological development. Chronologically, it begins a little earlier than the publication of his *Communist Manifesto* (1848). The major essential characteristic of this type of Marxism is that material activity had entirely replaced most of the earlier philosophical outlook. In Developed Marxism, it was no longer the *Geist* but material activity which determined all life. According to Marx, this material activity was nothing more than ordinary human activity, which in turn was elevated to the position of the essence of all reality. Thus, one might say that Developed Marxism is characterized by man's production of objects and, in fact, of the entire environment surrounding him.

In 1836 Marx enrolled at the University of Berlin to study jurisprudence. There are many indications that this field of study was, for Marx, only of secondary interest. His primary concentration was on philosophy and history. During his studies in law, Marx became acquainted with a limited number of professors and a large number of advanced students in philosophy who called themselves Young Hegelians. They all maintained that God was able to move toward His state of self-realization only when He was using man; that is, while God was self-realizing Himself, He was able to do it only through man. They also maintained that religion was something unreal, that it was nothing but a myth, and that everything important can be found in man alone. This latter concept happened to exercise a strong influence on Marx when he was writing the thesis for his degree. In it he stated that the next task of humanity should be the realization of philosophy, which will come about through: (a) a rejection of the assumption that man, in his present state, is a divine being, that he proceeds from God; (b) man can eventually become a divine being but only after a transformation, after a self-development, which will reflect man's own self-realization; (c) since man will be in a state of development which can bring about that transformation, the whole world, consisting of men, will also be transformed; (d) when this worldwide transformation has once taken place, this will bring the *self-realization of philosophy*.

The first Marxian idea was very much in step with the message being widely broadcast by German Philosophy. During his time, various philosophers in the country preached that God in reality was man and nothing else. Friedrich Engels was one of them.

Karl Marx also emphasized that there were a number of important points which could lead philosophy to leave its abstract and mystical form and enter a practical stage, a stage which would bring the present reality into harmony, that is, into the state of self-realization. In this regard, in order to promote the realization of philosophy, Marx declared unlimited war on what he called current reality. Therefore, one can deduce that Marx already, as a student, had conceived in general terms the idea of insurrection and revolution. His starting point was to change the world in a practical way. During the further development of this initial thought, Marx, while studying Hegelianism, came to the conclusion (obviously under Feuerbachian influence) that it was not God who alienated Himself into an object, but, contrary to Hegelian prescription, it was man who alienated himself from his own being and projects himself into a spiritual object, thus generating his own antithesis: the material substance was automatically generating its own opposite—the spiritual substance. In defending this point of view, Marx also stated that if all the ideas were brought into God, then nothing would be left for man. Feuerbach also came to Marx's assistance by sustaining the idea that man, when living in his current environment, is, indeed, an alienated man. Marx appreciated the help to such an extent that his next move was to become a loyal disciple of Feuerbach.

As an immediate result stemming from Feuerbach's influence, Marx quickly redefined his idea of realization of philosophy. He began to imply that there was no need at all for man to become "God," to become a divine being through his own self-realization. Instead, very Kantian-like, he stated that becoming just a *good man* by a degree of self-realization was enough. From that moment on, the entire concept of alienation was introduced by Marx into the domain of pure politics. He developed the idea that the State, as such, is just another form of man's alienation.

Having entered the domain of politics, Marx could not escape penetrating the realm of economics. However, Marx did not take this plunge by himself. It was another German, Moses Hess, who actually converted Marx to the economics of Socialism and Communism. Thus, Marx finally arrived at the idea that it was possible to have various kinds of alienation. However, the most important one, for his consideration, was economic alienation. Therefore, breaking away from Feuerbach as well as from Kant, Marx stated that man was not projecting himself into God, not into something spiritual (something opposite to him by substance), but he was projecting himself into money, through his own *labor*. Money, in this case, would be God in the sense that money appeared to be the essence of man's life; and, consequently, Marx implied that man worships it like he worships God. The whole Hegelian idea of spiritual alienation now became transformed in Marx's mind to the extent of taking the form of practical, natural alienation. In this respect, selling the products of labor was viewed by Marx as a particular practical form of alienation. This aspect of the Marxian idea of alienation was, thus, one of Marx's major differences from Feuerbach. Indeed, he stated that the substance which man was externalizing from his own being (what he was alienating from himself) was not a spirit or other abstract image, but purely and simply his own productive power. The products made by man's own hands were, indeed, a reflection of the real alienation. During the next step in his mental elaborations, Marx brought into the picture the idea of the proletariat. He said that the best example of an alienated man was, in fact, the proletarian man. The proletarian had no property, no money, nothing but his own labor power to sell to the capitalists in order to exist. Thus, the proletarian is the most alienated man. As a class in modern society, the proletariat is constantly fighting, trying to achieve nothing else but the overcoming of their own alienation. Subconsciously, Marx maintained that this was the *only real goal* of the proletarian class. All other goals were, then, only apparent—not necessarily real. Only when this alienation could be overcome would the proletariat become fully human and self-realized, that is, no longer alienated. This in turn, according to Marx, would be to realize philosophy. As one can see, although strongly Hegelian in structure, this Marxian understanding of the realizations of philosophy was an entirely new definition.

According to Marx, the practical workings of the overcoming process would first call for unmasking the idea of human alienation, stripping it from the holy shape that the earlier philosophy of Hegel has given it. Marx called, at this point, for the presentation of an alienation in its real shape, which is, according to him, a human shape, not a godly one. Thus, the earlier philosophic and mystical criticism of Heaven, or the Absolute, began to transform itself in Marx into a political and economic criticism.

In 1843 Marx departed for France. Establishing himself in Paris, he began to read the abundance of French literature on Socialism and Communism. During that particular period he also met Proudhon, with whom he became a close ideological friend. This friendship, however, as we have seen, did not last long.

When the economic theory of alienation was finally fully developed, Marx attempted to forge his criticism of political economy. In fact, he expressed this criticism in the three volumes of his major work, *Das Kapital* (1867, 1885, 1894). In reality, *Das Kapital* is a *criticism* of political economy, not a treatise on political economy, as it has been sometimes claimed. This is one important point that needs clarification. Marx came to the conclusion that logically one should look at theology in order to find grounds to criticize religion; by the same token one must look at economics in order to criticize political economy. This shows that, like Hegel, Marx consistently acted to preserve systematization in the building of his theory.

In summary, one can say that Marx began from the idea of the Hegelian phenomenology of the *Weltgeist,* which was in reality Hegel's great expression of philosophy. The essence of the Marxian point, however, was that Hegel was doing, in fact, nothing else but talking, in an abstract and mystified way, about economics. Thus, Hegelianism became in Marx a symbol of the money of the Spirit.

Marx maintained that nature could only be produced by history. One can see, at this point, constant repetition of the Hegelian impact on Marx. The latter had stated that the greatness of the notion of the Hegelian phenomenology was that its author, although unknowingly, was in reality grasping and speaking of: (a) the *process* of production; (b) the *essence* of labor; (c) man as a *result* of his own labor.

In reality, however, Hegel was not interested in economics at all. Nevertheless, this is what Marx maintained. In fact, the only labor which Hegel ever knew was the abstract notion of the spiritual labor of thought, a labor engaged in the process of its own self-realization. It probably helped Marx to grasp and realize what was, in fact, the essence of labor, but Hegel himself had nothing to do with economic labor.

Beginning from the Feuerbachian point that God is nothing but man himself, Marx came back to Hegel in reconstructing the Hegelian philosophy, but this time injected an economic touch into it. This was the manner in which *Marxism* came into being. It was by no means a result of one single proposition. The original Marxian basis was that history reflected the story of the Spirit and explained how this Spirit transformed itself, through the means of alienation, toward development. From this point on, Marx translated this mystical spiritual alienation into what he implied to be the harmony of a real alienation. In his first manuscript, dedicated to *alienated labor,* Marx made an attempt to translate this labor into the sphere of economics as a whole. In fact, in this early work, one can find no significant proof supporting his stand, but one finds, indeed, clearly enough, the excellent manner in which Marx posed the dilemma.

After reading Marxian theory as a whole, that is, Early and Mature Marxism taken together, one cannot but pose to oneself the question, "What would happen if man was not alienated; what would occur if man successfully overcame his alienation, and became a self-realized man?" In attempting to answer this question, one may run through the essential landmarks of Marxian thinking:

First, man is a creative being by nature. As such, he possesses vital and productive powers.

Second, it is natural for man to perform labor for the sake of producing things, for the sake of the joy of doing them and not for gaining his subsistence. One finds Fourier's earlier ideas well reflected in these two Marxian points.

Third, unlike animals, man has a consciousness of self-activity. This self-activity is performed by him spontaneously. Although one could again detect Fourieristic overtones on this point, it stems, in fact, from the Hegelian impact on Marx.

Fourth, in man's practical production of an objective work, he always has a tendency to shape his products according to what Marx calls the *Law of Beauty.* One might rightfully assume here that Marx was talking about esthetics and harmony.

Fifth, all the above-mentioned points are particles which, when put together in operation, help to make man prove himself.

Sixth, as a logical consequence of all this, that is, through man's activity, *nature* appears as a *creation* of man, as the work of man, and as the *object* of man. Indeed, this is exactly what Marx called *Objectification of Man.*

However, Marx realized that in the process of his labor, man duplicated himself, and logically then, his nature was escaping outside him, being expressed in the world of various objects all made by man. If all these objects, the result of man's labor, were preserved as man's own belongings, then he would be happy and he would not lose himself. However, since these objects usually become the property of someone else, man-producer loses himself; thus, he is alienated. Such alienation becomes much more pronounced when one realizes that man's labor was never free and spontaneous; on the contrary, it was a necessity for man's subsistence. Thus, from here one can see quite clearly the Marxist formula: the poorer man becomes, the more alienated he turns out to be.

However, Marx also posed the question: Why does man after having created all these beautiful objects, all around him, look at them as objects *alien* to him and to his activity? In answer, Marx explained that man looks at them as such only because he had *conceived* them as alien at the *moment* of their production. He conceived them as alien because he thought of them as a means of subsistence and not as an activity for his pleasure. Thus, the more unpleasant the labor of production was for man, the more alienated he became. Alienation, therefore, could be seen by Marx as crystallized only in the activity of labor. It clearly appeared that since man's nature is freely productive, the conditions of Civilization, which also had provoked Rousseau's stand, had changed that nature by compelling man to produce for his goal of subsistence. Indeed, for Marx, the whole point of the Revolution was to abolish, not labor as such, but *unpleasant* labor only. Here again one could clearly see the *evolutionary* Fourierism which Marx plans on a *revolutionary* foundation.

As one can obviously detect, Marxism is above all very closely related to the Philosophy of History of Hegel. In fact, Marx was doing nothing new. He was just decoding, in his own interpretive way, Hegelianism. The Objectification of Man appears in Marx as little more than labor which is used in the creation of the objects of the surrounding environment. It also appears, on the other hand, that labor, is some sort of externalization of man. However, according to Hegel, as seen by Feuerbach, the Spirit is all in man, the Spirit is all in the subject; but through alienation it also enters the object, thus the product. This is one of the essences of Marx's understanding and interpretation of Hegel. According to Marx, man feels disturbed, not because of the Spirit within him, but because of the existence of his Spirit outside him, that is, in the object, in a place where man's Spirit is transformed into something alien. Along with this, Marx maintained that it was in the nature of man to externalize himself. Therefore, Marx looked upon the world of man as a world of workers, as a world of workers constantly performing labor. Logically then, Marx conceived the world as characterized by externalization of the workers. Therefore, when the worker looks on the world, he cannot but discover his own alienation. Consequently, he would negate himself in the sense of not feeling satisfied with himself, because of his own externalization which he had discovered. The worker discovers his alienation because of the existence in the world of alienated, unfree, that is, *forced* labor. Labor was viewed by Marx as "forced" in the sense that it was performed for subsistence and not for pleasure, while the latter would be, indeed,—as Fourier has maintained—much closer to man's nature. In this respect, Marx maintained that this kind of labor is a *self-sacrificing* type of labor; and also that automatic forced labor in specialized factories was modifying man's body, but at the same time, it was completely ruining man's spirit. Thus, what in fact Marx was saying was that not God, not nature, but only man can be the power determining the alienation of another man. He continued by stressing that the man who determines this alienation is, in fact, the *master* of both the other man's labor and product. The master's power of making the other man produce was guilty of forcing this other man to alienate himself. Marx firmly maintained, therefore, that a man's self-alienation can appear, indeed, only in man's relationships with other men.

At this point, one might state that in a general sense modern psychiatry similarly maintains that insane people often look upon their own activity as not belonging to them, but to someone else. Schizophrenia could be taken as one of the most explicit forms of this syndrome.

Marx maintained the very materialistic view that *capital* is, in fact, the master of everything. He elaborated on this view by asking that if one has the capital, as the master does, then what would the capitalist be? In explaining the dilemma, Marx stated that the capitalist would be, in fact, the soul, the *personification* of the capital. Thus, the capital is transformed into man, or rather, it is transformed into *force* which is personified in man, which takes the form of man.

One may remind oneself, at this point, that the Hegelian *Weltgeist* too, was a force which, from time to time, took the form of a man "building history," such as Caesar, Napoleon, etc. If one looks at capital as a force causing conflicts in man's nature, then labor could also be looked upon as a kind of force. Marx, indeed, maintained exactly that, and came to the conclusion that there exist two important forces. First, there is an exploited force of the victim, the force of the alienated labor. Second, there is the exploiting force of the capitalist conceived through capital.

From this point on, the Marxian dilemma appears quite clear: one has labor versus capital equating, in a wider sense, the *workers' class* versus the *capitalist class* as a personification of the earlier forces. In Mature Marxism, this entire conception is modified still further. The modification consists of the fact that there were no more references by Marx to man as such because he presumed that man is already entirely alienated from himself. Based on the conviction that the act of alienation is accomplished through the unpleasant labor given in the moment of production, Marx also refrained from speaking about alienation. The Marxian explanation of this modification consists of the rationale that capital itself does not look upon labor as a man, but only as a power standing ready for various degrees of exploitation. Capital itself, being no longer man, is nothing but the force of exploitation. Labor and capital, therefore—two abstract forces— are both personified, Hegelian-like, in man; they have falsely taken the form of man, while in reality they are *not* man. They are only two different abstract forces. Striking indeed are the Marxian similarities with the basis of Hegelianism, especially the Hegelian definition of *reality* as opposed to the mere *appearance* of reality.

According to Hegel, history is the story of spiritual alienation. History will end when the spirit returns in himself through the dialectical process and the final synthesis, that is, when he will become the Absolute. This process, Marx maintained, is, in fact, the process of Communism. Communism will realize man, will cause his return in community and harmony with himself. This will be accomplished by bringing back into man his lost, alienated labor. In true Communism, however, there will be, according to Marx, another additional stage. The first stage will only be the *raw* stage. The final stage will still have to come in the future since in evolutionary progress everything cannot be accomplished at once. The goal of Communism appeared in Marx to be the goal of man reentering his self, that is, overcoming his alienation. This is referred to by Marx as the *reintegration of man* with himself which, in reality, will be to practice Communism.

The true meaning of this reintegration is aimed at private property. If there were no private propery, if it were abolished, man would stop producing for somebody else. The culmination of this idea would be reflected in the *abolition* of private property. Abolition of private property would mean, in fact, that man's alienation would cease because there would be no more production of objects conceived by the worker as destined to belong to someone else other than the producer. Thus, through his production, man would reenter himself because the products of his labor would remain his own. Therefore, one could clearly look at Communism as a transaction from a state of alienation toward a condition of *integration* of man with himself. The state of alienation could be characterized by the existence of private property and unpleasant, forced labor, while the condition of the integrated man will feature the abolition of private property as well as of unpleasant, forced production. In this respect, when Marx often uses the term *social man* he means a *human man,* a man in conformity with himself, a man no longer alienated or separated from his own being. The term *socialist* in Marx's view would then mean man determinedly engaged in the process of bringing humanity to that condition of conformity and harmony. Extending the scope of this process, which through Communism transforms an ordinary man into a human man, one could logically conceive the idea that through Communism nature too becomes human. By naturalism, Marx meant man's activity of creating objects, and also that a complete naturalism would equal complete humanism. Therefore, through the abolition of private property, nature, on the one hand (a nature which is freely created by man), and man himself, on the other, will blend together into total harmony. Therefore, society in Communism would be reflected by a complete unity of man with nature, a nature freely created by man, in fact, the final stage of the development of the Hegelian *Weltgeist* with the end of history. In this respect, Socialism and Communism were both regarded by Marx as the true expression of this harmony. Thus, one can again clearly see the Hegelian dialectics functioning. Man gets an appropriation of nature by getting to know it, but this is the nature which has first been produced by man. Although Marx could no longer speak of alienation which, in fact, implied religion or the spiritual fall of man, because he built his theory entirely on a materialistic basis, he still, in a material way, referred to alienation. This can clearly be seen in his elaborations on the specialized *division* of labor. He saw in this division a *true* alienation, which he defined this time through the division of labor. Thus, one of Marx's capital points is of a dual nature. It refers to the abolition of alienated labor, not only through the abolition of private property but also through the abolition of the division of labor. In fact, this is *the* crucial point in Mature Marxism.

In spite of the obvious relation of Marx to Early French Socialism and abstract German philosophy, he strongly criticized not only Hegel but also the French socialists, especially Fourier, whose ideas, in fact, Marx copied in presenting the concept of free labor in his final stage of Communism characterizing the harmonious society. It seems that by not admitting purposely outside influence in the building of his theory he attempted to vest it with some sort of personal identity. In reality, however, one can clearly detect that Marxism is not an original product of one man, so that Marx can only be credited mainly with having collected and systematized other people's ideas.

In criticizing evolutionary Socialism, Marx addressed himself to the following points:

First, he emphasized that the utopian schools, including those of Fourier, and the English Socialist, Robert Owen, fostered ideas of fantastic societies, unattainable castles in the air, with no realistic means for their achievement.

Second, Marx objected to the creation of small communities, while small communities were the basis of society for the evolutionary Socialists such as Fourier. Instead of their small-scale propositions, Marx advanced the idea that the new regime and the new social order would have much to do with the entire world on a global scale. This point was very clearly illustrated by Marx when he talked about a World Revolution, and not of local revolts or local changes.

Third, Marx also violently attacked the evolutionary Socialists because they abhorred the use of revolutionary tactics which, however, alone appeared to him realistic for the bringing about of fundamental change.

Fourth, Marx disliked the evolutionary Socialists, because they were not at all interested in, nor did they understand, the idea of the class struggle.

Fifth, one of the most important criticisms of the evolutionary Socialists was based on the fact that they wanted only to improve the conditions of the working man within the current state of society. Marx himself preferred the opposite. He wanted a temporary *worsening* of the workman's conditions because such a worsening would bring about the revolution in a much more imminent way. On that account, he became angry at every instance in which efforts were made locally or regionally to improve working conditions within the existing society.

Sixth, Marx also opposed the evolutionary Socialist tendency to moralize. Morals had nothing to do with a change in society since he conceived of a violent change resulting from the outcome of the struggle between two forces, capital and labor. In other words, Marx looked for power relations to decide the change in morals, or justice.

Seventh, Marx was also very much against the voluntaristic approach upheld by the evolutionary Socialists for the creation of the new society. Marx was against this voluntarism because it implied that whatever was to come about, would come only if there were enough good will for it. This also presupposes that if there were no good will, the change would not take place. This is, indeed, very much against Marx's *deterministic* belief in the Hegelian dialectics that change would come on a universal scale regardless of man's desire for it. Even if there were no revolution, change would still be imminent. The importance of the revolution, however, is to *shorten* the waiting period for that change.

The situation in Imperial Russia, prior to February, 1917, as well as the period between that date and the October Revolution of the same year, was character-ized by a long, gradually increasing discontent with national authority. The disastrous war against Germany, characterized by great inadequacies in strategy and logistics on the battlefields made this discontent crystallize to the point of no return. Thus, a domestic explosion seemed imminent. Various tactics to effect a radical change in existing conditions had been attempted in earlier times, starting with the creation of the *Narodniki* (a chiefly middle-class revolutionary organization), the *People's Will* party (a much more strongly radical wing based on the promotion of political assassinations and terrorism), the *Kadé* groups, and others. Thus, the basic motivation for the Russian Revolution while not Marxian in essence, did, in fact, attempt to devise the most suitable means for the achievement of the long-wanted change. Retrospectively, one may say that in reality various "experimentations" were continually being made, aimed at the discovery of the most efficient applicable method for disposing of the central autocracy which ruled by oppression and exploitation.

In brief, those were the circumstances among which the Marxian ideological explanations and predictions began to penetrate and grow amidst Russian society. Thus, one could look on Marxism in Russia as *only one* of the various attempts to devise and apply an efficient method for disposing of the central authority. This being the immediate objective, little critical and constructive thought was given to a decision on the type of regime that should, or would, follow the change. Only fragmentary, broad, and, indeed, vague ideas on Western European models of government made some isolated headway in a few circles. The government which resulted from the February, 1917, Revolution may be regarded as a perfect illustration of this. Sometime prior to that date, when the peoples in Russia became convinced that previous tactics—those of the Narod-niki, the People's Will, Kadé, and others—had in a sense failed, the teachings of German Marxism entered the scene. They presented the Russian intelligentsia with something quite innovative on the Russian scene. First of all, there was in it an impressive ideological systematization which appeared, on the surface, as "scientific." Second, it contained a series of convincingly logical predictions on the future development of society. Third, it proposed a definite form of political arrangement providing for a *Second Stage* of societal development, which was to follow the first, post-revolutionary, period of appeasement. This Second Stage was to be liberal to the point of preaching the withering away of the oppressive, for the Russians, State institution. Only one point in the newly introduced theory was lacking in innovation, namely the necessity of a *revolution*. This idea was not new; on the contrary, it had already been long accepted in the minds of the Russian masses. Thus, all they had to do was to make use of the weak governmental situation at the end of World War I and proceed with a revolution, a limited goal, but one which the people had already been conditioned to accept and anticipate. The three points mentioned above were new and impressive for the intelligentsia, especially the third point which answered logically the problems of the future.

Vladimir Ilich Ulianov Lenin (1870–1924) was one of the revolutionary leaders who was impressed by the Marxian propositions and at first *accepted them to the letter*. It does not seem probable that he had overlooked Marx's statements on the post-industrial and post-democratic prerequisites which were to guarantee the success of the Communist Revolution. Since they referred to the creation of necessary conditions for the launching of the Revolution, Lenin probably assumed that these conditions were not needed in Russia because, instead, the revolutionary spirit there was quite ripe, and in addition, unlike populations in the West, the Russian peoples in the provincial countryside were already used to communal life during the Czarist system: the "Dvor," "Mir," and "Zemstvo" communities. However, the chief contradiction between the prerequisite necessity related to the theory, and the reality in Russia (the country was in the pre-industrial and pre-democratic stage) must have occupied Lenin's mind to the point of devoting almost the entirety of his writings to the problem, "how to achieve the Revolution." While such ideas constantly obsessed him, the dilemma was equally real to other leading Russian Marxists. They, too, were preoccupied with the pre- and post-revolutionary issues at stake. Hence, one can observe all the differences and arguments between Lenin, on the one hand, and his Marxian companions, on the other. Hot debate among men such as Trotsky, Chernov, Plekhanov, Bakunin, and others—not to mention the leading Marxist of Europe, Karl Kautsky—freely swept across all of the Marxian logic and predictions. Although not openly admitting it, these men went to the extent of even attempting a reinterpretation of Marx's teachings and particularly adjusting them to the Russian heritage traditions, and reality. A quick rundown on the highlights of Lenin's explanations alone would be enough to illustrate the unsettledness and confusion of the issues related to the Russian application of Marxism. One important issue was the determination of the procedures for the building of Socialism, as reflecting the Marxian First Stage, Socialism, and then of Communism—that is, the Second Stage—symbolizing the perfectly harmonious society of Marx. On the general issue of the necessity for these two stages, Marxian logic seemed clear enough so that no significant disagreements occurred. However, sharp differences of opinion crystallized when attempts were made to define each one of these stages. For instance, in a dispute over that particular problem, Chernov disagreed with Lenin (and with Marx) on the matter by maintaining that the beginning of the First Stage should *not* necessitate the previous existence of a bourgeois class. Indeed, there was not such a class of any mentionable importance in Russia.

In terms of revolutionary tactics—while basing himself on the previous attitude of the Russian peasant class, and equally influenced by the reported earlier activities of Blanqui in post-revolutionary France (see pp. 163–164)—Lenin rejected the suggestion that the Russian peasant class could be useful for the Revolution. No earlier than 1905, however, he gradually began to modify this view. Lenin now began to envision a peculiar and useful role for the peasants in the Revolution. He thought that it would be good if he could secure their *neutrality* in the oncoming conflict, thus decreasing the potential strength of other competitive revolutionary groups in the country to which the peasant might lend support. Lenin thought that without peasant support their efforts would fail.

Lenin silently praised Marx for not having clearly defined the contours of the Second Stage. Had Marx done so, Lenin's task in converting the revolutionaries into Marxists and Communists would have been substantially more difficult. Now, through his own interpretation, he was able to adapt those teachings and make them appeal to the Russian mind. In this respect Lenin has implied that Marx never claimed that a new kind of society would emerge or that Socialism was in essence any different from capitalism itself. The latter will only appear in a new form, a form determined by the proletarian class. He clearly implied that capitalism, *achieved by the proletariat,* was in fact Socialism.

Gradually—mainly under the influence of the Russian utopian novelist Chernishewsky—Lenin began to understand the impracticality of Marxian theory. Thus he implied in 1917 that the framework of Socialism was, in a way, already built by the previous regime. All one had to do now was to take it over and place it at the service of the working class; the banks and the rest of the economic structure already existed in a centralized form, one only had to have workers operate them.

Finally, Lenin did realize that he had succeeded in preventing the emergence of capitalism in Russia, but he also was aware that he had failed to create Socialism in its place. Such an admission by Lenin is evident in another of his statements greatly emphasized on several occasions; namely, that the building of Socialism in "practice" was *one hundred times* more important than any theory. Indeed, it was quite a problem for Lenin to keep this "practice" within the directives extracted from the framework of Marxian theory. For instance,

Lenin's uncompromising accent placed on the necessity for a dictatorship of the proletariat emerged as a quite different proposition, when it was implemented, than the Marxian prophecy of dictatorship. In fact, after Marx, the dictatorship concept in his teachings began to decline. An interpretation made at that time even made allowance for the possibility of transformation of the dictatorship principle to the extent of permitting the creation of a Communist *democratic* republic. Karl Kautsky, who was the leading Marxist in Europe, did not much believe in dictatorship. Approaching Lenin directly on that issue, he explained that in fact there were two possible variations of Marxian theory: (a) a revolutionary variation; and (b) an evolutionary variation *not involving* a dictatorship. In responding, Lenin publicly called Kautsky a renegade.[28]

According to Lenin, the dictatorship was the foundation, the cornerstone, of Marxism. In reality, it seems that both Lenin and Kautsky exaggerated their respective views. In fact, neither dictatorship nor even the Revolution was the cornerstone of Marxian theory: it was the solution of the dilemma of *exploitation* of man by man. One may say in general terms that Lenin, by attempting to adapt and apply Marxism to the primitive characteristics of Russian society, was in fact "Russianizing" that highly philosophic German theory; he tried to give it a peculiar interpretation which would make it fit the underdeveloped Russian political, social, and economic conditions and mode of life.

In terms of the Communist Party itself, Lenin seems to have again backed away from most of the Marxian directions. Marx envisaged an enthusiastic *mass organization* voluntarily supported by the vast majority of the people. Lenin, however, in order to apply the idea to the Russian revolutionary political reality as referred to earlier, entirely embraced Blanqui's proposition of a *small*, elitist, and strongly militant type of organization—an organization of *professional* revolutionaries, disciplined, obedient, excellently trained in using small arms, and in promoting conspiracies. His practical idea was not at all the massive international revolt that Marx had predicted, but an efficiently executed *coup d'état*, limited to the Russian state. Therefore, unlike Marx, Lenin always thought of the Communist Party as a sort of efficient armed forces. He even referred to the Party in military language: "revolutionary attacks," "strategic retreats," "revolutionary shock troops," etc. In this respect he had the mentality of a war planner on a gigantic scale. He thought of himself as the supreme commanding general; of the Communist Party, as the general staff; and of the workers at large, as the soldiers ready to receive and obey orders. Normally, in the preparation of armed forces for war, the officers train the enlisted soldiers; in preparation for the revolution, the Communist Party members were to assume the role of those officers, while the workers were to perform the function of the

---

[28]V. Lenin, *The Proletarian Revolution and the Renegade Kautsky,* New York (1934).

enlisted men. The former had the responsibility of efficiently training the latter.

The Communist regime in the Soviet Union can so far be systematically studied through three different periods: 1917 to 1924; 1924 to 1953; and 1953 to the present.

1. Lenin was unquestionably the dominant political figure during the first period. This period was characterized *politically* by the building of an internally strong and efficient, all-powerful Communist Party which dominated the whole regime. The *economic* sector during that time was mostly agrarian-oriented, although there was much talk of initiating a sound industrial development.

2. The second period was overshadowed by the personality of Josef Stalin. It may be divided into two subdivisions: 1924–1938, which inaugurated and consolidated the Stalinist system of rule; and 1938–1953, which reflected the climax of the Stalinist regime.

From a purely *political* point of view, one may look on the second period as one of building a strong Soviet State institution at the *expense* of the Communist Party built previously by Lenin. In fact, during Stalin's regime, it seems quite clear that the Party was reduced to secondary rank. The *economic* sector during the second period shifted substantially from its previous goal and succeeded predominantly in creating the Soviet heavy industries at the *expense* of agriculture.

3. The third period may be characterized by the emergence and the rise of Khrushchev, his being ousted from the Party, and subsequent sociopolitical and economic developments leading to the current situation in the U.S.S.R. This whole period may be regarded *politically,* as well as from the *economic* point of view, as an attempt toward a general reversal back to the policies of Leninism. It should be noted, however, that neither under Khrushchev nor after his fall was this trend completed. All the attempts in that direction were either radical enough to provoke discontent among the group of leaders of the U.S.S.R. or were insufficiently promoted to weather severe criticism arising out of their implementation. In general, one may state that while the *economic* sector appeared to have achieved significant advancement in industry as well as in agriculture, the *political* realm was characterized by Khrushchev's attempts to rebuild the Communist Party, thus giving it back its Leninist status and prestige, a policy inherited and mantained by Brezhnev. This time it was done at the *expense* of the State institution. One might say that this was in general the meaning of the term "de-Stalinization." The other facets of post-Stalinist changes, although quite visible and spectacular, are chiefly related to strategy and tactics in accomplishing that goal.

A classical dilemma for the democracies (the U.S. type of Democracy included) is the controversy between "centralization of authority" and "decentralization." This dilemma, is, indeed, also present, though in a different form, in the Soviet

Union. In the United States one can detect this perpetual problem under the typically American guise of "States' Rights" versus "Federal Rights"—a problem dating back to the Constitutional Convention. In the Soviet Union one can see it as having strongly affected the country's sociopolitical life since the October, 1917, Revolution. The Soviet Union's top leadership positions—First Secretary of the Communist Party and Prime Minister—have at times been separated; at other times both have been combined in one man who is, in such cases, simultaneously the Party leader and the State (government) leader.

The pattern of such "centralization" and "decentralization" in the Soviet Union's hierarchy is observable at least once in each of the study periods suggested earlier, that is: 1917–1924; 1924–1953; and 1953 to the present. Lenin began as the Chairman of the Council of People's Commissars (the first government of the U.S.S.R.) and had simultaneous control over the Communist Party; then, after April, 1922, when his control weakened, Stalin became the Party Leader—Secretary General of the C.P.S.U.—while Lenin continued to retain his position as head of the government.

During the 1924–1953 period, Rykov served for a while as the U.S.S.R.'s head of the government, while Stalin held the first Secretaryship of the Communist Party; then, after the elimination of his political opponents and consolidation of his personal power, Stalin purged Rykov and assumed both positions.

As far as the third period is concerned, one can easily observe a continuation of the same pattern. In 1953, following a very short period of collective leadership, Malenkov succeeded Stalin as the head of the Soviet government, while Khrushchev inherited Stalin's first secretaryship of the Communist Party. Again, after Khrushchev's consolidation of power in 1957 (through the elimination of his political opponents, the so-called "anti-Party" group led by Molotov), he emerged as the leader of both the Communist Party and the government. The ousting of Khrushchev brought about a new period of "decentralization" during which Brezhnev succeeded him as the First Secretary of the Party, while Kosygin assumed the position of head of the Soviet government.

One major characteristic should be observed in this "centralization-decentralization" pattern in the Soviet Union, namely, during periods of weakness in the Soviet political leadership it is the "decentralizing" tendency which begins to prevail, while after each period of consolidation of power by one man, the centralizing phenomenon takes place.

Thus it becomes obvious that in spite of the apparent and widely advertised stability of the Soviet Union, controversial and damaging politics are ever a part of the picture; in spite of the loudly expressed unity which allegedly binds the Soviet citizenry together in their determination to build Socialism, diversionary politics are indeed always at large amidst Soviet political leadership. There are, however, four major differences between the Soviet type of domestic politics and the relatively free political competition for office in the democracies.

First: the decisive political struggles in the U.S.S.R. always take place on the top level, within the government or within the Party, or between the two.

Second: the political struggle is conducted in total secrecy, to the point of withholding from the Soviet masses any knowledge of its existence, or nature.

Third: after a particularly decisive political battle has been fought and won by one of the parties involved, the citizens are allowed to hear only the arguments of the victor. The defeated party is silenced indefinitely. For instance, an appropriate and illustrative case is the struggle that brought Khrushchev to ultimate power. It is known that during the summer of 1957, the old Bolshevik guard Molotov, accused by Khrushchev of being the leader of an allegedly "anti-Party" group, presented a lengthy and very significant defense of his actions before the Communist Party Central Committee. No one knows, however, (besides the Committee members) what exactly his defense was, what he actually did say, and on what he based his case. The Central Committee on its second ballot turned against him, and he simply disappeared from the Soviet Union's political scene until his death.

The *Fourth* important characteristic of Soviet politics that one should bear in mind is that when one leader loses a political battle of this sort, he loses out completely and indefinitely. He never returns to the political scene, nor has he any power to continue influencing Soviet political life.

This last characteristic, also shared by Fascism and National Socialism, is an additional element which is implicit in the idea of Modern Totalitarian Dictatorship.

The following charts, VI, VII, and VIII, illustrate respectively the structure of the Communist Party of the Soviet Union; the structure of the government of the U.S.S.R.; and the relationship between the government and the Soviets in the U.S.S.R. with the controlling role of the Communist Party.

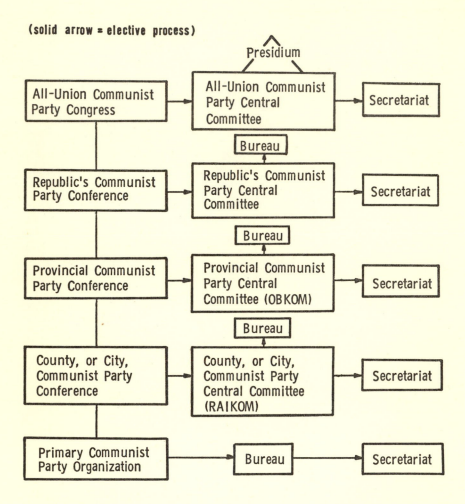

(solid arrow = elective process)

note: all secretariats are elected by the central committees and/or bureaus.

Yearly review reports are made by the central committees on the accomplished and pending party activity before the congress, the party conferences, or the primary party organization respectively.

Chart VI. The Structure of the Communist Party of the U.S.S.R.

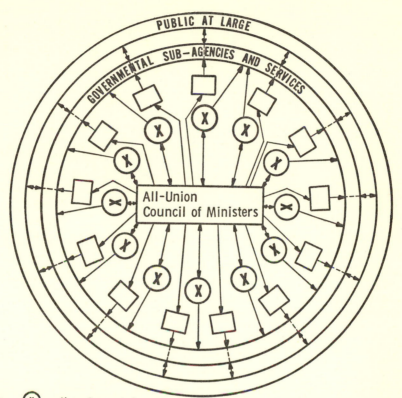

note: (X) = all-union ministries of the federal government/Moscow
         ☐ = union-republic's ministries

*Khrushchev's reform (February 1957):
        a large number of ministries of all-union and union-republic's
        levels were abolished and replaced by a larger number of
        "SOVNARKHOZES" (103), the latter not subordinated to the all-
        union council of ministers but to those on the union-republic's
        level alone, that number was to correspond to the number of
        the existing provincial communist party committees (OBKOMS),
        thus assuring the communist party control over the
        governmental agencies.

Chart VII. The Structure of the Federal Government of the U.S.S.R. (The Basic
Organization)*

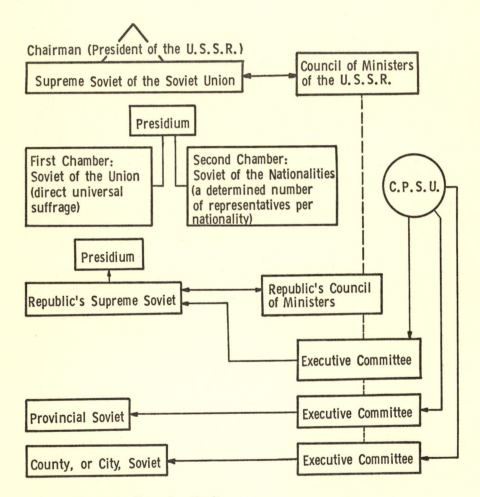

Chairman (President of the U.S.S.R.)

Supreme Soviet of the Soviet Union

Council of Ministers of the U.S.S.R.

Presidium

First Chamber: Soviet of the Union (direct universal suffrage)

Second Chamber: Soviet of the Nationalities (a determined number of representatives per nationality)

C.P.S.U.

Presidium

Republic's Supreme Soviet

Republic's Council of Ministers

Executive Committee

Provincial Soviet

Executive Committee

County, or City, Soviet

Executive Committee

note: solid arrow = flow of authority

Chart VIII. Functional Relations between the Government and the Soviets (U.S.S.R.), with the Controlling Role of the Communist Party

Bibliography

Part I: The Foundations

Barbu, Zevedei. *Democracy and Dictatorship.* New York: Grove Press, 1956.

Burch, Betty Brand. *Dictatorship and Totalitarianism.* New York: D. Van Nostrand Co., 1964.

Burnham, James. *The Machiavellians.* Chicago: Henry Regnery Co., 1943.

Friedrich, Carl J., and Brzezinski, Zbigniew K. *Totalitarian Dictatorship and Autocracy.* New York: Praeger Publishers, 1966.

————, ed. *Totalitarianism.* New York: Grosset & Dunlap, 1964.

Gilbert, G. N. *The Psychology of Dictatorship.* New York: Ronald Press Co., 1950.

Girvetz, Harry K. *Democracy and Elitism.* New York: Charles Scribner's Sons, 1967.

Gyorgy, Andrew, and Blackwood, George D. *Ideologies in World Affairs.* New York: Blaisdell Publishing Co., 1967.

Klausner, S., ed. *The Study of Total Societies.* New York: Doubleday & Co., 1967.

Laswell, Harold D.; Lerner, Daniel; and Rothwell, C. Easton. *The Comparative Study of Elites.* Stanford, Ca.: Stanford University Press, 1952.

Marcuse, Herbert. *One-Dimensional Man.* Boston: Beacon Press, 1964.

Moore, Barrington, Jr. *Social Origins of Dictatorship and Democracy.* Boston: Beacon Press, 1966.

Neumann, Franz., ed. *The Democratic and the Authoritarian State.* Preface by Herbert Marcuse. Glencoe, Ill.: Free Press, 1957.

Rejai, J., ed. *Democracy: Contemporary Democratic Theories.* New York: Atherton Press, 1967.

Spitz, David. *Patterns of Anti-Democratic Thought.* London: Collier-Macmillan Ltd., 1949.

Part II: Fascism

Ascoli, Max. *Fascism for Whom?* New York: W.W. Norton & Co., 1938.

Ashton, E. B. *The Fascist, His State, and His Mind.* New York: William Morrow & Co., 1938.

Bardet, Gaston. *La Rome de Mussolini.* Paris: Editions ch. Massin, 1937.

Beals, Carleton. *Rome or Death.* New York: Century Co., 1923.

Borgese, Guiseppe Antonio. *Goliath, the March of Fascism.* New York: Viking Press, 1937.

Borghi, Armando. *Mussolini, Red and Black.* New York: Freie Arbiter Stimme, 1938.

Burnham, James. *The Managerial Revolution.* Bloomington: Indiana University Press, 1966.

Cohen, Carl. *Communism, Fascism, and Democracy*. New York: Random House, 1962.

Colbert, Evelyn. *The Left Wing in Japanese Politics*. New York: International Secretariat, Institute of Pacific Relations, 1952.

Cole, George Douglas Howard. *The People's Front*. London: V. Gollancz, Ltd., 1937.

Colton, Ethan Theodore. *The Four Patterns of Revolution*. New York: Associated Press, 1935.

Crossman, Richard Howard Stafford. *Plato Today*. New York: Oxford University Press, 1939.

Davis, Jerome. *Contemporary Social Movements*. New York: Century Co., 1939.

Drucker, Peter F. *The End of Economic Man*. New York: John Day Co., 1939.

Dutt, Rajani Palme. *Fascism and Social Revolution*. New York: International Publishers Co., 1935.

Einzig, Paul. *The Economic Foundations of Fascism*. London: Macmillan & Co., Ltd., 1933.

Fascism in Action. Washington, D.C.: Library of Congress, 1947.

Finer, Herman. *Mussolini's Italy*. New York: Grosset & Dunlap, 1965.

Finer, S. E., and Mirfin, D., ed. *Vilfredo Pareto Sociological Writings*. New York: Praeger Publishers, 1966.

Florinsky, Michael T. *Fascism and National Socialism: A Study of Economic and Social Policies of the Totalitarian State*. New York: The Macmillan Co., 1936.

Gibson, Hugh, ed. *The Ciano Diaries: 1939–1943*. New York: Doubleday & Co., 1945.

Greene, Nathanael. *Fascism, an Anthology*. New York: Thomas Y. Crowell Co., 1968.

Greenfield, Kent R. *Economics and Liberalism in the Risorgimento: A Study of Nationalism in Lombardy. 1814–1848*. Baltimore, Md.: The Johns Hopkins Press, 1966.

Haider, Carmen. *Capital and Labor Under Fascism*. New York: Columbia University Press, 1939.

Halpern, William S. *Mussolini and Italian Fascism*. New York: D. Van Nostrand Co., 1964.

Harris, H. S. *The Social Philosophy of Giovanni Gentile*. Urbana: University of Illinois Press, 1960.

Heimann, Edward. *Communism, Fascism, or Democracy?* New York: W. W. Norton & Co., 1938.

Herridge, William Duncan. *Which Kind of Revolution?* Boston: Little Brown & Co., 1943.

Hibbert, Christopher. *Mussolini, une force de la nature*. Paris: Editions Robert Laffont, 1963.

Hoover, Calvin Bryce. *Dictators and Democracy*. New York: The Macmillan Co., 1937.

Hostetter, Richard. *The Italian Socialist Movement, Origins 1860–1862*. New York: D. Van Nostrand Co., 1958.

Johnsen, Julia Emily. *Selected Articles on Capitalism*. New York: H. W. Wilson Co., 1933.

Josephs, Ray. *Argentina Dairy*. New York: Random House, 1944.

Laski, Harold Joseph. *Where Do We Go From Here?* New York: Viking Press, 1940.

London, Kurt. *Backgrounds for Conflict.* New York: The Macmillan Co., 1945.

Lopreato, Joseph, ed. *Vilfredo Pareto.* New York: Thomas Y. Crowell Co., 1965.

Loucks, William Negele. *Comparative Economic Systems.* New York: Harper & Bros. 1952.

MacGregor-Hastie, R. *The Day of the Lion: the Life and Death of Fascist Italy, 1922–1945.* New York: Barnes & Noble, 1963.

Matthews, Herbert Lionel. *The Fruits of Fascism.* New York: Harcourt Brace & World, 1943.

Mayer, J. P. *Political Thought in France from Sieyès to Sorel.* London: Faber & Faber, 1943.

Meisel, James H., ed. *Pareto and Mosca.* Englewood Cliffs, N.J.: Prentice-Hall, 1965.

————. *The Myth of the Ruling Class: Gaetano Mosca and the Elite.* Ann Arbor: University of Michigan Press, 1962.

Mussolini, Benito. *Fascism: Doctrine and Institutions.* Rome: Ardita Publishers, 1935.

————. *My Autobiography.* New York: Charles Scribner's Sons, 1928.

Mussolini, Rachele. *Le duce mon mari.* Paris: Editions Fasquelle, 1958.

Nolte, Ernst. *Der Faschismus in seiner Epoche.* Munich: R. Piper & Co., 1963.

Norlin, George. *Fascism and Citizenship.* Chapel Hill: University of North Carolina Press, 1934.

Oakeshott, Michael Joseph. *The Social and Political Doctrines of Contemporary Europe.* London: Cambridge University Press, 1940.

Page, Kirby. *A New Economic Order.* New York: Harcourt Brace, 1930.

Pareto, Vilfredo. *Traité de sociologie générale.* Lausanne-Paris. 1917.

Paris, Robert. *Histoire du fascisme en Italie: des origines à la prise du pouvoir.* Paris: François Maspero, 1962.

Parmelle, Maurice Farr. *Bolshevism, Fascism, and the Liberal-Democratic State.* New York: John Wiley & Sons, 1934.

Pomba, Giuseppe Luigi. *La civiltà fascista: Illustrata nelle dottrina e nelle opere.* Introduction by Benito Mussolini. Torino: Unione Tipografico-editrice torinese, 1928.

Prezzolini, Giuseppe. *Fascism.* New York: E. P. Dutton & Co., 1927.

Raushenbush, Helnar Stephen. *The March of Fascism.* New Haven: Yale University Press, 1939.

Rossi, Angelo. *The Rise of Italian Fascism.* London: Methuen & Co., 1938.

Salvadorci, Massimo. *Cavour and the Unification of Italy.* New York: D. Van Nostrand Co., 1961.

Salvemini, Gaetano. *Under the Axe of Fascism.* New York: Viking Press, 1939.

Schmidt, Carl T. *The Corporate State in Action, Italy Under Fascism.* New York: Oxford University Press, 1928.

Schneider, Herbert Wallace. *Making Fascists.* Chicago: University of Chicago Press, 1929.

————. *Making of the Fascist State.* New York: Oxford University Press, 1928.

————. *The Fascist Government of Italy.* New York: D. Van Nostrand Co., 1936.

Seldes, George. *Sawdust Ceasar: The Untold History of Mussolini and Fascism*. New York: Harper & Bros. 1935.

————. *You Can't Do That*. New York: Modern Age Books, 1938.

Seton, Watson Christopher. *Italy from Liberalism to Fascism*. London: Methuen & Co., 1967.

Sharp, Roland Hall. *South America Uncensored*. Toronto: Longmans Canada Ltd., 1945.

Sorel, Georges. *Reflections on Violence*. London: Collier-MacMillan Publishers, 1950.

Steiner, H. Arthur. *Government in Fascist Italy*. London: McGraw-Hill Publishing Co., 1938.

Stowe, Leland. *While Time Remains*. New York: Alfred A. Knopf, 1946.

Strachey, Evelyn John St. Loe. *The Menace of Fascism*. New York: Friede Covici, Inc., 1923.

Swing, Raymond Gram. *Forerunners of American Fascism*. New York: Julian Messner, div., Simon & Schuster, 1935.

Tassinari, Giuseppe. *Ten Years of Integral Land-Reclamation under the Mussolini Act*. Feanza, Italy: Fratelli Lega, 1939.

Van Til, William. *The Danube Flows Through Fascism*. New York: Charles Scribner's Sons, 1938.

Weber, Eugene. *Varieties of Fascism*. New York: D. Van Nostrand Co., 1964.

Weiss, John. *The Fascist Tradition*. New York: Harper & Row, 1967.

Welk, William George. *Fascist Economic Policy*. Cambridge, Mass.: Harvard University Press, 1938.

Wittke, Carl Frederick. *Democracy is Different*. London: Harper & Row Ltd., 1941.

Woolf, Leonard Sidney. *Quack Quack*. New York: Harcourt, Brace and Company, 1935.

Part III: National Socialism

Abel, Theodore. *Why Hitler Came to Power*. Englewood Cliffs, N.J.: Prentice-Hall, 1938.

————. *The Nazi Movement*. New York: Atherton Press, 1965.

Allen, Wm. Sheridan. *The Nazi Seizure of Power*. Chicago: Quadrangle Books, 1965.

Angress, Werner T. *Stillborn Revolution*. Princeton, N.J.: Princeton University Press, 1963.

Barzun, Jacques. *Darwin, Marx, Wagner*. New York: Doubleday & Co., 1958.

Becker, Howard. *German Youth: Bond or Free*. London: Kegan Paul Trench, Trubner & Co., 1946.

Berndt, Alfred-Ingemar. *Gebt mir vier Jahre Zeit! Documente zum ersten Vierjahresplan des Führers*. Introduction by Joseph Goebbels. Munich: Zentralverlag der N.S.D.A.P. Franz Eher Nachf G.m.b.H., 1937.

Biddiss, Michael D., ed. *Gobineau: Selected Political Writings*. New York, Harper & Row, 1970.

Bossenbrook, Wm. J. *The German Mind*. Detroit: Wayne State University Press, 1961.

Boveri, Margaret. *Treason in the Twentieth Century*. New York: G. P. Putnam's Sons, 1961.

Brady, Robert A. *The Spirit and Structure of German Fascism*. London: Victor Gollancz Ltd., 1937.

Bramsted, Ernest K. *Goebbels and National Socialist Propaganda*. East Lansing: Michigan State University Press, 1965.

Brennecke, Fritz. *The Nazi Primer*. New York: Harper & Bros., 1938.

Bullock, Alan. *Hitler, A Study in Tyranny*. New York: Bantam Books, 1958.

Burden, Hamilton T. *The Nuremberg Party Rallies 1923–1939*. New York: Praeger Publishers, 1967.

Burnham, James. *The Machiavellians: Defenders of Freedom*. Chicago: Henry Regnery Co., 1963.

Butler, Rohan D. O. *The Roots of National-Socialism 1788–1933*. New York: Howard Fertig, Inc., 1968.

Cameron, Norman and Stevens, R. H., trs. *Adolph Hitler. Secret Conversations 1941–1944*. Introduction by H. R. Trevor-Roper. New York: Farrar, Straus, 1953.

Cranshaw, Edward. *Gestapo, Instrument of Tyranny*. New York: Viking Press, 1957.

Demeter, K. *The German Officer Corps in Society and State, 1650–1945*. New York: Barnes & Noble, 1965.

Devel, Wallace R. *People Under Hitler*. New York: Harcourt, Brace and Company, 1942.

Dorfalen, Andreas. *Hindenburg and the Weimar Republic*. Princeton, N.J.: Princeton University Press, 1964.

Ebenstein, William. *Nazi State*. New York: Farrar & Rinehart, 1943.

Engels, Friedrich. *The German Revolutions: The Peasant War in Germany* and *Germany: Revolution and Counter-Revolution*. Chicago: University of Chicago Press, 1967.

Fichte, Johann G. *The Vocation of Man*. New York: Bobbs-Merrill Co., 1956.

Florinsky, Michael. *Fascism and National Socialism: A Study of Economic and Social Policies of the Totalitarian State*. New York: The Macmillan Co., 1936.

Glock, Charles Y. *Christian Beliefs and Anti-Semitism*. New York: Harper & Row, 1966.

Grunberger, Richard. *Germany 1918–1945*. New York: Harper & Row, 1964.

Guderian, Heinz. *Panzer Leader*. New York: Ballantine Books, 1952.

Hagen, Lewis. *The Mark of the Swastika*. New York: Bantam Books, 1965.

Hale, Orton J. *The Captive Press in the Third Reich*. Princeton, N.J.: Princeton University Press, 1964.

Heller, Erich. *Thomas Mann, the Ironic German*. Boston: Little, Brown & Co., 1958.

Hitler, Adolph. *Mein Kampf*. New York: Reynal & Hitchcock, 1941.

————. *My New Order*. Edited by Raoul de Roussy de Sales. New York: Reynal & Hitchcock, 1941.

Jäckel, Eberhard. *Hitler's Weltanschauung: A Blueprint for Power*. Translated by Herbert Arnold. Middletown, Conn.: Wesleyan University Press, 1972.

Jarman, Thomas L. *The Rise and Fall of Nazi Germany*. New York: New American Library, 1961.

Kamenetsky, Ihor. *Secret Nazi Plans For Eastern Europe*. New York: Bookman Associates, 1961.

Keitel, Wilhelm. *The Memoirs of Field-Marshal Keitel.* New York: Stein & Day, 1966.

Kelly, George A., ed. *Johann Gottlieb Fichte, Addresses to the German Nation.* New York: Harper & Row, 1968.

Kirkpatrick, Clifford. *Nazi Germany.* New York: Bobbs-Merrill Co., 1938.

von Klemperer, Klemens. *Germany's New Conservatism, Its History and Dilemma in the Twentieth Century.* Princeton, N.J.: Princeton University Press, 1957.

Koehl, Robert Lewis. *RKFDV: German Resettlement and Population Policy.* Cambridge, Mass.: Harvard University Press, 1957.

Kohn, Hans. *Revolution and Dictatorships: Essays in Contemporary History.* Cambridge, Mass.: Harvard University Press, 1950.

————. *The Mind of Germany: The Education of a Nation.* New York: Charles Scribner's Sons, 1960.

Konai, Aurel. *The War Against the West.* New York: Viking Press, 1938.

Konvitz, Milton. *Essays on Political Theory.* Ithaca, N.Y.: Cornell University Press, 1948.

Langham, Walter. *Historic Documents of World War II.* New York: D. Van Nostrand Co., 1958.

Laqueur, Walter. *Young Germany: A History of the German Youth Movement.* New York: Basic Books, 1962.

Lerner, Daniel. *Nazi Elite.* Stanford, Ca.: Stanford University Press, 1951.

Lewis, Cleona. *Nazi Europe and the World.* Washington, D.C.: Brookings Institution, 1941.

Lewy, Guenter. *The Catholic Church and Nazi Germany.* New York: McGraw-Hill Book Co., 1964.

Lichtenberger, Henri. *The Third Reich.* New York: Greystone Corp., 1937.

Lochner, Louis P., ed. *The Goebbels Diaries: 1942–1943.* New York: Doubleday & Co., 1948.

Lowis, Robert. *Toward Understanding Germany.* Chicago: University of Chicago Press, 1954.

Lytton, Edward B., Lord. *Rienzi: The Last of the Roman Tribunes.* Boston: Little, Brown & Co., 1893.

McGovern, William M. *From Luther to Hitler.* Boston: Houghton Mifflin Co., 1941.

Marx, Fritz Morstein. *Government in the Third Reich.* New York: McGraw-Hill Book Co., 1937.

Massing, Paul. *Rehearsal for Destruction: A Study of Political Anti-Semitism in Imperial Germany.* New York: Harper & Bros., 1949.

Mayer, Milton. *They Thought They Were Free: The Germans, 1933–1945.* Chicago: University of Chicago Press, 1955.

Meinecke, Friedrich. *The German Catastrophe: Reflections and Recollections.* Cambridge, Mass: Harvard University Press, 1950.

————. *The German Catastrophe.* Boston: Beacon Press, 1963.

Merkl, Peter H. *Origin of the West German Republic.* New York: Oxford University Press, 1963.

Moeller van den Bruck, Arthur. *Germany's Third Empire.* London: George Allen & Unwin Ltd., 1943.

Mosse, George L. *The Crisis of German Ideology: Intellectual Origins of the Third Reich.* New York: John Wiley & Sons, 1964.

————. *Nazi Culture*. New York: Grosset & Dunlap, 1968.

Muhlen, Norbert. *The Survivors: A Report on the Jews in Germany Today*. New York: Thomas Y. Crowell, 1962.

Nazi Conspiracy and Aggression. Washington, D.C.: U.S. Government, 1946–1947.

Nazi-Soviet Relations. Washington, D.C.: Department of State, 1947–1948.

Nolte, Ernst. *Der Faschismus in seiner Epoche*. Munich: R. Piper & Co., 1963.

Pfeiler, Wilhelm K. *War and the German Mind*. New York: AMS Press, 1966.

Poliakov, Leon. *The Study of Anti-Semitism*. New York: Vanguard Press, 1965.

Pulzer, Peter G. J. *The Rise of Political Anti-Semitism in Germany and Austria*. New York: John Wiley & Sons, 1964.

Rauschning, Hermann. *The Revolution of Nihilism; Warning to the West*. New York: Longmans, Green & Co., 1939.

Reitlinger, Gerald. *Final Solution: The Attempt to Exterminate the Jews of Europe*. New York: Barnes & Noble, 1961.

Rogger, Hans, and Weber, Eugene, eds. *The European Right: Historical Profile*. Berkeley: University of California Press, 1965.

Rossi, A. *Russo-German Alliance 1939–1941*. London: Chapman & Hall Ltd., 1950.

Schlabrendorff, Fabian von. *The Secret War Against Hitler*. New York: Pitman Publishing Corp., 1965.

Schoenbaum, David. *Hitler's Social Revolution*. New York: Doubleday & Co., 1966.

Schopenhauer, Arthur. *Essay on the Freedom of the Will*. New York: Liberal Arts Press, 1960.

————. *On the Basis of Morality*. New York: Bobbs-Merrill Co., 1965.

————. *The World as Will and Idea*. New York: Doubleday & Co., 1961.

Schuman, Fredrick Lewis. *The Nazi Dictatorship: A Study in Social Pathology and Politics of Fascism*. New York: Alfred A. Knopf, 1935.

Schweitzer, Arthur. *Big Business in the Third Reich*. Bloomington: Indiana University Press, 1964.

Sington, Derick, and Weidenfeld, Arthur. *The Goebbels Experiment: A Study of the Nazi Propaganda Machine*. New Haven: Yale University Press, 1943.

Smith, Bradley F. *Adolf Hitler*. Stanford, Ca.: Stanford University Press, 1967.

Snell, John L. *The Nazi Revolution, Germany's Guilt or Germany's Fate*. Boston: D. C. Heath Company, 1959.

Snyder, Louis L. *The Idea of Racialism*. New York: D. Van Nostrand Co., 1962.

————. *German Nationalism: The Tragedy of a People*. Harrisburg, Pa., Stackpole Co., 1952.

————. *The Weimar Republic*. New York: D. Van Nostrand Co., 1966.

Stein, George. *The Waffen SS: Hitler's Elite Guard at War, 1939–1945*. Ithaca, N.Y.: Cornell University Press, 1966.

Stern, Fritz. *The Politics of Cultural Despair*. Berkeley: University of California Press, 1961.

Stoddard, Theodore Lothrop. *Into the Darkness*. New York: Duell, Sloane & Pearce, 1940.

Tenbrock, Robert Hermann. *A History of Germany*. Munich: Hueber, Paderborn, Schöningh, 1968.

Tennenbaum, Joseph. *Race and Reich*. New York: Twayne Publishers, 1956.

Tobias, Fritz. *The Reichstag Fire*. Translated by Arnold J. Pomerans. New York: G. P. Putnam's Sons, 1963.

Trevor-Roper, H. R., ed. *Hitler's Secret Conversations*. New York: New American Library, 1953.

Turner, Henry A., Jr. *Stresemann and the Politics of the Weimar Republic*. Princeton, N.J.: Princeton University Press, 1963.

Vermiel, Edmond. *Germany in the Twentieth Century: A Political and Cultural History of the Weimar Republic and the Third Reich*. New York: Praeger Publishers, 1956.

Vogt, Hannah. *The Burden of Guilt*. New York: Oxford University Press, 1964.

Wagner, Richard. *The Ring of the Nibelungs*. New York: E. P. Dutton & Co., 1960.

Waldman, Morris. *Sieg Heil!* Dobbs Ferry, N.Y.: Oceana Publications, 1962.

Walzel, Oskar. *German Romanticism*. Translated by Alma Louise Lussky. New York: G. P. Putnam's Sons, 1932.

Zahn, Gordon. *German Catholics and Hitler's Wars: A Study in Social Control*. New York: Sheed & Ward, 1962.

Part IV: Marxian Communism

Adorastskii, Vladimir V. *Dialectical Materialism*. New York: International Publishers, 1934.

Anderson, Thornton. *Masters of Russian Marxism*. New York: Appleton-Century-Crofts, 1963.

Apter, David E. *Ideology and Discontent*. New York: Free Press, 1964.

Baldelli, Giovanni. *Social Anarchism*. Chicago: Aldine-Atherton, 1971.

Barker, Ernest, Sir, ed. *Social Contract; Essays by Locke, Hume, and Rousseau*. London: Oxford University Press, 1948.

Beck, Lewis White. *Studies in the Philosophy of Kant*. New York: Bobbs-Merrill Co., 1965.

Beer, Max. *The General History of Socialism and Social Struggles*. New York: Russell & Russell Publishers, 1957.

Behrens, C. B. A. *The Ancient Regime*. London: Thames & Hudson Ltd., 1967.

Berdiaev, Nicolai, A. *The Origin of Russian Communism*. Translated by R. M. French. London: Geoffrey Bles, Ltd., 1948.

Berdiajew, Nikolai. *Wahrheit und Lüge des Kommunismus*. Darmstadt: Holle-Verlag, 1953.

Berlin, Isaiah. *Historical Inevitability*. London: Oxford University Press, 1954.

————. *Karl Marx. His Life and Environment*. London: Oxford University Press, 1963.

Bernstein, Eduard. *Evolutionary Socialism*. New York: Schocken Books, 1961.

Bober, M. M. *Karl Marx's Interpretation of History*. Cambridge, Mass.: Harvard University Press, 1948.

————. *Karl Marx's Interpretation of History*. New York: W. W. Norton & Co., 1927.

Boswell, James. *Jean-Jacques Rousseau*. New York: McGraw-Hill Book Co., 1953.

Bottomore, T. B. *Karl Marx—Early Writings*. New York: McGraw-Hill Book Co., 1963.

Bowers, David F. *The Heritage of Kant.* New York: Russell & Russell Publishers, 1962.

Boyd, William. *Jean-Jacques Rousseau.* New York: Russell & Russell Publishers, 1963.

Brinton, Crane. *The Anatomy of Revolution.* New York: Random House, 1965.

Broome, J. H., and Arnold, Edward. *Rousseau, A Study of His Thought.* London: Edward Arnold Publishers, Ltd. 1963.

Buber, Martin. *Paths in Utopia.* Boston: Beacon Press, 1958.

Carter, April. *The Political Theory of Anarchism.* New York: Harper & Row, 1971.

Cassirer, Ernst. *The Question of Jean-Jacques Rousseau.* Bloomington: Indiana University Press, 1963.

Caute, David. *Communism and the French Intellectuals.* New York: The Macmillan Co., 1964.

Cohen, Jim. *The Confessions.* Baltimore, Md: Penguin Books, 1953.

Cole, George Douglas Howard. *A History of Socialist Thought: The Forerunners.* London: Macmillan & Co., Ltd. 1957.

————. *A History of Socialist Thought: Marxism and Anarchism.* London: Macmillan & Co., Ltd. 1957.

————. *The Meaning of Marxism.* Ann Arbor: University of Michigan Press, 1964.

Cooper, Rebecca. *The Logical Influence of Hegel on Marx.* Seattle: University of Washington Press, 1925.

Croce, Benedetto. *Historical Materialism and the Economics of Karl Marx.* London: Macmillan & Co., Ltd. 1914.

Crossland, C. A. R. *The Future of Socialism.* New York: Schocken Books, 1963.

Daniels, Robert V. *Marxism and Communism.* New York: Random House, 1965.

De George, Richard T. *Patterns of Soviet Thought.* Ann Arbor: University of Michigan Press, 1966.

Dodge, Guy H., ed. *Jean-Jacques Rousseau: Authoritarian Libertarian?* Lexington, Mass: D. C. Heath Co., 1971.

Drachkovitch, M., ed. *Marxism in the Modern World.* Stanford, Ca.: Stanford University Press, 1965.

Durkheim, Emile. *Montesquieu and Rousseau.* Ann Arbor: University of Michigan Press, 1960.

————. *Socialism and Saint-Simon.* Translated by Charlotte Sattler. Kent, Ohio: Kent State University Press, 1958.

Easton, L. D., and Guddat, K. H., eds. *Writings of the Young Marx on Philosophy and Society.* New York: Doubleday & Co., 1967.

Elzbacher, Paul. *Anarchism.* New York: Libertarian Book Club, 1960.

Engels, Friedrich. *Socialism, Utopian and Scientific.* New York: International Publishers Co., 1935.

————. *The Origin of the Family, Private Property and the State.* New York: International Publishers Co., 1942.

Ewing, Alfred Cyril. *A Short Commentary on Kant's Critique of Pure Reason.* Chicago: University of Chicago Press, 1938.

Federn, Karl. *Materialist Conception of History.* London: Macmillan & Co., Ltd. 1939.

Feuer, Lewis S. *Marx and Engels.* New York: Doubleday & Co., 1959.

Foxley, Barbara, ed. *Emile*. New York: E. P. Dutton & Co., 1963.

Franklin, Julia. *Selections From the Works of Fourier*. London: Swan Sonnen-schein & Co., 1901.

Freeman, Robert, ed. *Marxist Social Thought*. New York: Harcourt Brace & World, 1968.

Fried, Albert, and Sanders, Robert, eds. *Socialist Thought: A Documentary History*. Chicago: Aldine-Atherton, 1964.

Fromm, Erich. *Marx's Concept of Man*. New York: Frederick Ungar Publishing Co., 1961.

————. Socialist Humanism: *An International Symposium*. New York: Doubleday & Co., 1965.

Gray, Alexander. *The Socialist Tradition, Moses to Lenin*. London: Longmans, Green & Co., 1946.

Grebanier, Bernard D. *Jean-Jacques Rousseau*. New York: Barron's Educational Series, 1964.

Greene, Frederick Charles. *Jean-Jacques Rousseau, A Critical Study of His Life and Writings*. New York: Barnes & Noble, 1969.

Greene, Theodore M. *Kant*. New York: Charles Scribner's Sons, 1957.

Gregor, James. *A Survey on Marxism*. New York: Random House, 1965.

Guehenno, Jean. *Jean-Jacques Rousseau*. New York: Columbia University Press, 1966.

Haimson, Leopold. *The Russian Marxists and the Origins of of Bolshevism*. Cambridge, Mass.: Harvard University Press, 1955.

Hanfi, Zawar. *The Fiery Brook: Selected Writings of Ludwig Feuerbach*. New York: Doubleday & Co., 1972.

Hegel, Georg. *Reason in History*. New York: Liberal Arts Press, 1953.

Hendel, Charles William. *The Philosophy of Kant and Our Modern World*. New York: Liberal Arts Press, 1957.

Henderson, W. O., ed. *Engels' Selected Writings*. Baltimore, Md.: Penguin Books, 1967.

Hook, Sidney. *From Hegel to Marx*. Ann Arbor: University of Michigan Press, 1966.

————. *Marx and the Marxists*. New York: D. Van Nostrand Co., 1955.

————. *Reason, Social Myths and Democracy*. New York: John Day, 1940.

Horne, A. *The Fall of Paris: The Siege and the Commune, 1870–1871*. New York: Barnes & Noble, 1966.

Iggers, Georg, and Cole, George Douglas Howard. *Doctrine of Saint-Simon*. Boston: Beacon Press, 1958.

Jackson, John Hampden. *Marx, Proudhon, and European Socialism*. New York: Collier Books, 1962.

Johnson, Chalmers. *Revolutionary Change*. Boston: Little, Brown & Co., 1966.

Joll, James. *The Anarchists*. Boston: Little, Brown & Co., 1964.

Jordan, Z. A. *The Evolution of Dialectical Nationalism*. New York: St. Martin's Press, 1967.

Kant, Immanuel. *Analytic of the Beautiful, From the Critique of Judgment*. New York: Bobbs-Merrill Co., 1963.

————. *Critique of Practical Reason and Other Writings in Moral Philosophy*. Chicago: University of Chicago Press, 1949.

————. *Foundations of the Metaphysics of Morals*. New York: Bobbs-Merrill Co., 1959.

————. *The Metaphysical Principles of Virtue*. New York: Bobbs-Merrill Co., 1964.

————. *The Metaphysics of Morals*. New York: Bobbs-Merrill Co., 1965.

————. *On History*. New York: Bobbs-Merrill Co., 1963.

————. *Perpetual Peace*. New York: Bobbs-Merrill Co., 1957.

————. *Prolegomena to Any Future Metaphysics*. Chicago: Open Court Publishing Co., 1902.

Kautsky, Karl. *The Economic Doctrines of Karl Marx*. London: A & C Black Ltd., 1925.

Kelsen, Hans. *The Political Theory of Bolshevism*. Berkeley: University of California Press, 1948.

Knox, T. M., ed. and trans. *Hegel's Philosophy of Right*. Oxford, England: Clarendon Press, 1949.

Kohn, Hans. *The Mind of Modern Russia*. New Brunswick, N. J.: Rutgers University Press, 1955.

Krimerman, L. I., and Lewis, Perry, eds. *Patterns of Anarchy: Collection of Writings on the Anarchist Tradition*. New York: Doubleday & Co., 1966.

Kropotkin, Peter. *The Place of Anarchism in Socialistic Evolution*. London: New Temple, 1886.

Lakoff, Sanford A. *Equality in Political Philosophy*. Cambridge, Mass.: Harvard University Press, 1964.

Lange, O., and Taylor, F. M. *The Economic Theory of Socialism*. New York: McGraw-Hill Book Co., 1964.

Lenin, V. *The State and Revolution*. New York: Vanguard Press, 1929.

Lichtheim, George. *Marxism: An Historical and Critical Study*. New York: Praeger Publishers, 1962.

Lokkowicz, N. *Marx and the Western World*. South Bend, Ind.: University of Notre Dame Press, 1967.

Lowenburg, Jacob, ed. *Hegel-Selections*. New York: Charles Scribner's Sons, 1957.

MacDonald, James Ramsay. *The Socialist Movement*. New York: Henry Holt & Co., 1911.

McLellan, David. *Marx before Marxism*. New York: Harper & Row, 1970.

Maksimov, Gregory, ed. *The Political Philosophy of Bakunin*. Glencoe, Ill.: Free Press, 1953.

Manuel, Frank E. *French Utopias*. New York: Free Press, 1966.

————. *New World of Saint-Simon*. Cambridge, Mass.: Harvard University Press, 1963.

Marcuse, Herbert. *Reason and Revolution: Hegel and the Rise of Social Thought*. New York: Oxford University Press, 1941.

————. *Soviet Marxism*. New York: Columbia University Press, 1958.

Martin, Kingsley. *The Rise of French Liberal Thought*. New York: New York University Press, 1954.

Marx, Karl. *Capital*. Chicago: Britannica, 1955.

————. *The Communist Manifesto*. Edited by Friedrich Engels. New York: New York Labor News Co., 1888.

————. *Critique of Political Economy* (preface only). London: J. M. Dent, 1930.

————. *Early Writings*. London: C. A. Watts & Co., 1963.

————. *The Eighteenth Brumaire of Louis Bonaparte.* New York: International Publishers Co., 1963.

————. *Pre-Capitalist Economic Formations.* London: Lawrence & Wishart, Ltd., 1964.

————. *Theories of Surplus Value.* New York: International Publishers Co., 1952.

Marx, Karl, and Engels, Friedrich. *The Russian Menace to Europe.* Glencoe, Ill.: Free Press, 1952.

————. *Writings on Politics and Philosophy.* New York: Doubleday & Co., 1959.

Mayo, Henry B. *Introduction to Marxist Theory.* New York: Oxford University Press, 1960.

Mendel, Arthur P., ed. *Essential Works of Marxism.* New York: Bantam Books, 1961.

Meyer, Alfred G. *Communism.* New York: Random House. 1962.

Niebuhr, Reinhold. *Marx and Engels on Religion.* New York: Schocken Books, 1964.

Osborn, Ann Marion. *Jean-Jacques Rousseau.* New York: Russell & Russell Publishers, 1964.

Owen, Robert. *A New View of Society and Other Writings.* London: J. M. Dent & Sons, 1927.

Parkes, H. B. *Marxism: An Autopsy.* Chicago: University of Chicago Press, 1964.

Petrovio, Gajo. *Marx in the Mid-Twentieth Century.* New York: Doubleday & Co., 1967.

Plamenatz, John. *German Marxism and Russian Communism.* New York: Harper & Row, 1965.

Polin, Raymond. *Marxian Foundations.* Chicago: Henry Regnery Co., 1966.

Prest, Oskar, ed. *Hegel: Reason in History.* New York: Bobbs-Merrill Co., 1953.

Proudhon, Pierre-Joseph. *Qu'est-ce que la propriété?* Paris: Garnier-Flammarion, 1966.

Rousseau, Jean-Jacques. *Discourse Upon the Origin and the Foundation of Inequality Among Mankind.* New York: Collier, 1961.

————. *Les reveries du promeneur solitaire.* Paris: Editions Gallimard, 1965.

————. *The Social Contract and Discourses.* New York: E. P. Dutton & Co., 1947.

Ruhle, Otto. *Karl Marx.* New York: Viking Press, 1929.

Saint-Simon, Henri Count de. *Social Organization, the Science of Man and Other Writings.* New York: Harper & Row, 1964.

Schaff, Adam. *Marxism and the Human Individual.* New York: McGraw-Hill Book Co., 1970.

Scott, Anthony John, ed. *The Defense of Gracchus Babeuf Before the High Court of Vendome.* Amherst: University of Massachusetts Press, 1907.

Shatz, Marshall S., ed. *The Essential Works of Anarchism.* New York: Bantam Books, 1971.

Simkhovitch, Vladimir G. *Marxism Versus Socialism.* New York: Columbia University Press, 1913.

Talmon, J. L. *The Origins of Totalitarian Democracy.* New York: Praeger Publishers, 1961.

Trotsky, Leon. *The Revolution Betrayed: What is the Soviet Union and Where is it Going?* New York: Doubleday & Co. 1937.

Tucker, Robert C. *Philosophy and Myth in Karl Marx.* London: Cambridge University Press, 1961.

Ulam, Adam B. *The Unfinished Revolution: An Essay on the Sources of Influence of Marxism and Communism.* New York: Random House, 1964.

Vardys, V. Stanley. *Karl Marx: Scientist? Revolutionary? Humanist?* Lexington, Mass.: D. C. Heath Co., 1971

Vossler, Otto. *Rousseaus Freiheitsletter.* Gottingen: Vandenhoeck & Ruprecht, 1963.

Wetter, Gustav. *Dialectical Materialism.* New York: Praeger Publishers, 1959.

Winwar, Frances. *Jean-Jacques Rousseau.* New York: Random House, 1961.

Wolfe, Bertram D. *Marxism.* New York: Dial Press, 1965.

―――――. *Three Who Made a Revolution.* New York: Dial Press, 1948.

Woodcock, George. *Anarchism.* Cleveland: World Publishing Co., 1962.

Wright, Ernest H. *The Meaning of Rousseau.* New York: Russell & Russell, Publishers, 1963.

Zeitlin, Irving M. *Marxism: A Re-Examination.* New York: D. Van Nostrand Co., 1967.

Zimand, Savel. *Modern Social Movements.* New York: H. W. Wilson Co., 1921.

Zimmermann, Friedrich. *Das Ende des Kapitalismus.* Jena: E. Diederichs, 1931.

Index